# AN UNAMERICAN BUSINESS

## The Rise of the New EUROPEAN ENTERPRISE

DONALD KALFF

KOGAN
PAGE

London and Philadelphia

**Publisher's note**

Every possible effort has been made to ensure that the information contained in this book is accurate at the time of going to press, and the publishers and authors cannot accept responsibility for any errors or omissions, however caused. No responsibility for loss or damage occasioned to any person acting, or refraining from action, as a result of the material in this publication can be accepted by the editor, the publisher or any of the authors.

First published in Dutch in the Netherlands in 2004 by Uitgeverij Business Contact, Amsterdam

Editor original English manuscript: Abi Daruvalla

First published in English in Great Britain and the United States in 2005 by Kogan Page Limited
Reprinted in 2006

120 Pentonville Road
London N1 9JN
United Kingdom
www.kogan-page.co.uk

525 South 4th Street, #241
Philadelphia, PA 19147
USA

© Donald Kalff, 2006

ISBN 0 7494 4490 8

**British Library Cataloguing-in-Publication Data**

A CIP record for this book is available from the British Library.

**Library of Congress Cataloging-in-Publication Data**

Kalff, Donald.
    An unamerican business : the rise of the new European enterprise / Donald Kalff
        p. cm.
    Includes bibliographical references and index.
    ISBN 0-7494-4490-8
    1. Industrial management—United States. 2. Business enterprises—United States. 3. Industrial management—Europe. 4. Business enterprises—Europe. I. Title.
HD70.U5K35 2005
658.4′00973—dc22
                                                                    2005019183

Typeset by Digital Publishing Solutions
Printed and bound in the United States by Thomson-Shore, Inc

# Contents

Introduction and Summary 1

1 **The revolution of the 1990s** 15
The empire strikes back 16
Confidence restored 17
The American view of the world 19
The American Enterprise Model 20
A second look 23
Wrapping up 27

2 **The 1990s were not what they seemed** 29
The US economy performed poorly 31
US corporate results were dismal 35
A legacy of vulnerabilities 42
Sacrificing the shareholder 48
An indictment 53

3 **The end of the road** 55
Economic policies in the US and in the EU 57
The corporate gloss loses its shine 63
Can the franchise be renewed? 78
In summary 83

4 **Unintended consequences and unaccounted costs** 85
The hero of the 1990s 86
Corporate head office 95
Battlegrounds 103
The Gulag Archipelago 118

**5**   **A European Enterprise Model**                              **121**
       The foundations of growth                                    121
       Ownership, control and economic benefits                     127
       Governance                                                   132
       The European manager                                         138
       The management agenda                                        143
       A sense of inevitability                                     155

**6**   **The competitiveness of Europe**                           **157**
       Rekindling internal growth                                   159
       A world of partnerships                                      171
       The new foundations                                          178
       Taking stock                                                 185

       **Epilogue**                                                 **187**

       *Notes*                                                      *205*
       *Index*                                                      *215*

# Introduction and Summary

*An UnAmerican Business* is a fresh and agnostic look at the past, present and future performance of companies that have embraced the American way of conducting business. Many believe in the virtues of this approach and all European companies with a stock market listing belong to the converts, but this book comes to the conclusion that their faith is misplaced. It turns out that the performance of these companies is below their own standards. It also becomes clear that the American way of doing business limits a company's growth potential, does not take into account certain costs and leads to unintended consequences. Moreover, the foundation for cooperation (both within and between companies) that is crucial for the next round of economic development is severely damaged.

More importantly, the book draws attention to Europe's independence and its capacity to develop its own brand of capitalism. *An UnAmerican Business* takes issue with the notion that globalization forces harmonization of the ways companies conduct their business. To the contrary, Europe is large and strong enough to go its own way and to become the most successful region in the world.

In economic terms, the fact that Europe can support many different approaches to business – depending on specific market requirements and regulatory contexts – is an advantage. Choosing the right combination of governance, management, organization, planning, performance evaluation and remuneration for private companies becomes a source of competitive advantage. New models are emerging and will spur Europe's economic growth. This book sketches the contours of one such alternative – and highly competitive – European model for large companies. It is based on the notion that the quality of people and the quality of their cooperation are replacing finance and technology as the main factors that limit successful corporate development.

## THE DEMISE OF THE AMERICAN ENTERPRISE MODEL

Chapter 1 concludes that even under the greatest possible pressure, the US private sector and the institutions connected to it are incapable of profound change.

Enron seemed to mark the beginning of the end. One of the icons of the Roaring Nineties, a company that had capitalized on the liberalization of the US energy markets and whose innovative trading practices and rapid expansion were the envy of the world's business community, was unmasked as the epitome of deceit. The affair pushed the accountancy industry into an unprecedented crisis and accountancy firm Arthur Andersen disappeared altogether. At about the same time it became apparent that the largest and most reputable investment banks in the country – Merrill Lynch, Citigroup and JPMorgan among them – had been guilty of stock market manipulations. Scandal after scandal followed, spreading to encompass a wide array of sectors all the way from the New York Stock Exchange to mutual funds, from the telecommunications to pharmaceutical industries.

Naturally, a wave of remedial action was launched: law enforcement was stepped up and companies and their CEOs throughout the United States were prosecuted. The New York state attorney general led the charge in the all-important financial sector and new regulations were introduced by the Securities and Exchange Commission (SEC), the New York Stock Exchange (NYSE) and Congress (the Sarbanes-Oxley Act) – all this with full support from President George W. Bush and his cabinet.

Huge interests were at stake. Following the burst of the internet bubble and the subsequent gradual decline of the stock market, further damage to confidence in the US economy had to be controlled at all costs. The country longed for a return to the 1990s, which had been the longest period of economic expansion in history, a time during which high economic growth was accompanied by low unemployment and a surprisingly low level of inflation. As far as the private sector was concerned, it had been an era characterized by high levels of investment, high productivity growth and high profitability.

The fierce reaction by law enforcement agencies, regulators and Congress was also intended to defend the legacy of the Reagan/Thatcher revolution and its 'world-view'. This is the set of notions, beliefs and ambitions that guided those who aimed for success throughout the 1990s. In this world-view, the empowered, confident and ambitious citizen takes centre stage. He is fully prepared to take responsibility for his actions, but expects to be rewarded for his efforts. He is accompanied by the shareholder, who is willing to put his hard-earned financial resources at risk, and the entrepreneur who battles it out with his competitors. The government's role is to create the conditions for the proper functioning of capital and labour markets, as markets are considered the superior way to allocate resources in the interest of the economy at large.

At corporate level these principles translated into the pursuit of share-holder return on investment as the dominant purpose of the company, belief in a strong CEO and the creation of independent business units that could operate close to their markets. In the interest of transparency and to ensure control of corporate processes, management focused on setting and evaluating progress against financial targets. Companies made sure that financial incentives were in place at every organizational level to assure compliance with shareholder interest. All these changes were accompanied by a shift in culture that was personified by the new manager who was prepared to fight for his shareholder, believed in competitiveness as the key to success and always focused on the big leaps forward.

This American Enterprise Model was exceptionally successful. It was emulated by virtually all large public companies in Europe and there seemed no limits to its applicability. Outside its own realm, the model set standards for the organizational structure and culture of large parts of the public sector, such as energy supply and public transport, and even education and health care.

As the true believers in the American Enterprise Model predicted, the US economy perked up in the course of 2002, productivity resumed its above-average growth and corporate profitability improved significantly. Doubters were confronted with compelling evidence that even the greatest of shocks could be absorbed by the US economy. The American Enterprise

Model had once more proved its resilience. It could be improved and it should be refined, but tinkering with its core was considered unwarranted, undesirable and, because of the absence of an alternative, dangerous.

Yet, for those who want to see it, the public prosecutors, the SEC and the NYSE got bogged down. Each case of wrongdoing by the largest and most reputable banks in the country was settled in return for high or low fines, but always without admission of guilt. The leadership of the SEC was undermined by fights over its management and it took two years before the accounting industry had an overseeing board with teeth. The NYSE was distracted by the forced withdrawal of its chairman. Congress passed new and supposedly far-reaching legislation but left considerable holes in the patchwork of regulations. The real battles with those who had very considerable interests to defend – CEOs, investment bankers and accountants – were lost.

The response of corporate America to the stock market crash, the scandals and the recession reflected rigidity. The US world-view and the American Enterprise Model increasingly acted as a straitjacket. The combination of past success, a deeply rooted ideology and the premium that financial markets put on quick and tangible results could only produce the same responses albeit more vigorously. Such stubbornness in a changing world carries a price.

When the past performance of the US economy and US companies is reassessed in Chapter 2, it turns out that the 1990s were not what they seemed. Economic growth, productivity, employment, inflation and reduction of poverty were far less impressive than generally assumed. This was particularly disappointing in light of the information and communication revolution which should have brought economic development to a higher plane. American companies made surprisingly little progress in improving productivity, despite sustained growth in demand. Profitability was modest and needs to be corrected significantly downwards in light of the dubious and illegal corporate bookkeeping practices that were revealed in the 1990s. Ill-conceived investments caused overcapacity in many sectors which led to considerable write-offs. Contrary to what many prefer to believe, the differences in macroeconomic performance in comparison with Europe were small or non-existent. European companies clearly fared better than their American competitors in terms of both profits and competitiveness in world markets.

On top of this, the 1990s left an impressive legacy of vulnerabilities, most of them American-made. The twin deficits of the early 1990s – the federal government deficit and the trade deficit – came back with a vengeance, accompanied this time by the biggest crisis in state finances ever. Corporate and private debt too approached historically high levels, while at the same time the quality of that debt deteriorated. All in all the exposure to interest rate increases, inevitable in light of the historically low rates, had increased. With poor corporate financial reporting, plenty of bills still to settle and exploding but unregulated derivative markets, even the resilience of the American banking system was called into question.

The irony is that the 1990s saw the destruction of shareholder value by the vigorous pursuit of higher share prices. Investors, led by analysts, brokers and the media, continued to focus on past, present and future profitability and not on future cash flows as the only rational approach for management and for the valuation of stocks. Many decisions to improve profitability reduced future cash flows and therefore destroyed value.

Chapter 3 provides the evidence that the cherished notions developed and nurtured during the 1990s as an integral part of the US world-view and the American Enterprise Model have run their course. But this is not accepted in the United States. The Bush administration is still rejuvenating the Reagan revolution by introducing tax reductions, privatizing a range of government services and more union bashing. But European politicians have started to distance themselves from the US agenda. Tax reduction and tax reform are part of a broader programme to reform the welfare state, but the aim is to safeguard its future. Overhaul of social security systems is inevitable but social cohesion remains important. With respect to privatization, resistance has grown and pragmatism is starting to prevail over ideology.

In the corporate context, financial markets (represented by financial analysts, investment bankers and journalists) continued to push for steps with a direct and immediate impact on the share price during the 1990s. Policies such as the purchasing of corporate shares, corporate restructuring, cost cutting and outsourcing were particularly popular. The cost of this straitjacket was considerable. Many opportunities to create value were ignored. Moreover all these policies either fell victim to the law of diminishing returns or were outright counterproductive.

Companies that bought their own stock to support their share price sooner or later undermined their financial resilience. Poorly performing business units could only be sold or dismantled once. Friend and foe now agree that corporate mergers and acquisitions destroy shareholder value for the acquiring company. Less well known is that, in many instances, cost synergies did not materialize and that productivity suffered. Outsourcing of corporate activities was popular, but with each step the risks increased: there was less flexibility in terms of meeting changes in demand and specifications. On top of this, the supply, production and distribution chain became vulnerable. Reduction of staff was often presented as unavoidable to remain competitive, but each new round either yielded less or came at a higher cost in terms of the coherence and viability of the organization and the morale of its survivors.

Truly new ideas were in short supply. Academia and the consultancy industry did not deliver. Business schools belonged to the most ardent supporters of shareholder return on investment. They increasingly depended on corporate sponsorships and had to pave the way to lucrative positions for their students. The consultancy industry had no interest in demonstrating independence; business was flourishing and ideological purity was considered important. The shortage of fresh ideas was particularly felt by the many companies that operated in saturated markets. Sales and marketing efforts became less and less effective.

Chapter 4 deals with the unintended consequences and unaccounted cost of the American Enterprise Model. The CEO, the hero of the 1990s, was put on a pedestal by financial markets and the media. Inside companies, CEOs needed maximum control to deliver on ambitious commitments to shareholders and to provide comfort to the many who wanted a strong leader. Belief in the omnipotence of the CEO proved to be costly. In many companies he became a source of destabilization. His personal preferences had undue influence on the appointment of managers and corporate partnerships. In his attempts to please financial markets he often raised expectations that his company could not fulfil. Increasingly CEOs had to step down, taking many managers with them. The consequences were far-reaching, disruptive and expensive.

Drives to reduce overheads deprived head offices of much technical and commercial experience. As a result more and more companies had to rely on external help, in particular from strategic advisors and investment bankers. These were of course stout defenders of their clients, but the interests of the shareholders were never far away when it came to advising on mergers, divestment of business units, corporate financing and other major corporate decisions. The advisors' financial interests reached levels that called their independence into question.

The emphasis on the business unit as the workhorse of the company caused fault lines. Business units needed a separate identity and their own charismatic leader. They also needed corporate support and money to realize their ambitions in the best interest of their customers and the business unit. This meant companies had to learn to live with tensions between the CEO and business unit managers, between a financially oriented head office on the one hand and commercially and operationally oriented business units on the other hand. There was also tension among business units. All these strains were compounded by growing divergence between the personal financial interests of managers and the achievement of corporate financial objectives. This was in turn fuelled by higher, and increasingly variable, remuneration. Furthermore the competitive attitude of managers, highly appreciated in terms of keeping competitors at bay, proved a doubled-edged sword when it came to dealing with colleagues. More than ever managers felt compelled to defend their positions against real and imaginary attacks. Distrust and caution became essential for survival.

Increased tensions and the inevitable rise in the frequency and severity of conflicts had a major and negative impact on the quality of corporate decision making. Operational and strategic decisions that are wholly or partially taken to strengthen managers' personal positions destroy value.

At a time when cooperation between increasingly specialized experts and business units had become essential to make progress, it turned out that the American way of doing business had well and truly destroyed the trust upon which all forms of cooperation are founded.

All in all, there is ample reason to break away from the American Enterprise Model. The conclusion is that the model is inflexible, that it delivers much less than assumed, that the law of diminishing returns is in full force. The few new ideas that did emerge face a bleak future. The dedicated application of the American Enterprise Model leaves a trail of unintended consequences and unaccounted costs.

## THE RISE OF EUROPEAN ENTERPRISE MODELS

Despite all its shortcomings, the American Enterprise Model will survive. In the United States there is no alternative and US companies have no choice but to refine the model. They will also continue to benefit from a benign business environment: a single integrated and relatively homogeneous market place; flexible labour markets; a widely spread entrepreneurial spirit; a high level of investments in research and development; good cooperation between universities and the private sector; and an abundance of venture capital.

The American Enterprise Model will also survive in Europe for a considerable time to come. Most European public companies have passed the point of no return. Their organizational structures and procedures reflect American principles. They have attracted management that support the model wholeheartedly. They are caught in the web of financial markets and the media and have fixed their policies accordingly. European managers that believe in the American Enterprise Model skilfully deflect the criticisms levied against the too powerful CEO, his remuneration and the corporate governance structure. They distance themselves from the unethical behaviour of their American counterparts and soothe nerves by stressing the social responsibilities of their companies. Their instinct for survival is well developed and much can be done to satisfy critics without compromising the basic principles.

Yet support for the existing alternative European Enterprise Models (such as family businesses, co-operatives and privately owned firms) and the design and implementation of new ones based on different principles provide huge opportunities. This is so particularly if companies are built to create economic value and not to optimize profit per share, and if they are founded on the notion that the quality of people and the quality of their cooperation are now the constraining factors for corporate development rather than technology or finance. Social innovation, new forms of organization and new ways to assess and improve performance with help of indicators that reflect the real world will take centre stage. This holds true both inside companies and among partners.

One such new and radically different European Enterprise Model that is particularly suited for large companies is presented in Chapter 5. This model covers the following crucial areas: company ownership, governance, management, the management agenda, organizational development and, finally, performance evaluation and remuneration.

Under this model, corporate ownership has a different basis. As a matter of principle, those who have conceived of the business idea that underpins the company own it. The underlying consideration is that there is no fundamental difference between business ideas and scientific findings, brands or works of art. They are all forms of intellectual property and inalienable rights are established at the moment of creation.

In a going concern where many business ideas are developed, tested and implemented, these rights migrate to the company as a whole, and to management who are the corporate representatives. This ties in with the special responsibilities of management to build a viable portfolio of business ideas, including the abolishment of existing and the creation of new ones.

Ownership and control overlap completely as long as companies finance their growth from their cash flow. If companies want to accelerate growth they have to enter the market for money, commitment, risk and the various ways financiers could exercise control over the company. Additional money is cheap for firms with a solid cash flow that pursue truly inspiring business ideas: firms that have installed first-class managers, have obtained solid market positions and can rely on a core of outstanding experts and employees that are highly productive. In the case of loans, interest rates will be low, repayment flexible, the bank's collateral reasonable and the bank's control over the company modest or even non-existent. In the case of financing with private equity, investors will take their fair share of the economic profit of the company and secure their interests in areas that are important to them, including the possibility to capitalize on the value created by the company at some point in the future. Part of the equation is also consensus regarding corporate strategy and governance. Crucial to all investment decisions is investor confidence in management. Good managers with an entrepreneurial spirit can lock in investors for a long time without having to yield too much control while protecting their solvency.

Clearly, when companies are less than outstanding the price for money goes up – in terms of interest rates and other conditions, and in terms of the degree of control that has to be yielded to the financiers.

All these arrangements, custom-made for each individual company, are laid down in shareholder and loan agreements and in the company's articles of association. All contracts can be changed if and when, over time, the capital requirements of the company increase or decrease. Every day, all over Europe, hundreds of contracts are completed – far from the glare of equity markets – with the creation of economic value the shared concern of all involved.

Companies that for whatever reason cannot withdraw from the stock market and companies that find the demands of the private equity houses in their sector too onerous could adopt a common European enterprise standard as a basis for a separate stock market index. This would flush out investors that are after above-average returns in the medium and long term.

In the proposed European Enterprise Model small, professional boards, with a full-time chairman, govern the company. Given the fact that value creation is in the hands of experts and battle-hardened middle managers, representatives of these personnel categories have to approve new members of the board nominated by their chairman.

Some of the board members have a deep understanding of the company and the sector in which it operates; others bring insights into the workings of large companies and political and regulatory knowledge. The board appoints and dismisses a CEO and the members of the executive management team and determines their remuneration. It sets corporate targets and evaluates corporate performance. It approves investments, partnerships, changes in the financing of the company and other major decisions. It advises and supports management in every way possible.

Under this model, a board approves and evaluates the implementation of plans developed by the CEO and his team. These plans include targets and programmes to make progress in three different areas.

The first area concerns the company as a going concern: that is to say, given its people, activity portfolio, assets, partnerships and financing. The focus is on safeguarding the integrity of the company. It implies compliance with all internal and external rules and regulations, and the dutiful application of best operational and commercial practices. It also involves the optimization of the results and the development of existing partnerships. It involves the management of the shareholder and loan agreements. In financial terms this is the area of the cash flow statement.

In the second area, the objective is to increase the value of the company structurally, again given its existing portfolio of activities. This includes changes in management and management structure, changes in the composition of the workforce, the introduction and the integration of new equipment and improvements in the portfolio of partnerships. It also includes lasting reductions in the cost of money. This is the area of the balance sheet, not only in the financial sense of the word, but also in the sense of a company's inherent capacity to improve its free cash flow in the years to come.

The third area concerns the quality of the corporate activity portfolio. The focus here is on structural improvement in the company's free cash flow by changing the portfolio of activities. It is the area of strategic positioning. It involves the pursuit of new business ideas with different staff and different partners. It includes the cessation of some existing activities.

The European CEO and his management team have to strike a balance between the pursuit of these three different corporate objectives, all essential in the pursuit of corporate continuity.

In the arena of cash flow optimization, the management team leads not by exercising control but by setting standards and by ensuring that the appropriate control mechanisms are in place. When it comes to the balance sheet, the management team's role is not primarily to decide on investments, personnel and other proposals designed to increase the economic value of the company, but to concentrate on the quality of decision-making processes, from the inception of ideas to board approval. Management must study investment, budgeting, hiring and firing criteria and procedures. They must look at the consistency of procedures, at the behavioural consequences of rules and at potentially counterproductive incentives.

The CEO and his team are personally involved in all initiatives that relate to the renewal of the company. They are directly responsible for the generation and identification of new business ideas that can underpin internal growth, and growth with the help of partnerships. They bring together, lead and protect teams of specialists that have to test and develop these new ideas. They are there when new partners have to be found and contacted. Management must create the conditions for internal change and build and defend their company's reputation as a partner. They have a special responsibility when it comes to calling a halt to projects that – despite the best efforts of all involved – can no longer be expected to yield sufficient value. And naturally, the CEO and his team have a special responsibility in dealing with the company's financiers. Corporate independence is a precious commodity that is worth defending in the interest of value creation.

Organizational and management development permeates throughout the company. Managers and employees are not 'human resources': they are the company. They need a structure and a cultural environment that enables them to trust their managers, colleagues and subordinates. Trust manifests itself in the form of openness; openness means informed debate and improving decision making.

Management does not 'fill vacancies' but 'builds teams'. Teams need team leaders that stand up for their troops. Team members must feel capable of speaking their minds at the risk of embarrassing their superiors, peers, subordinates or themselves.

The business unit remains the workhorse of the company. Any conflicting interests among corporate and business unit managers are resolved by alignment around economic value. Planning, performance evaluation and remuneration are brought in line with the new principles. To avoid conflicts of interest, neither managers nor employees possess shares in the company. Everyone receives a salary, a share of the free cash flow the company generates and part of the extra economic value the company creates by investing in people and fixed assets.

The key question is whether or not companies that embrace such a model can compete with competitors that are guided by the American model. This issue is addressed in Chapter 6. The battlefield is Europe. The protagonists are European companies with a stock market listing and European private companies.

European Enterprise Models will gain the upper hand for a variety of reasons. Confidence in the American Enterprise Model has already been eroded. European investors have sold US shares in considerable quantities. The problems that European companies encounter in managing their US interests have become more apparent and the reputations of some eye-catching European managers determined to follow in the footsteps of their US counterparts have been destroyed.

The advantages European companies enjoy as a result of flexibility in governance and management have already been mentioned. Furthermore, checks and balances are an integral part of decision making in European companies. Inside the company interests are aligned and as a result many of the counterproductive internal conflicts that are so typical for the American model can be avoided.

Even more important is flexibility in terms of policy making. Circumstances and markets change all the time and companies that have implemented this European model can apply a broader range of policies. They also avoid the destruction of economic value that comes with the pursuit of short-term profitability at the expense of future cash flows.

Performance evaluation does justice to the multifaceted world that managers face and the inescapable trade-offs between the short and the long term, and between performance and the creation of potential. Cooperation between increasingly specialized experts and middle managers is the key to value creation, and the European Enterprise Model provides the context in which the trust that is required for productive cooperation can be built.

The European Enterprise Model is much better suited than the American model to breaking new ground to achieve internal growth. The new European managers are well placed to clean up after the merger craze. Attention for, affinity with, and skills to improve innovation processes and procedures will also create value. Great strides can be made by improving productivity other than by investing in new plant and equipment and by the development and delivery of sophisticated services in a consistent manner.

In the world of partnerships, the European Enterprise Model is equipped to build a wide range of relationships: short term and long term, superficial and profound, limited and extensive, bilateral and multilateral. In this way companies can tap many different sources of value at the right time. Ventures are based on framework agreements, joint management and a degree of trust. Such an approach avoids the very detailed and constrictive contracts that are required under the American Enterprise Model.

In this European model, mergers find their justification in the value that is created by joining activities and combining assets and not by optimizing financial parameters. Managers of both companies create the conditions for joint efforts by their experts and middle managers. They make sure that the identified potential can be realized by designing and manning the project's organization, building support in both companies and steering the new entity past the regulators. It is only when additional value is identified and it is reasonable to expect plans to be implemented that negotiations start to distribute the jointly created additional value in a fair and equitable way.

Values, skills and social virtues that are conducive to the forging of partnerships also pay off handsomely in joint innovation efforts. Large companies that resist the temptation to buy small innovative companies but strike new forms of cooperation are bound to do much better. Pre-competitive research and research cooperation across industry boundaries provide many opportunities.

The biggest bounty is to be found in the world of information and communication technology (ICT). New opportunities are of a fundamentally different nature when data processing and storage becomes a commodity. The creation of the smart home, the integration of ICT with the entertainment and media infrastructure and the provision of security will all require intense cooperation beyond traditional industry boundaries, and all this is playing into the hands of companies that have embraced the European Enterprise Model.

## THE CONDITIONS ARE IN PLACE

Europe can develop its own brand of capitalism. Globalization is largely a myth. Trade between the European and American regions as a percentage of economic output has not increased since the 1980s and direct foreign investment outside the regions remains small as a percentage of total investment. Crucially, only 25 per cent of the capital needs of European companies is met by stock markets. Financing from a company's own cash flow, bank loans and private equity are far more important. As a result the majority of European companies could enjoy tailor-made governance and management structures and support from knowledgeable and committed financiers. They would also be relieved of the web of unrealistic expectations spun around stock market listings and the policy limitations that come with them.

European Enterprise Models are firmly rooted in European values. They do justice to the European predilection for comprehensive solutions, for working in teams, and for the fullest possible participation by all members of the organization.

A European world-view is slowly but steadily unfolding. It will mould the political and institutional context of companies in ways that are conducive to the flourishing of European Enterprise Models. Conversely, truly European companies will feed the emerging world-view.

The European way of conducting business is competitive and the introduction of more advanced models will strengthen European companies. Its foundations are becoming more and more solid. Profound change is inevitable. A new US economic recession – quite possible in light of its dismal legacy from the 1990s and US policies since – could accelerate the migration to European Enterprise Models.

# 1

# The revolution of the 1990s

The end of capitalism was nigh, or so it seemed. In the summer of 2002 the foundations of the US economy were shaking. The demise of Enron and Arthur Andersen during the autumn of 2001 proved to be the prelude to a number of sinister events. In addition to Enron and Andersen, criminal charges were brought against executives of WorldCom, Adelphia Communications, Tyco and ImClone Systems, while icons such as AOL Time Warner, Computer Associates, Global Crossing and Qwest Communications were put under investigation.[1] Scores of other companies had to restate their accounts from previous years to fend off sanctions from the Securities and Exchange Commission (SEC).

Two common threads were apparent. The managements of the most renowned companies in the United States had conspired to inflate reported profits to stay in tune with market expectations. And they had also protected private financial interests before or during the downfall of the companies for which they were responsible.

The role of Arthur Andersen in the Enron scandal came to light in excruciating detail and destroyed the hard-won reputation of the accounting industry which was the guardian of US-style capitalism.

Equally shocking were the problems in the financial community. The most prestigious banks in the United States ignored their own golden rules. Analysts (Merrill Lynch) helped to manipulate stock prices; rose-tinted research reports and bullish stock ratings helped to sell investment banking services (Credit Suisse First Boston, Goldman Sachs and Citigroup, among many others).

The knock-on effect was in line with the severity of the revelations. Stock markets crashed, pension funds were wiped out and lay-offs were inevitable to salvage the remains of once proud companies. And the most precious of all commodities – trust in financial markets and the economy – evaporated. All this took place at the end of a two-year period during which the internet bubble burst, big media conglomerates went from riches to rags and cable and telecommunication companies stared into the abyss.

## THE EMPIRE STRIKES BACK

The reaction seemed swift and determined. Investigations were pursued with vigour. The US Justice Department, the SEC, stock exchanges and Congress all moved into the fray.

Eliot Spitzer, the New York state attorney general, carved out a special role for himself in cleaning up Wall Street. Using the criminal investigations of individual banks as leverage, Spitzer and Stephen Cutler, head of enforcement at the SEC, worked with 12 financial institutions for total separation of business research and investment banking by reinstating the once impenetrable Chinese walls.

In addition to the companies that were attracting most of the headlines because of criminal investigations, many more were put under scrutiny by the SEC. Among these were many of the industry's big names such as Halliburton, Kmart, Xerox, Dynegy, Duke Energy, Computer Associates, Network Associates, Peregrine Systems, Rite Aid and Enterasys.

As part of the SEC drive to bring the crisis under control, chief executives and chief financial officers of 700 listed US companies signed off on their accounts. A legal loophole for irresponsible executives – the possibility of denying knowledge of transgressions by employees – was closed and minds were put to rest.[2]

The New York Stock Exchange (NYSE) and NASDAQ introduced new listing requirements including the need for shareholders' approval for stock option plans, the presence of a majority of independent directors on the corporate board and the obligation to have only independent directors on audit and remuneration committees.

As early as 25 July 2002 the Senate and the House of Representatives approved the Sarbanes-Oxley Bill with overwhelming majorities and just five days later President George W. Bush signed the bill into law. In an effort to set the accountancy industry straight and to strengthen control over CEOs and CFOs, the law included an outright ban on nine non-audit services including the building of financial information systems, legal services and investment banking services. The law also called for the introduction of an independent regulatory board operating under the auspices of the SEC with the power to investigate and fine auditors and, to the dismay of many, the power to set auditing standards. The position of executives was significantly affected by a ban on subsidized personal loans, new rules concerning share dealings and the strengthening of the position of corporate lawyers. There was also a new obligation to certify the accuracy of corporate accounts with draconian penalties in cases of wilful violation. The law applied to all 14,000 American companies with a stock market listing.[3]

## CONFIDENCE RESTORED

The closing of ranks as a reaction to the crisis was entirely predictable. The broad consensus was that the 1990s were unprecedented in terms of corporate and economic success. It was an era of high economic growth and low unemployment combined with low inflation, all fuelled by a private sector that kept increasing productivity, profitability and investment. In the pursuit of shareholder value it was an era of 'virtuous' circles as consumers and employees took their cues from a positively charged atmosphere and continued to borrow and spend, increasing corporate turnover and efficiency and triggering product development and investment.

Although scandals continued to break in the first half of 2002, there was evidence of the economic system's resilience. Corporate profits were up, the stock market was recovering and the housing market remained strong. The third quarter of 2002 was even better. The economy grew by an extraordinary 4 per cent and productivity unexpectedly swelled by the same percentage. The increase in labour costs per unit of production came down significantly, reducing the risk of inflation. The NASDAQ was rallying. The chairman of the Federal Reserve Board referred to the fact that management and information technology investments were working their way through business processes.

Census data published in August 2002 provided an update of the American Dream. Throughout the 1990s standards of living increased markedly with gains in income, housing, education and mobility. Dynamism was everywhere. The south-eastern and western regions of the United States thrived, 13.3 million new Americans arrived from abroad and the percentage of Americans that graduated from high school rose by 82 per cent, while those with at least a bachelor's degree was up by 25 per cent.[4]

In a major address, Bush emphasized the soundness of the vast majority of American companies and expressed his faith in the American people in general and the American consumer in particular. The chairman of the Federal Reserve Board soothed nerves too by telling the nation: 'the effects of recent difficulties will linger for a bit longer, but as they wear off and in the absence of significant adverse shocks, the US economy is poised to resume a pattern of sustainable growth'.[5]

There was therefore every reason to assure the business community and the public at large that the fundamentals of American capitalism were sound and that all necessary measures had been taken to prevent fraud and all other forms of manipulation that threaten the proper functioning of markets.

Although some accused the president of concentrating on quick fixes, the consensus was that the checks and balances built into the US political system guaranteed a proper mix of immediate action and fundamental reform. Some believed this was proof of the fundamental soundness of the system, and unflattering comparisons were made with Japan and Germany, countries that for decades had failed to address structural weaknesses in their economies.

Two years of extraordinary events in the financial world were also notable for the absence of any form of scrutiny into the fundamental reasons for the humiliating exposure to the dark side of American business. The consensus was that the evil had been identified, the rotten apples removed and damage contained. Business ethics and corporate responsibility suddenly appeared high on the agenda but nobody delved deeper, nobody expressed any qualms about the future. The discussion was restricted to the depth and duration of the recession and these came to a natural end when the economy recovered in 2002. The superiority of the American way of doing business was considered self-evident as was its unlimited potential. European companies were perceived to perform poorly and were looked upon with amazement and disdain. Even if one was to admit to certain shortcomings in the American way of doing business, any discussion about its merits as a comprehensive set of goals and tools was considered totally superfluous: there was simply no alternative.

## THE AMERICAN VIEW OF THE WORLD

The resistance to change was partially politically motivated. Those in power in the United States, including the many businessmen in George W. Bush's administration, had a vested interest in continuity. In addition, many regulators and government agencies were implicated in the failure of so many companies, accountancy firms and banks and therefore had every reason to avoid discussions about flaws in the system as a whole. For example the SEC was taken to task by the Senate Governmental Affairs Committee for the 'systematic and catastrophic failure' in its regulation of Enron. The discovery that the SEC had not reviewed any of Enron's annual reports since 1997 was particularly damaging, but nonetheless a diagnosis of the reasons for this failure was not forthcoming.

Another explanation for the closure of ranks is the dominance of the strongly held and widely spread US world-view. This is a comprehensive set of beliefs, assumptions, experiences and aims about the world. This helps to interpret events and is needed to chart a path forward. A world-view acts as a filter for unwanted information – in this case about fundamental flaws in the system – and serves as a guide in the quest for corroborative evidence. If challenged, a world-view is defended, sometimes at considerable cost to the holder.

This prevailing world-view is embraced by the powerful and the successful, by politicians, government officials and corporate executives. It appeals to them and does justice to the fundamental values held by the vast majority of Americans. Its roots are in the Thatcher revolution and the Reagan revolution of the 1980s. Both leaders captured the mood of the time by redefining the role of government and restoring what they saw as the proper relationship between the individual and the state. The government needed to be treated with suspicion; 'the nation' was considered a crucial binding element and patriotism was considered natural. Unilateralism was not only defensible but also justified because it was based on the moral and material capacity to lead.

Great faith was put in an individual's right to choose, in accountability, reward and punishment. Individuals needed to be empowered to fend for themselves as members of the community, shareholders, consumers and employees. Individuals had to be able to reap the benefits of their pursuits for themselves and for their children. Dependence was considered inconsistent with human dignity. Markets were not only always right; they were also fair. Competition and risk taking were the new foundations for economic and social development. The shareholder, the risk taker *pur sang* and the successor to the old-style entrepreneur, became the personification of this view of the world.

Style, the way things were done, also changed fundamentally. Social inhibitions and self-restraint became things of the past. The concept of the common good lost its shine. Competition is about winning: winning by the widest possible margin and total victory. The reward for victory must be now and not in the future. The world is seen as full of diverging interests and conflicts are considered unavoidable. The idea is that conflict mobilizes creativity and generates commitment, both conditions for mutually beneficial and fair agreements. In this brave new world, an agreement without conflict is hardly worth having; opposition is virtuous. It is only fitting that in the pursuit of one's interests everything is allowed that is not legally or contractually excluded. Since everybody is playing according to the same rules, no fight can do lasting damage. History is irrelevant the moment a deal is struck or even when it has failed. Dwelling on the past is a waste of energy and creates unwanted barriers to future, potentially profitable, initiatives by parties that were at odds.

This world-view underpins the choice of political priorities such as tax reduction, stimulation of home ownership, the creation of a society made up of shareholders, reduction of union influence, privatization of state assets, deregulation of markets (including financial and labour markets), the facilitation of international trade and foreign investment and, finally, a foreign policy geared to national interests. These policies left the political opposition in disarray and Reagan and Thatcher were both re-elected by a wide margin. Convictions ran deep, resulting in a fierce drive to export the US world-view and its accompanying political priorities. Enemies were crushed, friends exasperated.

## THE AMERICAN ENTERPRISE MODEL

Corporate America and Britain played a crucial part in this revolution. In the first place, this was because the corporate world benefited directly from new government policies designed to support the economy. Corporate taxes were reduced, labour laws were reviewed to provide companies with more flexibility, and environmental and other constraining legislation was less stringently applied. Privatization and deregulation provided new opportunities.

After a period of initial caution, companies became active supporters of the revolution. They grasped the opportunities brought by the shift in political climate to revamp industrial and government relations. The withdrawal of government, trust in the benign role of markets, reliance on competition and the emphasis on rewards and punishment played very much into the hands of the private sector. Different ways of conducting business converged into one American Enterprise Model with the following characteristics:

1. An emphasis on risk taking, believed to be the essence of entrepreneurship. Corporate employees receive salaries, suppliers and customers operate under the protection of enforceable contracts, the tax code secures the interests of government and bondholders enjoy a fixed income irrespective of corporate performance. The only party that is exposed is the shareholder. Risk taking has to be rewarded and pursuit of shareholder value is therefore the right thing to do.

2. A strong and solo leadership. In the interests of transparency, fast decision making, proper implementation and accountability, the company has to be led by one person: the CEO. To secure their interests, shareholders link CEO and management remuneration to profitability and the creation of shareholder value.

3. Decentralized decision making. This is necessary if companies are to react quickly and adequately to changing customer preferences and the action of competitors. Companies need to be split into divisions, divisions into business units and business units into product/market combinations.

4. Tight financial controls. The decentralization of decision making needs to be accompanied by tight financial control, based on unambiguous targets, at all levels. Management remuneration depends on the achievement of set targets. Transfer prices between units need to reflect market prices so that the profitability of units and their market value can be determined. On this basis, organizationally and operationally

independent units can be bought and sold to optimize the corporate portfolio.

5. Financially oriented head offices. At corporate level, finance and control capacity is adapted to the growing needs of management and the financial community. The need to reduce costs and to avoid overlap with business unit activities leads to fewer commercial and technical experts at head office level, leaving these as lean as possible.

6. A flexible relationship between management and employees. In many companies personnel planning is replaced by internal labour markets.

7. New-style management. Companies select gifted managers that are mentally equipped to concentrate on big leaps forward and to impose radical change. These managers operate on the verge of aggressiveness, no mercy is given and no mercy is asked for; only results count and these have to be tangible. The new rules of the game are easy to understand and everybody is aware that personal sacrifices are inevitable.

Eventually, in the euphoria of corporate success, the company as an institution became a culturally dominant force, the embodiment of US virtues and the benchmark for management standards in public services ranging from health care, education and social security to the military.

The US media sang the praises of the United States, the US economy and the US enterprise culture, with Fox, CNN and *BusinessWeek* the most vocal of all supporters. US business schools made a major contribution. Intentionally or not, they selected students who believed in shareholder value and who were sensitive to financial incentives. Curricula reinforced the need for the 'right' attitudes and equipped students with skills that enabled them to demand and to receive high starting salaries.[6] This drew more applicants which enabled the business schools to raise tuition fees which in turn helped to attract better faculty.

The American Enterprise Model also proved to be a highly successful export product. Increases in foreign trade, investment and international stock trading all played a part. As a result, virtually all listed European companies emulated what were generally considered as best management practices.

A natural desire to return to the glorious 1990s coupled with a well-developed instinct to defend powerful positions and large financial interests and the existence of shared beliefs is an extremely powerful force.

It creates a world in which the triumph of liberal democracy is inevitable. Attempts by British prime minister Tony Blair and other politicians to create a 'Third Way' by propagating the stakeholder – as opposed to the shareholder – economy led to nothing and liberal democracy became indistinguishable from the American world-view and the American Enterprise Model.[7] A world is created in which the then US Treasury secretary Paul O'Neill called business honesty 'the new patriotism'[8] and President Bush presented spending as a national duty. It is a world in which those in charge consider criticism of the US's social inequality, its inefficient use of energy or the fact that it gives economic growth priority over environmental protection as 'anti-American'.

# A SECOND LOOK

For those who want to see it, it is clear that the response of Congress, NYSE, SEC and public prosecutors to the scandals was timid in places. Moreover the impact of their actions suffered as a result of different interpretations of the new legislation, problems in implementing new procedures and the skilful manoeuvring of the parties involved.

The 107th Congress passed the Sarbanes-Oxley Act but could not agree on bankruptcy reform and failed to address the problem of option schemes. It did not pass legislation to protect pensions and did nothing to prevent US companies from avoiding taxes by incorporating offshore.[9]

CEOs and CFOs did indeed give in to the SEC's demands (later included in the Sarbanes-Oxley Act) that they sign declarations to guarantee the quality and truthfulness of their corporate accounts. But *BusinessWeek* pointed out that these declarations were riddled with holes. In particular it drew attention to the fact that no organizational provisions had been made to ensure compliance and bring wrongdoers to justice. *The Economist* commented that terms such as 'wilfully' and 'knowingly' appear in enough places to provide escape routes for clever executives. And most executives covered themselves by forcing their middle managers to sign comparable documents guaranteeing the truthfulness of their submissions to the CEO – setting off a whole trail of declarations throughout the company.[10]

The Sarbanes-Oxley Act called for the foundation of a Public Company Accounting Oversight Board (PCAOB). Operating under the auspices of the SEC, this body was charged with setting up new accounting rules and supervising the accounting industry. The start-up of the new board was mired in difficulties. And despite the fact that the reputation of their sector was in shreds, the remaining four big accountancy firms fought tooth and nail against the setting up of new rules. Everything was done to limit the mandate of the PCAOB.

On top of this, there was much squabbling among SEC commissioners about how they should proceed, and the nomination of the PCAOB's first chairman. For a variety of reasons, including his choice for the PCAOB chairmanship, the position of SEC chairman Harvey Pitt came under pressure. He eventually lost support from the White House and had to resign.

All this took place at the worst possible time for the SEC as it struggled to cope with a rapidly growing workload, an inadequate budget, severe understaffing, low morale and a Wall Street that exerted (with the help of well-placed allies in Congress) enormous influence on the rule-making process.[11]

The White House reneged on earlier commitments and reduced the promised increase in funding for the SEC – which has been assigned to police corporate America – by 27 per cent. This turned out to be the start of a long and dirty fight between the White House and Congress. In the end little was left of the early atmosphere of standing shoulder to shoulder in going after the reckless individuals who had brought the American Enterprise Model into disrepute.

It was only in the spring of 2003 that William Donaldson was confirmed as the new SEC chairman. His priorities were shoring up its management, improving the agency's morale, the hiring of staff and, most important of all, appointing a new PCAOB chairman. No new policies were announced.

Shortly thereafter, William McDonough was lured away from the Federal Reserve Board to become PCAOB chairman.[12] Only then could the PCAOB start its review of interim accounting standards, which over time were adopted, replaced or modified. At last the specific audit standards required by Sarbanes-Oxley could be implemented, and work on improving the efficiency of public companies' internal controls could finally start.[13]

To improve the governance of US companies, a committee was appointed of the great and the mighty. After much internal strife which undermined its authority, the committee made a number of recommendations. Some were obvious: internal and external accountants should come from two different audit firms and the employment of an outside audit firm should be limited to 10 years. Others did not reflect much insight into the way companies operate: employees were to be encouraged to raise ethical issues and to report violations of corporate standards and the CEO and executive board were encouraged to emphasize the importance of ethical conduct. On the central issue of separating the role of company chairman and CEO, the committee was split and the recommendation to separate the two functions was qualified by merely obliging companies to explain their choice for a particular supervisory structure.

Moving on to business analysts and investment bankers, the third and fourth group of professionals under scrutiny (after management and accountants), New York state attorney general Eliot Spitzer found overwhelming evidence of wrongdoing.[14] Analysts paved the way for investment banks' acquisition of new assignments by issuing buy recommendations for the companies targeted by the bankers. His investigation covered 10 top US investment banks.

The first out-of-court settlement was struck between Spitzer and Merrill Lynch and met with serious criticism. Many commentators felt the outcome was in favour of the bank. The bank was quick to note that the settlement 'represents neither evidence nor admission of wrongdoing or liability'. It paid a $100 million fine, and agreed to separate analyst compensation from investment banking fees and to create a committee that would oversee analysts' recommendations.

Only in October 2002, more then a year after the first scandal broke, did the SEC, the National Association of Securities Dealers (NASD) and the NYSE follow Spitzer's lead and agree to coordinate their investigations to protect the investor and to bring matters to a close.[15] The final settlement was announced at the end of April 2003. The banks agreed to a $1.4 billion fine, composed of penalties, restitution to investors and the financing of independent research and investor education. They further committed to an impenetrable firewall between bankers and analysts.[16] It is in itself revealing that the presence of analysts at meetings of bankers and clients was only now explicitly forbidden, that the offices of bankers and analysts have to be physically separate, and that analyst remuneration can no longer be linked to the turnover of investment bankers.

As in the earlier case involving Merrill Lynch, the banks were adamant that this payment did not reflect admission of any wrongdoing and only two individuals agreed to leave the industry as part of separate settlements.

Many argued that the agreement would do nothing to protect the small investor. Large investors would continue to buy their own research. High-quality, and therefore expensive, reports would continue to be made available to clients who brought a minimum amount of business to a bank. It is difficult to see how the average discrepancy (entrenched over decades) of

40 per cent between analysts' forecasts of corporate earnings versus actual reported earnings could be improved.

Then there is JPMorgan Chase and Citigroup who, according to the SEC and the New York district attorney, actively helped Enron to lie to investors. They assisted Enron in dressing up loans as liabilities related to trading activities and even found ways to account for the borrowing of money as cash flow. In one transaction, buying and selling Treasury bills with borrowed money boosted operating cash flow by $500 million. Some observers find it puzzling that the SEC settled for an administrative procedure against Citigroup which ended up with a modest fine of $126.5 million.

The overall impression is that CEOs (with the possible exception of those who were involved in criminal activities), accountants, analysts and bankers were only slightly affected in the aftermath of the greatest corporate and banking scandals of the century.

Remarkably, CEO incomes continued to go up. In 2002, a recession year with corporate earnings and stock prices way down and workers laid off in record numbers, some of the unattractive option schemes disappeared but, according to a survey of 200 large companies, the median amount of direct compensation, cash, shares and prerequisites increased by 17 per cent.[17]

For most accountants, it was back to business as usual. The process of divesting non-accountancy activities is running smoothly. Most transactions concern recent acquisitions that were never organizationally integrated with the accountancy practice and can as a result be spun off with ease. Day-to-day activities are not affected. In a study of 1,240 US companies, the Investor Responsibility Research Center in Washington found that only nine companies changed auditor in 2001 and only six did so during the first half of 2002. Even when Arthur Andersen was dissolved, its chartered accountants had no problem in finding their way into the four remaining major accountancy firms.

As the proponents of the American Enterprise Model would stress, the best proof that corporate America has moved beyond the incidents of 2001 and 2002 is provided by the stock markets. By the end of March 2003, stocks in Standard & Poor's 500 stock index were trading at a price equal to about 30 times their earnings per share over the previous year. At the end of the 1990–91 recession, that multiple was 18. Individual investors, and with them speculation fever, have returned to the stock markets. Institutional investors were more optimistic than ever. And finally, research cannot discern any impact on the stock price of companies that failed to provide affirmation of their accounts as required by the Sarbanes-Oxley Act.[18]

# WRAPPING UP

Power coupled with an appealing ideology and large financial interests constitutes an insurmountable barrier to change. Actions that hurt are avoided. In the words of Jim Peterson, columnist of the *Herald Tribune*: 'The participants [in the system] are inextricably intertwined with each other: companies, accountants, analysts, advisors, investors and their lawyers. Although in their own self interest none are saying so, no adjustments of the expectations and the behaviour of any of them can be successfully imposed that does not address and modify them all.'[19]

Prophetic words in light of the increasing amount of wrongdoing that emerged in the years after the initial flurry of scandals. Hardly any area remained untouched: the NYSE, mutual funds, the pharmaceutical industry and the mortgage sector were all found to be misbehaving.

The memory of the 1990s with its unprecedented progress lingers on and the concept of sustainable growth based on perpetual productivity improvement is alive and well. Once the rotten apples had been removed, it was business as usual and there was no reason why the good old days could not return.

Sophisticated companies strive to enhance their credibility by engaging in discussions about business ethics, corporate responsibility, stricter regulations and adjustment of governance. But at the end of the day, nothing changes. The American Enterprise Model can be refined and smoothed at the edges, but all this serves only to protect its core. Even if major companies or other participants in the system wanted to break away, there is no escape.

The American Enterprise Model will increasingly become a straitjacket and there is a price to be paid for overconfidence. The cost of inflexibility becomes apparent when the performance of the model is assessed and found wanting, when the limitations of doing more of the same become visible and when unintended consequences and unaccounted costs are revealed. These are the subjects of the next three chapters. The final two chapters will be devoted to an alternative approach.

In Europe, history and cultural diversity have produced an abundance of alternative and successful enterprise models. As a result, Europe has a repertoire of responses available to counter commercial threats and to exploit a variety of opportunities. One such advanced and competitive model, geared to the needs of large companies, will be presented.

# 2

# The 1990s were not what they seemed

US politicians, civil servants, entrepreneurs and bankers – all those who shape the US economy – look back on the 1990s with pride. They want everybody to know that they presided over an economic miracle. US economic growth hovered around 4 per cent while inflation remained under control, which in turn enabled the Federal Reserve Bank to keep interest rates low. Employment surged and, in the course of 2000, unemployment fell to 4 per cent. For the first time, the whole American population participated in what turned out to be the longest economic expansion in history. Income distribution improved and poverty was rolled back. The private sector flourished, the level of investment was high and profitability soared. Booming stock markets reflected improvements in the structure of the US economy. American pride was ignited; Americans walked tall. A vibrant US economy outperformed its European and Japanese counterparts by a wide margin. Everything pointed to the continuation of rapid growth. A large increase in direct European investment in the United States and in US companies was convincing proof of the superiority of the American Enterprise Model.

The considerable progress of the United States in so many fields was to a large extent attributed to the capacity of US companies to achieve and sustain remarkable increases in productivity. The consensus was that continuous improvements in management and major investments in information and communication technology (ICT) had put productivity growth at a structurally higher level. Until the mid-1990s productivity had grown on average by 1.5 per cent per year. In 2000 productivity growth had risen to 3.4 per cent. The acceleration of the growth rate to 4.3 per cent during the final quarter of 2000 supported the belief that rates of between 3 and 4 per cent were here to stay and that the new economy, despite the collapse of the dot.com sector and the prolonged stock market downturn, had well and truly arrived.

The 1990s acquired mythical proportions. The shallow recession of 2001 was seen as an unfortunate interlude and in quarter after quarter the pundits announced that a recovery was just around the corner. Everything and everybody was mobilized to return to the growth paths of the previous decade. The recipes of the 1990s were followed with even more vigour than before. The federal government lowered taxes twice and by doing so injected another $117 billion and $200 billion into the US economy in 2003 and 2004. The Federal Reserve Bank reduced interest rates by an incredible 5.5 per cent to 1 per cent. Companies went further and faster down the dual road of shedding staff and outsourcing activities. It was hardly a surprise that the combination of these unprecedented measures produced a recovery from 2002 onwards.

However, look beyond the headline figures and a fundamentally different picture emerges. The 1990s were not what they seemed, and the security, comfort and guidance many decision makers derive up to this day from this era are ill founded.

The 1990s were not as glorious as many believe in at least four respects. The US economy performed less well than headline figures suggested at the time, both historically and in comparison with Europe. Contrary to popular belief American companies fared poorly, and far worse than their European counterparts. By the end of the 1990s it became clear that progress had carried a price in the form of greatly enhanced risk throughout the economy. Finally, it became apparent that shareholders too had paid dearly for management attempts to improve their return on investment.

# THE US ECONOMY PERFORMED POORLY

The real picture starts unfolding if changes in the key US macroeconomic indicators are scrutinized: economic production, individual wealth (and the distribution thereof), inflation, job creation and unemployment.

## Economic production

In a study comparing the performance of economies in the United States and the euro countries during the critical 1996–2001 period, the Deutsche Bundesbank estimated that the average annual growth of real gross domestic product (GDP) was 3.6 and 2.4 per cent respectively (GDP is the grand total of personal consumption, gross private domestic investment, net exports, and government purchases). This is a significant difference but not as large as US rhetoric suggests. Of this 1.2 per cent gap, half can be explained by differences in the growth rates of the two populations. The US population grew annually by 1 per cent as a result of a high birth rate and a sizeable influx of immigrants, compared to a 0.25 per cent growth rate in the euro area.

The calculation of economic growth in the US was further influenced by the application of the so-called hedonic method in estimating inflation. Widely used in the United States but rarely in Europe, this method takes the ongoing quality improvement of durable goods such as cars, TVs and PCs into account and this leads to lower estimates of inflation and hence higher estimates of real GDP. The Bundesbank estimated that annual economic output in Germany would have been almost 0.25 per cent higher between 1996 and 1999 if the hedonic method had been used. Comparable conclusions can be drawn for other European economies.[1]

Another difference between the United States and Europe is the way company spending on software is entered onto the national accounts. In the United States, acquisition of software is seen as an investment. This is a contribution to capital formation, one of the components of GDP. Put differently, US companies put software on the balance sheet and depreciate the investment over a number of years. European companies book these expenses as cost that does not show up in GDP numbers. According to a study by INSEE (France's Institut National de la Statistique et des Etudes Economiques) this difference explains another 0.3 per cent in the growth rates in the two areas. Again, similar conclusions can be drawn for other European countries.[2]

## Individual wealth

Focusing on individual prosperity, NDP (net domestic product) is the appropriate basis for comparison. 'Net' refers to the net additions to the capital stock: total gross domestic investment minus an allowance for depreciation. In the late 1990s US companies had to depreciate far more ICT investments (in addition to software, investment in computers and data transmission capacity) than their European counterparts. This again puts the European economic performance in a more favourable light.

If NDP per capita is compared, it turns out that between 1996 and 2001 the average American became wealthier at a rate of 2.2 per cent per year, compared to 1.9 per cent for the average inhabitant in the euro area. This difference is smaller than many assume and is even smaller if the effect of the application of the hedonic method of inflation calculation on the US NDP number is taken into account.

The performance of the US economy is cast in an even less flattering light when mean values, rather than average income and wealth, are taken into account. It turns out that the mean income (corrected for inflation) rose by just 5 per cent over the whole 1989 to 1998 period. Net wealth – that is cash, stocks and real estate minus debt – increased by no more than 4 per cent.[3]

The way in which income and wealth is distributed in the US and Europe is of course very different. Income and wealth distribution in the US has always been skewed and the perception that, unlike during previous periods of economic upturn, the 1990s contributed to a more even distribution of income and wealth is wrong. Economic disparity in 2000 was greater than ever. In that year, the wealthiest 1 per cent earned an average $862,700 after tax, three times more than in 1979 and up 37 per cent from 1997. The same group also benefited from tax reductions and rapid increases in the value of real estate and shares. By 2000 the richest 1 per cent of Americans owned more than the poorest 40 per cent, twice as much as in 1979.[4]

Poverty is another measure of individual wealth and it is clear that poverty in the US came down during the second half of the 1990s. The incomes of ethnic minorities grew by 16 per cent for African-American families and 25 per cent for Hispanic households while white families saw an increase of 11 per cent. So poverty among black and Hispanic communities fell by 7.9 per cent and 1 per cent respectively. However it is a sobering thought that despite this progress and a period of substantial economic growth, the overall poverty rate in 2000 was 13 per cent of the total US population, comparable with the late 1960s. Obviously, with a growing population, the absolute number of poor Americans increased considerably over the period.[5] Part of the explanation is that many of the jobs that were created at the low end of the labour market did not pay enough to rise above the poverty threshold.

How much of the progress during the 1990s was structural remains to be seen. Once the economy stopped growing in 2000, unemployment among the poor increased rapidly. Even with a slight increase in unemployment from 4 per cent in 2000 to 4.8 per cent in 2001, people in all income groups lost out except the wealthiest 20 per cent of the population.

## Inflation

Looking at the history of inflation in the US, it is clear that the 1990s were much better than the 1980s. In 1991, the Consumer Price Index (CPI) dropped, on an annual basis, from more than 6 per cent to 3 per cent as a result of a sharp economic downturn and this level was maintained until 1997 when it fell to 1.6 per cent. However, by the end of the decade, inflation had accelerated. It rose from 1.6 per cent in 1998 to 3.4 per cent in 2000. Looking at the components of the CPI, the picture is more blurred than is generally assumed. By the end of 2000, inflation in the services sector had risen to 4.5 per cent (year on year). The Non-Durables Index reached 7 per cent, after hitting a high of 12 per cent towards the end of 1999. A decrease in the prices for durables such as washing machines, PCs and cars saved the day. In 1997 and 1998 the Durables Index was negative to the tune of 1.5 per cent, only rising to plus 0.5 per cent by the end of 2000. These numbers show that, unlike in the glowing reviews of the 1990s, indigenously produced inflation was considerable. It was only by importing an increasing quantity of ever cheaper durables that prices were kept in check.

The growth of the Producer Price Index (PPI), a leading indicator of the CPI, was even more pronounced and rose from minus 3.2 per cent in 1998 to 6.6 per cent in 2000.[6] This acceleration took place despite the above-average growth in productivity, low energy prices and a temporary pause in the perpetual increase in the cost of medical care. It took the recession in 2001 to break these inflationary trends.

The strong dollar played a pivotal role in keeping import prices low throughout the period. The favourable exchange rate was partly supported by a perception of low US inflation which, as the figures presented above demonstrate, was not supported by the facts.

## Employment

Another feature of the 1990s, etched on the minds of many, was the creation of a large number of jobs. In 1992, US unemployment stood at 7.6 per cent, falling to 4.1 per cent eight years later.[7]

This chapter of the US success story needs to be rewritten for at least three reasons. Firstly, it has to be noted that throughout the 1990s millions of people dropped out of the labour market. Surveys show that at the height of the boom, in 2000, 11 per cent of all men between the ages of 18 and 54 had no work. This finding was supported by the resurfacing of many 'missing' workers as disability payment claimants. The number of people receiving disability pay rose from 3 million in 1990 to 5 million in 2000.[8] Obviously, such a rise cannot be explained by deterioration in the health of the average American.

Secondly, in interpreting the official unemployment statistics, the large – and rising – number of Americans in prison was ignored. The total number of inmates rose from 1.1 million in 1990 to 2 million in 2000,[9] which represented approximately 0.6 per cent of the labour force. This shrank the ranks of the unemployed who are well represented among convicts, and created artificial vacancies. Given the high risk of unemployment after release from prison, US unemployment will be adversely affected again when these inmates are released. The situation in Europe is spectacularly better both in terms of absolute numbers and in terms of the growth rate of the prison population.[10]

Thirdly, while glorifying the US job machine, most policy makers remained oblivious to the fact that by 1997 employment in the United States and in the euro area grew at the same rate. And from 2000, the euro area actually outperformed the United States. In the five years to the end of 2002, US employment increased by an average of 0.8 per cent per annum, compared to 1.4 per cent in the euro countries.[11]

## On reflection

The conclusion is that, in macroeconomic terms, both the US and the eurozone countries (taken as a single unit) progressed at the same rate during the 1990s. The same holds for the income and wealth of the average individual on both sides of the Atlantic although the gap between rich and poor is greater in the United States.

All this runs counter to the perception of most political and business leaders. It is definitely at odds with the economic victory US politicians and businessmen declared on behalf of their nation.

These finding are remarkable in light of the competitive advantages the United States enjoyed throughout the 1990s: large, homogeneous and well-functioning markets, a structurally higher level of spending on research and development, availability of an abundance of venture capital, streamlined procedures for starting businesses and liberal bankruptcy laws.

Meanwhile, Europe did not yet have a common currency and European markets for labour, insurance, financial services and energy were not liberalized. On top of this, European companies had no choice but to struggle with 11 languages, significantly different business practices and 15 legal and regulatory systems. Full integration of financial markets alone would have added 0.7 per cent per annum to Europe's GDP.[12]

# US CORPORATE RESULTS WERE DISMAL

This section scrutinizes the performance of the large American companies, measuring them against their own standards of success: productivity growth, profit and preparation for the future in the form of high-yielding investments.

## Productivity growth

The very heavy emphasis on productivity figures is not without danger because measurement has become increasingly difficult in modern economies which mostly produce services. Stephen Roach, chief economist of Morgan Stanley, points to the technical difficulties in determining the productivity of the 42 million American 'knowledge workers', among them managers, advisors and specialists with a variety of pedigrees who operate alone or in very small companies. He also draws attention to the blurring of the line between work and leisure which is driven by rapidly expanding ICT facilities. He attributes part of the productivity growth that has been measured to an increase in the number of unregistered hours.[13]

Ignoring these warnings, American politicians, bankers and managers keep pushing productivity as the most important economic parameter. In a complicated world, this single figure is used to reflect the dynamism of the American economy (unequivocally).

However, given that productivity statistics are used as a vital indicator for success, it is important to realize that here too perception and reality diverge. To start with, what many people do not realize is that US productivity growth has been lagging behind that of Europe for decades. This has changed since 1995 but it is not true that European productivity growth was running behind to any significant degree.

During the second part of the decade, politicians, regulators, business leaders and investors became accustomed to annual increases in productivity of 4 per cent and started to assume that this was sustainable.

Then, early in 2001, three reports were published that started to shed a different light on productivity growth in the US economy. Firstly, the US Bureau of Labor Statistics revised its 1999/2000 growth rate from 3.4 to 2.6 per cent.[14] Secondly, Goldman Sachs estimated the structural annual increase of productivity (ie without the effects of the business cycle) at 2.25 per cent, only 0.75 per cent higher than the long-term historic trend.[15] But the most disconcerting evidence was presented in a McKinsey report on productivity growth per economic sector.[16]

According to McKinsey, nearly all post-1995 productivity growth (from a baseline of 1 per cent annual growth between 1987 and 1995) can be attributed to just six sectors: retail, wholesale, securities, telecoms, semiconductors and computer manufacturing. In a number of other economic sectors productivity deteriorated. Of the total 1.33 per cent extra productivity growth between 1995 and 1999, 0.96 per cent was achieved in retail, wholesale and securities, sectors in which higher consumer spending and increased sharetrading helped to improve efficiency. Since consumer spending cannot rise forever and the stock market crash reduced turnover, sustainability of productivity growth in these sectors is questionable. The net contribution of the other three sectors, representing 70 per cent of the US economy, turns out to have been nil. In terms of ICT (presumed to be the bedrock of improvements in productivity), the study points to the introduction of advanced technological applications in the securities industry but most of the developments in inventory control and material handling in the retail and wholesale sectors were less exciting. Three case studies (hotels, retail banking and telecommunications) revealed that substantial investment in ICT is no guarantee for productivity improvement.

Robert Gordon of the National Bureau of Economic Research came to an even more pessimistic analysis. He showed that the extra productivity improvement of 1.35 per cent during the late 1990s over and above the historic long-term trend had two causes. Economic growth, the impact of higher production and sales volumes, contributed 0.54 per cent. Only the remaining 0.81 per cent was structural in nature. Subsequently he presented evidence that the latter improvement was due to higher multi-factor productivity growth in the production of computers, peripherals, telecommunication equipment and the like. This is the improvement in productivity that results from intangibles such as better management, better integration of ICT and more training rather than the installation of new plant and equipment. In looking beyond this sector Gordon concluded: 'There is no revival of productivity growth in the 88 per cent of the private economy lying outside of durables; in fact when the contribution of massive investment in computers in the non durable economy is subtracted, multi-factor growth outside of durables has actually decelerated.'[17]

In comparing the growth of American productivity with developments in Europe, it should be noted that the definition of productivity used in US statistics boosts reported growth rates to the maximum extent possible. US policy makers concentrate on output per man-hour in all non-farming sectors. Many Europeans use GDP per worker. This covers the whole economy – including the public sector where it is notoriously difficult to improve productivity – and is therefore bound to show lower growth. Comparing like with like (GDP per man-hour) results in average growth of 2.2 per cent in the United States versus 1.4 per cent in the euro area, a much smaller gap than is generally assumed. This narrows further if differences in the US and EU calculation of GDP (outlined above) are taken into account.[18]

Credit Suisse First Boston (CSFB) corrected two of these anomalies by taking NDP per hour worked as a basis for comparison. Looking at the period from 1996 to 2001, CSFB maintains that the United States holds a modest advantage over the euro area: an average per year of 1.8 per cent versus 1.5 per cent.[19]

This difference has to be seen in light of the rapid increase in part-time work in Europe; although a welcome sign in terms of greater labour market flexibility, this had a negative impact on output per worker. In addition, European productivity figures were negatively influenced by the absorption of the former DDR into the German economy. At the beginning of the 1990s, the West German economy had closed the productivity gap with the United States to a modest 5 per cent. At the end of the decade this had widened to 15 per cent.[20]

## Profitability

Throughout the 1970s and the 1980s the profitability of US non-financial companies, as expressed as a percentage of GDP, remained fairly constant and fluctuated around 10 per cent. This came down substantially in the early 1990s but rose to 12.5 per cent in 1997. From that point, the share of profits in the economy dwindled to approximately 7.5 per cent in late 1999.[21]

Taking the most-favoured measure of corporate profitability, profit per share, the picture is less grim but still very different from what many want to believe. Looking at the period from 1997 to 2000, years during which the US economy grew on average by more than 4 per cent per year, the average reported profit per share of companies in the Standard; & Poors (S&P) 500 index remained constant at $38 per share.[22] This was exactly the time that the ICT breakthroughs from earlier in the period should have produced high-margin products and thus higher profitability. Lack of progress is equally remarkable in light of the major share-purchasing programmes offered by a considerable number of companies, a trend that should have affected this parameter positively.

Another angle was adopted in a study by UBS Warburg but produced comparable conclusions. The bank used operational profit as a better measure to assess corporate performance than overall profitability. It took the period between1988 and 2000 (two economic peak years to circumvent the effects of the business cycle on profitability) and calculated that the profits of companies in the S&P 500 index grew by an annual 9.1 per cent. This percentage proved equal to the annual average profitability growth between 1960 and 2000. The conclusion that the 1990s were not necessarily more successful than other decades rings very different from the usual exuberant pronouncements.

In comparing corporate profitability in the United States and the euro area on the basis of percentage share of the GDP, the surprising but inescapable conclusion is that the US was lagging throughout the 1990s. It is even more remarkable that the gap with Europe widened during the last three years of the decade.

All studies cited point to mediocre performances by US companies in spite of the highly favourable economic circumstances at the time. Furthermore, in light of everything that has come to the surface in recent years the profitability statistics of the 1990s need to be revised downwards in a very substantial way.

First there was the purge in the summer of 2002 when the SEC cordially invited corporate America to come clean on deviations from the accounting rules and to revise their corporate accounts. Some adjustments of profitability were sizeable, some modest, but all negative.

Profitability in the 1990s was also flattered by excluding the costs of elaborate option schemes maintained by virtually all US companies. The vast majority of US companies opted for the possibility, available throughout the 1990s, of accounting for the cost of option schemes in a footnote in their annual reports. The London-based research bureau Smithers & Co calculated that, if the 500 US companies in the S&P index had been obliged to deduct the total costs of their option schemes from their pre-tax profits, results for 1998, 1999 and 2000 would have been 13, 14 and 24 per cent lower.[23] These numbers are modest in comparison to the outcome of analyses by Dresdner Kleinwort Wasserstein. This bank estimated that the inclusion of the costs of option schemes would require a downward revision of reported profitability in 2001 to the tune of 30 per cent for all companies – and 75 per cent for technology companies. The technology sector is a special case where options were granted in such quantities and allowed to be exercised at such low levels that, for example in the case of Microsoft, reported profitability of $9.4 billion in 2000 would have to be adjusted to just $2.1 billion.

The growing cost of option schemes was a major problem for US companies only. In 2000, the average S&P 500 CEO earned more than $6 million, of which two-thirds consisted of variable pay. This level of remuneration was far higher than in Europe and the package was much more options-based.[24] Dresdner Kleinwort Wasserstein calculated that, for 2001, the profitability of European companies would have to be reduced by only 10 per cent, or 20 per cent for technology companies. This points to an even wider gap in the performance of American and European companies.

Further downward revision of the profitability of US firms comes from the substantial number of S&P 500 companies that reported pension fund income on their financial statements. This number increased from 70 in 1997 to 155 in 2000. CSFB estimates that 12 per cent of the earnings growth registered by those companies in 2000 came from pension income.[25]

Throughout the latter part of the 1990s a number of companies succumbed to the temptation of assuming unrealistically high returns on investment by their pension funds. As a result they reduced employer contributions and thereby overstated corporate profitability by a substantial margin. For General Electric and Boeing the day of reckoning came in the fourth quarter of 2002. General Electric had to announce that it projected a shortfall in its pension fund that could reach $23 billion and Boeing had to take a $4 billion charge against its fourth-quarter results to plug holes in its pension fund. The total impact of these rosy projections on profitability throughout the 1990s is estimated at 10 to 15 per cent.

The US Treasury estimates that the total underfunding of pensions by the S&P 500 firms came to $300 billion, which amounts to an impressive drain on future profitability. This liability may yet be dwarfed by corporate promises to provide retirees with the same health benefits they had while working. These obligations are 'unfunded', unregulated and unpredictable.

Finally, historic profitability will have to be adjusted downwards as a result of shareholder lawsuits that are now making their way through the courts. In the autumn of 2002, Stanford Law School estimated that 724 class actions awaited trial, with an unknown number of further actions in the pipeline.[26] These include claims against fraudulent companies such as Enron, Dynegy and Global Crossing, but also reputable firms such as Bank of America, Bristol-Myers and Intel.[27] There are also specialized law firms that design tailor-made approaches. Instead of class actions, they assist pension funds and other big investors that have the largest axes to grind and have the resources to follow through to the very end. Instead of shareholders, they concentrate on bondholders. And instead of the federal courts they bring their cases to the state courts. They sue blue-chip banks such as Citigroup, JPMorgan Chase, Lehman Brothers, CSFB, Goldman Sachs and others, not for fraud – which is difficult to prove – but for issuing misleading statements in underwriting, for example, bond issues.[28] The impact on profitability is significant. Pension funds like CalPERS for example accused JPMorgan Chase and Citigroup, the underwriters of WorldCom's last $11 billion bond issue, of lack of proper due diligence, eventually forcing the banks to take provisions of billions of dollars.

And finally, nobody will ever know how much damage was done to corporate profitability by outright criminal offences.

## Preparing for the future

Yet another supposed achievement of US companies during the 1990s was their high level of investment. Investment is, of course, the foundation of future profitability. As a percentage of GDP, US companies' investments rose from approximately 12 per cent in 1991 to 18 per cent in 2001. However, if these numbers are examined, it becomes apparent that the entire increase is accounted for by expansion in a limited number of sectors: information technology hardware, telecommunications, cable companies, software and the media. These were all the recipients of one of the most grotesque misallocations of funds in economic history. Capacity was increased to cope with exponential growth that never came. The pace of software development was such that poor quality and insufficient security are now major factors. The US's National Institute of Standards and Technology estimates that software errors cause approximately $60 billion damage to the US economy each year and computer crime remains a fast-rising phenomenon.

Investment in ICT was rarely in support of truly new business ideas. Obvious uses of the internet to sell to consumers and to organize tenders and auctions were very slow getting off the ground. Success was more dependent on old-fashioned warehousing and logistics than dazzling new software. The big idea of the late 1990s, combining the provision of internet facilities and the production of 'content', proved to be badly conceived. For example, AOL's acquisition of Time Warner and Telefonica's takeover of Endemol failed very quickly.

In addition to the creation of overcapacity, and the failure of new business concepts, goodwill payments (the difference between the book value of an acquired company and the actual price that was paid) became totally detached from commercial reality. Moreover many huge commercial and service departments that were established in the 1990s had to be abolished within two to four years.

All in all, the performance of US managers as investors can be gauged by looking at the write-offs that had to be taken into account for their failed projects. Between 1995 and 2001, the real depreciation ratio (the ratio of real macroeconomic depreciation to real GDP) in the United States went up by 20 per cent compared to 6 per cent in the euro area. And the end is not yet in sight as many companies can only survive if recent acquisitions can be sold – which will produce further write-offs. At one point, AOL Time Warner, Vivendi Universal, Walt Disney and Bertelsmann were all trying to sell units in a very weak market, a direct consequence of decisions taken during the 1990s.

## The broad picture

In summary, the performance of the US economy and of US companies during the 1990s – measured against their own standards – falls far short of the headline figures that shaped perceptions and helped to build seemingly unassailable reputations.

European politicians trying to whip up support for restructuring their economies by pointing at American performance should think twice. The EU's Lisbon strategy has to be cast in a different light.

The conclusions of Robert Gordon amount to a serious indictment of the majority of US managers and the information technology consultants they employed. Riding the crest of a technological wave, companies bought revolutionary new information and communication equipment but apparently destroyed value in the process of integrating this new equipment in their organizations.

# A LEGACY OF VULNERABILITIES

The 1990s should also be judged in light of the inheritance they passed on. It turns out that a number of developments during this period severely undermined the conditions required for corporate development and economic growth.

## Triple deficits and more

During the 1990s, the US trade deficit remained stubbornly high and a source of uncertainty. More importantly, the way the deficit was financed changed fundamentally during these years. During the early part of the decade, the deficit was largely financed by the sale of government bonds, solid investments that drew investors from all over the world. They could rely on the creditworthiness of the US government and were protected against the ups and downs of the US economy. The only risk was a possible decline of the dollar but there was no direct exposure to the performance of the US private sector.

By 2000 all this had changed. That year, the trade deficit of the US economy amounted to $420 billion or 4 per cent of GDP. The largest part of this, $239 billion, was financed by foreign purchases of long-term company bonds. The second-largest source of finance was direct foreign investment. Foreign companies invested $129 billion more in the United States than US companies abroad that year. The third largest, the net acquisition by foreigners of US shares, amounted to $88 billion.[29] All these investments were based on confidence in the future viability and profitability of corporate

America. Any change of perception, or genuine deterioration of performance could lead to a withdrawal of funds.

Almost from the start of the first George W. Bush administration, the federal deficit of the early 1990s returned with a vengeance. Government revenues decreased. The 1990s had already seen a persistent decline of corporate tax payments as tax management became increasingly sophisticated. At the outset of the recession, profits – and therefore tax payments – came down further. The loss of confidence in the US economy had to be countered.

The subsequent two rounds of tax reductions, designed to kick-start the economy, greatly increased the deficit. At the same time, US government expenditure grew rapidly as a result of the war in Iraq and the cost of homeland security, but also due to the more generous funding of social programmes. In less than three years the government went from a budget surplus of 2 per cent of GDP to a deficit of 4 per cent.

As a consequence, the US would have to rely more on short term financing. This is exactly what happened from 2002 onwards. As a result of a fall in takeovers of US companies by foreign firms and a sharp decline in interest for US shares, long-term financing of the deficit was cut in half, greatly increasing the vulnerability of the US economy.

The result in 2003, with interest rates still low, was a decline in the value of the dollar and, more importantly, uncertainty regarding its future value. The supposed benefit, improving the position of American companies on world markets in order to reduce the larger-than-ever trade deficit (to the tune of $60 billion per month in the course of 2004), did not materialize and this added greatly to the uneasiness of the financial markets.

The void was filled by the central banks of China, South Korea and Japan. They invested heavily in US bonds to protect the favourable exchange rates of their own currencies which were the basis for their fast-growing exports to the United States. As a result, the United States became exposed to both commercially and politically inspired changes of policy in those countries.

The situation is much riskier now than in the early 1990s, since trust in the US economy has become synonymous with continued growth in consumer spending, while the Bush administration and the Federal Reserve are running out of options to prop up consumer demand. See also Chapter 3.

Moreover, it is very difficult to justify that more than two years into the recovery the US interest rates are still negative, and that such lax monetary policy is being exported to the euro zone and to East Asia. It is being exported to Europe because the decrease of the value of the dollar forces the ECB to keep interest rates for the euro zone lower than they otherwise would have been, and to East Asia because the central banks in the area print local money to finance the purchasing of US Treasury bonds. As a result in 2004 the global supply of dollars rose by an amazing 25 per cent. Inflation remained tame but there are now three bubbles that threaten the world economy: house prices in certain areas in the United States, in the UK and countries such as Spain; bonds, as a result of unusually low long-term interest rates; and stocks despite big jumps in corporate profits.

A final, new and negative feature of economic life is the deterioration of the finances of most of the 50 states – in fact the third deficit. Their administrations often preside over economies that dwarf those of many European nations. They are trapped by lower tax income, the need and often the legal obligation to balance their budgets, and the political death of officials who suggest raising taxes. The states are a new source of instability and risk, with California as the unenviable frontrunner.[30]

## Corporate debt

Between 1995 and 2001, the much-flaunted American entrepreneurial spirit did not permeate everywhere. Non-financial corporations, apparently short of investment opportunities in the midst of an economic boom, acted in the name of shareholder interest and supported their stock price by stock buy-backs to the tune of $870 billion. This, in combination with a borrowing spree of $2.1 trillion (in part to finance the stock buy-backs), led to an increase of corporate debt from 39 per cent of GDP in 1995 to 47 per cent in 2001.[31] The resilience of American companies suffered as a result. The capacity of large companies (that is to say those that are still in business) to service their debt had not been eroded and their solvency appeared reasonably satisfactory, but all of this was courtesy of the aggressive monetary policy of the Federal Reserve Bank that lowered the official interest rates from 6.5 per cent to a new historic low of 1 per cent with unprecedented speed.[32]

With economic recovery under way since 2002, the Federal Reserve Bank now has to proceed with extreme caution so as not to spoil the party, and has been preparing markets carefully for very modest interest rate increases. The fact that the official rate in 2004 was still negative in real terms cannot be seen as a sign of good health.

Many companies will prove to be vulnerable when at some point in the future interest rates will have to rise more quickly to finance the triple deficit, prevent inflation or finance investment increases.

It is significant that the shallow recession of 2001 caused the failure of many companies. In 2001, companies with total assets of more than $260 billion filed for bankruptcy protection. During the first eight months of 2002 the pace of filings accelerated to an accumulated total of $250 billion of asset value. With bankruptcies acting as the tip of the iceberg, it has to be assumed that many companies were hovering on the brink of financial collapse.

Another indication that the American private sector is not the epitome of strength it is perceived to be is the rapid deterioration in the quality of debt. A study by the Federal Reserve Bank, the Federal Deposit Insurance Corporation and the Office of Comptroller of the Currency concluded in 2002 that about 13 per cent of the $1.9 trillion in bank loans and credit lines might not be paid back. This is the highest level since 1992. Risky loans rose to $236 billion in June 2002 from $193 billion a year earlier, a 9 per cent increase.

Finally, it must be noted that many invoices from the 1990s remain outstanding. Corporate obligations to pension funds have been mentioned.[33] Many US executives will at some point call in their deferred remuneration. But these shortfalls might be small compared to corporate commitments to pensioners' healthcare insurance. No reserves have been allocated, supervision to ensure that the necessary steps are taken is lacking, and the size of the damage to future profits is simply unknown.[34]

## New financial products

Another product of the 1990s was the tremendous growth in the trade of over-the-counter derivatives. These instruments were increasingly used to hedge foreign exchange, interest rates and credit risks, but the trade in derivatives has now taken on a life of its own, independent of transactions in the real economy. To this day, these markets are largely unregulated although the potential consequences of a default are considerable. This became clear as early as 1990 when Drexel Burnham Lambert, an important trader in derivatives, went bankrupt. The US Treasury, the Federal Reserve Bank and the largest commercial banks in the country had to work closely together, putting up billions of dollars in loans to prevent other banks from collapsing. Ten years later the risks were far greater. According to Morgan Stanley, the runaway growth of credit derivatives, from $50 billion in 1998 to an estimated $2.4 trillion in 2002, was of particular concern.[35] In its 72nd annual report, the Bank for International Settlements drew attention to dealer-specific risk, citing a considerable reduction of credit ratings and referring to ongoing industry consolidation. It pointed out that in 2001 in the United States only three banks held 89 per cent of the outstanding stock of foreign exchange derivative contracts. The same vulnerability existed in the market for interest derivatives, again with three banks accounting for most of the total notional amount outstanding. JPMorgan Chase seemed particularly vulnerable. In the nine months to 30 June 2001 the bank had to write off $3.3 billion in bad loans and it was estimated that the bank nurtured a derivatives portfolio of $25 trillion.[36]

The trade in these financial products – which enable parties to leverage their investment without any limit but are not fully understood by most managers or even financial experts – remained completely unregulated. The *International Herald Tribune* (*IHT*) warned that the collapse of one or two banks could cause a cascade, pulling down many others. Stopping such a chain reaction would be beyond the means of the Federal Reserve Bank and the remaining banks. The result would be a full-scale crisis involving the whole financial system. The newspaper took the Bush administration to task for not taking action. In 1998, Wall Street banks evaded legislation by imposing stricter internal standards for risk management. Since then, the political will to take on the bank lobby has been lacking. The *IHT* asserted that the government did not want to face the bureaucratic nightmare that would result from involving the Federal Reserve Bank, the Treasury, the SEC and the Commodity Futures Trading Commission.

With the stock markets moving sideways, the search for above-average returns by all investors, from speculators to highly respected pension funds, guarantees the unabated and accelerated growth of hedge funds.

In another development, the 1990s witnessed a very strong growth of so-called syndicates. Commercial banks reduced their exposure (ie the risk that their customers would default on their loans) by selling off corporate and consumer debt, such as mortgages, to smaller banks, insurers and mutual funds. This created a $9 trillion so-called securitization market. By selling off these loans, banks no longer had to meet regulatory requirements to reserve a portion of their capital to cover the risk associated with them. This sum could then be leveraged in more profitable ways.

This fast-growing business makes the financial system more vulnerable in three ways. Banks who have built up client portfolios over many years have a detailed insight into the quality of these loans. In packaging and selling them on they are released from passing judgement on the risks involved – leaving these assessments to the purchasers of the debt, parties who by definition have far less insight into the portfolios. Some of these parties repackage these loans and sell them on to an anonymous and even less-informed market of individual investors. Secondly, in selling on loans, banks stop providing a financial buffer during bad times. Finally, in building these markets, banks removed substantial areas of business from supervision by the monetary authorities.[37]

## A grim assessment

The performance of the US economy during the 1990s was below par, the performance of large US companies poor. The post-millennium recession was long overdue. The legacy inherited from the problems of the 1990s was compounded by the truly extraordinary measures that were taken to pull the US economy out of the doldrums. A rapid increase in government spending, substantial tax reductions and the lowering of interest rates were some of the moves introduced. Companies did their bit by axing 3.3 million jobs between early 2000 and August 2002, pushing up the unemployment rate to 5.9 per cent and boosting the number of those unemployed for longer than 27 weeks by 800,000. This cost cutting was so ferocious that the mere threat of more kept the real income of the average American constant.

American policy makers allowed confidence in the continual rise in consumer spending to become synonymous with confidence in the economy as a whole. Consumers with big debts could no longer turn to the stock market for extra income; they had already refinanced their houses and wage increases seemed to be a thing of the past. Many of those who were made redundant found new jobs, but were paid lower wages. The US consumer could not reduce savings further.

The only way forward was to encourage consumers to start saving, not least because the cost of the things that traditionally matter to them – such as college and health care – was rapidly increasing. But increasing savings means that consumer spending will fall. The resulting loss of confidence in the US economy combined with the exploding trade in derivatives puts the US banking sector at very serious risk.

The US economic recovery of 2002 was bought with borrowed money, adding greatly to the weaknesses of the US economy that resulted from the government and corporate policies of the 1990s.

# SACRIFICING THE SHAREHOLDER

In the 1970s, the so-called Chicago school of economists laid the foundation for a totally new approach to the management of enterprise: the pursuit of shareholder value as the sole corporate concern. They felt this was not only economically correct, but also morally justified as shareholders run by far the largest risk of all those (management, employees, suppliers, customers and the Internal Revenue) with a vested interest in the well-being of a company. Empirical research seemed to support the notion that the pursuit of shareholder value was the best way to serve the interests of all corporate constituents and this suited the mood of the times. To make this philosophy work, capital markets needed to be liberalized to guarantee the most effective allocation of funds throughout the economy. Pushing the interest of the shareholder further by reducing shareholder exposure as much as possible (the concept of shareholder value) was gradually and insidiously replaced by shareholder return on investment. In addition it was premised that a persistent increase in profit per share would be seen and rewarded by the stock markets and lead to higher share prices. This line of argument is fundamentally flawed as outlined in the remainder of this chapter.

## The right thing to do

The concept of shareholder value is deceptively simple. The value of a share is nothing more and nothing less than the sum of future cash flows (ie the net result of all revenues and all costs the company will generate and incur year after year). The value of these future cash flows needs to be discounted in three ways. Clearly, because of inflation, future cash flows are worth less than cash flows today. Moreover, potential investors always have risk-free opportunities, for example government bonds, and companies have to offer a risk premium over and above this risk-free alternative. On top of this, the discount factor should contain an industry-specific risk premium. Future cash flows are more unstable in the semiconductor business than in the brewing business and this uncertainty carries a price. Applying these corrections produces the so-called free cash flow. The net present value of all future free cash flows is the true economic value of the company.

Crucial in this approach is that the cost of financing the business, interest rates on bank loans, leasing and the cost of equity, is treated as any other cost a company incurs. There is no difference between the cost of raw materials, labour cost, maintenance cost and the cost of money.

There is no question that concentration on free cash, also called value-based management, is fundamentally better than the use of indicators such as accounting profit, operating results, return on investment or all the other refinements and ratios that have been developed over the years to evaluate corporate performance. In accounting terms, the profit and loss statement looks back while the balance sheet represents the present. Even in combination these two provide a very poor basis for decision making. Companies have, for example, a tendency to invest in their profitable lines of business. Managers of profitable business units are in a better position to obtain fresh funds for renewal and expansion than their counterparts that are responsible for poorly performing units. But the fact is that the predictive value of past performance is very poor. Moreover it is very difficult to determine profitability. Despite gargantuan efforts to formalize and standardize profit reporting, subjective judgement continues to play an important role.

Value-based management forces managers to concentrate on the future and to confront the uncertainties inherent in business. Unfounded certainties need to be banned. Some uncertainties can be removed. The management of risk needs to take centre stage. Emphasis on economic value provides the basis for this, by for example using different rates of inflation in different countries and by assigning different risk to different activities. By allocating investments to business units and charging them for the cost of capital, it becomes possible to identify corporate activities that create and those that destroy value. Value-based management helps to weigh the different costs of various forms of financing.

Finally, value-based management, which concentrates on easily traceable cash, provides transparency and makes fraud far more difficult. Most companies already apply value-based management when making investment and takeover decisions, but use accounting methods to monitor their new investments and acquisitions. This means original intentions are lost in the process and moves to improve monitoring suffer as a result. Curiously enough, most companies live happily with the inconsistency of value-based and accountancy-based decision making.

Concentration on economic value with the free cash as an important measure of performance is essential in the pursuit of corporate continuity. It is one of the building blocks of the European Enterprise Model that will be presented in Chapter 5.

## A task beyond management

As with any other fundamental shift, choosing shareholder value as the main corporate yardstick needs the introduction of a different mode of thinking throughout the organization. It also needs a major overhaul of many corporate systems, procedures and practices.

In 2001, the *Harvard Business Review* (*HBR*) reported on the conditions for the successful transformation to value-added management.[38] The analysis was based on a survey of 117 companies (out of an original sample of 1,862 large firms in North America, Europe and Asia) that had recently introduced a form of value-based management.

Corporations that were successful had committed themselves to their investors early on in the process. They had invested in massive training programmes throughout the organization. They had made sure that financial incentives worked in the way desired and that business unit managers had received the authority to take, or at least to propose, steps to improve return on capital employed. Finally, these corporations had revamped their budgeting and planning systems and had invested in the appropriate management information systems.

It is remarkable that the majority of US companies did not embark on this route, despite their espoused desire to act in the best interest of their shareholders. Of those that did, many (50 per cent according to some estimates) failed to fulfil the conditions necessary for successful implementation and had to abandon the project. AT&T is one of the more conspicuous failures. Even companies that persevered achieved less than expected. The real success stories are few and far between. The *HBR* survey highlights the achievement of Dow Chemical, Lloyds Bank, Siemens and Cadbury.

It would seem that, by failing to introduce value-based management and the appropriate definition of share value on which it is based, the CEOs of the 1990s have not acted in the best interest of their shareholders. Serious as this may be, there is more.

## Damage without limits

The vast majority of US companies chose a far more limited definition of shareholder value. Shareholder return on investment became the overriding goal. This is the difference between the sale and purchase price of the stock, corrected for dividends over a well-defined period of time. Institutional investors with obligations to pensioners and widows in the distant future exercised some counterpressure but an overwhelming majority of managers, investment bankers, financial analysts and journalists agreed on this simplest definition of value. In the US, support of the stock price became less and less dependent on the absolute level of profitability, or even profitability in relation to the amount of capital employed. A consensus developed that the pursuit of profit per share was the way to higher stock prices. A constant increase in profit per share, which of course implied exponential growth, came to be seen as a minimum. Far preferable was a rise in growth.

The damage to shareholder interest caused by this limited view is difficult to gauge. How much has Royal Dutch Shell saved by overhauling its geology department in the second half of the 1990s? What was the impact on profit per share and how were future cash flows affected in a company where 80 per cent of its performance depends on the discovery and exploitation of oil and gas fields? What did Shell achieve by implementing an extensive share – purchasing programme? What was the impact of speeding up production from existing wells in terms of profit per share, but what about the oil that was left behind due to accelerated production? How was the total amount of winnable reserves – and therefore the economic value of the company – affected?

The next chapter will assess the effectiveness of some of the most popular steps that are inherent in the American Enterprise Model to improve profit per share.

Companies like Shell made themselves very vulnerable by including a comparison with the profitability of their competitors and the performance of their stock among their measures of corporate success, and by linking results in these areas to executive remuneration.

It is a major and very costly misjudgement of the workings of stock markets to assume a causal link between corporate initiatives, profit per share and stock price. But the belief that market parties – each with limited insight into how a company operates, its competitors and market mechanisms – will arrive at the right stock price by some magic process is unshaken. This belief is fundamentally flawed. Trade exists by grace of the fact that two parties assume that an existing price is incorrect: one considers it too high, the other too low. On top of this, neither is in the position to pass judgement on the value of the company, because in the real world the stock price is affected by many forces that have nothing to do with the value of the company.

Time and again, research proves that most private investors are financially illiterate. In one study, 70 per cent of the respondents did not appreciate the inverse relation between interest levels and the value of bonds, and 60 per cent did not know what the expiration of bonds meant.[39] When it comes to stock markets, unfounded optimism is followed by unfounded pessimism. The impact of the media, with its predilection for news that can be explained to mass audiences and news with a high level of human interest, is big.

Behavioural economists present overwhelming empirical evidence that investors are not rational. Loss weighs heavier that profit. The format in which information is moulded and the order in which it is presented greatly influence which decisions are made. The impact of recent events is disproportional and individual investors overestimate their capacity to interpret new developments by a wide margin.

Financial analysts and stockbrokers add insult to injury: buy recommendations prevailed over sell recommendations to a huge extent. Outperforming the indices was, for the majority among them, too much to ask.[40]

Many large funds play a guessing game by trying to predict how their rivals will react to economic and social developments. All of them are under pressure from their shareholders to show good results quickly and are forced to concentrate on companies that hit the headlines at the expense of companies that produce steady results year after year.

American finance professors Chris Levy and Christopher Linden draw the conclusion that there is no relationship between the price and the value of a share and that the share price says very little about a company's state of health. The ultimate measure of success, the share price, produces false readings with major and very costly consequences.

Take for example a decision about the future of a CEO and his plan for the company. Dirk Jager of Procter & Gamble came under fire for the introduction of a long-term programme to increase internal growth. A mishandled acquisition undermined his position further – but his fate was only sealed when the company's share price dropped.

Another example concerns decisions on governance and management in the wake of acquisitions. Market capitalization determines the balance of power. When AOL took over Time Warner in 2000, Time Warner managers were removed from top executive levels. It took five years of poor decision making by AOL managers who lacked media and publishing experience before the company appointed a CEO from the Time Warner stable and business started to recover.

The same applies to policy making following an acquisition. Because Dutch steel manufacturer Hoogovens had a low market capitalization (unjustifiably as it happens) it was swallowed up by British Steel to form Corus – and has been stymied in its development ever since.

It is tragic and ironic that managers and bankers destroyed economic value in the name of the shareholder throughout the 1990s and ever since.

## AN INDICTMENT

Looking back, it is difficult to escape the feeling that opportunities of truly historic proportions were missed during the 1990s. Peace, technological breakthroughs and prosperity hardly ever occur simultaneously as they did during this period. Economic growth in the United States should have been higher and expansion should have lasted longer given the impressive competitive advantages the country enjoyed throughout the decade. Extra economic value could have been used to solve society's problems in the United States and elsewhere. Instead the believers in the American Enterprise Model destroyed value by pursuing shareholders' return on investment.

By 2001, a poisonous brew had formed. Its ingredients were the mistaken belief that the 1990s were a golden decade and the conviction that the US world-view, economic policy and American Enterprise Model could withstand any challenge and were superior to European alternatives.

This restricted response to the recession of 2001 to 'more of the same': lower taxes and interest rates, more dismissals and outsourcing. This was the price at which an economic recovery was bought and it only compounded American woes.

Subsequent generations have inherited a much riskier economic and corporate world. It is the result of slash-and-burn economics hidden under the cloak of creative construction. The after-shocks of the greatest speculation wave ever can still be felt. Debt is rampant and the recipes of the 1990s are no longer effective: this is the subject of the next chapter.

# 3

# The end of the road

As highlighted in Chapter 1, the idea that the US version of free market capitalism has proven itself a successful concept is well entrenched. Evidence to the contrary, summarized in Chapter 2 and all in the public domain, has so far been ignored. Whistle-blowers place themselves outside mainstream America. Those who argue that historical and cultural differences produce different forms of capitalism, and that these can be equally effective, belong to a tiny minority.

Free-market capitalism, US style, and its flag carrier, the American Enterprise Model, are the most successful US export products. In continental Europe in particular, many corporate, government and EU policies are modelled on their Anglo-Saxon forerunners. Despite these successes, the US government, US companies and the US media have lost very little of their zeal and appear determined to go even further in conquering the world, country by country if necessary. There is a deeply held conviction that this is important not only for the United States and corporate America, but also in the best interests of other countries. The scandals and the recession of 2001 did not result in a rethink of this belief. To the contrary, when a true believer is confronted with setbacks, he only pushes harder in the same direction and becomes more assertive in the defence of his ideology.

These basic instincts manifested themselves throughout the 1990s but acquired an extra dimension in the wake of the election of President George W. Bush and the Congressional election in autumn 2002.

The tone of US criticism against Europe became increasingly shrill. The feeling was that Europeans are, sadly enough, incapable of setting financial markets free and reforming labour markets. European employees work an amazingly small number of hours for too much pay and enjoy far too much protection against dismissal. It is clear that Europeans refuse to rein in welfare spending and remain incapable of bringing national legislation and regulations into line. Europe is running far behind in essential areas such as financial services, information technology and, in particular, biotechnology. Europe lacks the leadership and the will to spur on its atrophying economies.

The drive to export the US view of the world can be seen everywhere and the country's willingness to compromise in international negotiations is greatly reduced.

Despite mounting criticism, the US Treasury, the IMF and the World Bank as separate institutions and collectively as the 'Washington Consensus' are driven and inspired by US policies and the efficiency of the American Enterprise Model. Political, legal and economic restructuring by recipient countries is invariably part and parcel of IMF assistance packages. Financial help is available in exchange for commitments to privatize state-owned companies, reduce government subsidies for food and other basic needs, lower import tariffs and liberalize markets. Of course, the liberalization of financial markets is the jewel in the crown.

Nowhere is the drive to export the US view of the world more visible and tangible than in its support for the Third World. Net US development assistance dropped from 0.21 per cent of GNP in 1990 to 0.11 per cent in 2001. Under considerable pressure to do more, the Bush administration announced a $2 billion increase in the course of 2002, bringing the new total to $13.5 billion. This package was accompanied by an unprecedented set of conditions. Receiving governments have to demonstrate their ability to control corruption, invest in education and health care and promote market liberalization, deregulation and privatization. The United States and the recipient country sign multi-year contracts; progress is monitored and there are regular financial audits.

The first two sections of this chapter are devoted to exploring the limits of US economic policies in support of the American Enterprise Model and the limits of the American Enterprise Model itself. In a third and final section new ideas that could help to lengthen the life cycle of the US model are investigated.

# ECONOMIC POLICIES IN THE US AND IN THE EU

As outlined in Chapter 1, the Reagan revolution was based on five pillars: a reduction in the role of government; the privatization of state assets and the outsourcing of non-essential government activities (leading to substantial and lasting tax reductions); deregulation of markets; the support of free trade; and the reduction of trade union power. The belief was that governments should leave the allocation of economic resources to the market place and should stop meddling in the private lives of their citizens. The pursuit of happiness would produce a nation of shareholders and homeowners. The Clinton years provided ample evidence of the wisdom of these choices and continuity was assured when the Bush administration took over. Very few observers expected what followed: a feverish extension of the revolution, the proud floating of the ideology and an impatient eagerness to take the fight to the opponent.

It was at this point that the United States and Europe went their own separate ways. In Europe the revolution had run out of steam. What was easy and obvious had been done; more of the same proved to be difficult and the price of further progress along the same track went up. The political leadership at the time saw the danger, and the best and the brightest were mobilized to rejuvenate the agenda and expand the franchise. Despite a combination of power, financial interests and creativity, it proved to be very difficult to bring the corporate revolution to welfare, education, health care and security services. Even established and successful government policies such as privatization and market liberalization appeared to be losing their lustre.

## The withdrawal of government

The tax rate has always been the most important measure of government involvement in economic and private life. Proposals for tax cuts were easy to explain and had universal appeal. The rejuvenated revolutionaries in the United States never ceased to push for more. Tax reduction was an important plank in the Bush/Cheney election platform and they delivered immediately after being elected in 2001 with a $1.4 billion package of cuts. These were designed to apply for a set period but calls to make them permanent were heard from day one and the political need to counter the recession of 2001 produced fresh proposals for the abolition of the dividend tax as its centrepiece.

Many economists considered this second package reckless in light of the impact on government revenues, the rapidly rising cost of homeland security and the price of wars in Afghanistan and Iraq. They did not think it opportune to swell an already growing federal deficit. Political resistance to this second package was also considerable. The impact on income distribution was severely criticized. Many did not consider the abolition of the dividend tax an effective tool for turning the economy around. Yet the administration stayed the course and Congress followed suit.

Europe followed a different path. In the UK in 2002, the Labour government made a complete turnaround by submitting a budget to parliament that called for higher taxes and substantial increases in spending on health care, public transport and education. This amounted to tacit acknowledgement that the fiscal policies of the 1990s had reached their limits.

On the Continent too the tide was turning. After significant reductions in corporate and income taxes throughout the 1990s, many countries shelved further plans to reduce taxation. However, national elections in France and Germany in 2002 and 2003 respectively plus the need to react to a drawn-out recession brought fresh commitments. Yet the context was different from the 1990s. Tax cuts in both countries were now part of a much delayed overhaul of the welfare state, including revisions of unemployment and disability benefits and attempts to improve the flexibility of labour markets. Political support for further tax cuts dwindled in light of rising spending on pensions, health and care for the elderly and the need to curtail government budget deficits.

Another marker of government involvement in the economy is the absolute size of its budget. Here, even in the United States and despite claims to the contrary, ideology and political power were never sufficiently forceful to achieve a reduction, neither over time, nor in any single year. This was true both for the statutory programmes such as health care and welfare entitlements, and for discretionary spending. The budget of the US federal government rose continuously from $1,324 billion in 1991 to $2,011 billion in 2001 and has risen faster since.[1] New and very expensive commitments to Medicaid and the war in Iraq are even kept out of the projections of government spending. The federal budget as a share of GDP has remained remarkably constant, hovering at around 20 per cent since 1962. The Bush administration had to resort to very creative bookkeeping, including the shifting of expensive programmes to the state level, to show a slight decrease.

Exactly the same phenomena can be observed in all European countries, including the UK. Despite all the rhetoric and spin-doctoring, the call on government services and investment continues to increase and no austerity measure can break this trend.

## Privatization

Privatization of state-owned companies and outsourcing of government tasks, the second pillar of the Reagan revolution, proceeded differently in the United States and Europe.

In the United States, federal and state governments had always been far in advance of other members of the Organisation for Economic Co-operation and Development (OECD). US governments had never owned (parts of) manufacturing companies and banks, and their privatization of the railways and utilities set an example for the rest of the world.

Neither the California electricity crisis in 2001 nor the power blackout in Canada and the north-east of the United States in August 2003 could undermine the belief in privatization. Evidence that the liberalization of electricity and natural gas markets produced a shortfall in investments, which over time translated into energy shortages and highly disruptive price hikes, was ignored.

Nothing could stop the Bush administration. Ideology prevailed over analysis. From its inception the administration broke new ground by testing the waters for the privatization of social security. After the 2004 elections it became one of the defining plans of the Bush presidency. Outsourcing of government services took on a very different meaning. New tender procedures were designed to transfer the work of 850,000 federal employees (from a total 1.8 million) to the private sector.[2]

In Europe, the end of government ownership of industrial companies proved to be relatively easy. The privatization of banks and telecommunication companies was more complicated because privatization and deregulation had to go hand in hand. In the water, gas and electricity markets government divestments were only possible after highly complicated deregulation processes.[3]

Regulators, politicians and the public at large still critically monitor the privatization of utilities. Mistakes are openly discussed and the energy crises in the United States have had an impact on the ongoing privatization processes of European utilities.

In the Netherlands – in many ways the most Anglo-Saxon country on the European continent – railway privatization has come to a grinding halt and the Dutch government is only likely to sell off part of its 100 per cent ownership of Schiphol Airport under the most severe conditions. Meanwhile, plans for the privatization of the country's electricity and gas companies met stiff resistance.

In the UK, the government's privatization policy was undermined by a number of serious train accidents and the bankruptcy of Railtrack, the company that owned and managed the infrastructure of British railways (formerly British Rail). In the end the government had no choice but to retake full control.

In France, the government embarked on a major privatization programme in the 1990s, withdrawing from many banks and manufacturing companies. Under considerable pressure to curtail its budget deficit to comply with the European Stability Pact, the government announced a fresh initiative in the summer of 2002. This included the sale of power and gas utility EdF/GdF, Air France, France Telecom and nine other state-owned companies. Reactions were hardly encouraging and counterforces were mobilized. The pension rights of EdF/GdF employees proved to be a formidable hurdle, plans to reduce the government stake in Air France could only be packaged in a takeover of KLM and the difficult financial position of France Telecom made it a risky proposition for any potential buyer.[4]

Germany was never a frontrunner. The privatizations of Deutsche Telekom and Deutsche Post were only concluded in 2000 and the government continues to struggle with the privatization of airports.

Europe's struggle reflects the erosion of ideology and the rise of the pragmatists.

## Market liberalization

In the United States, liberalization reached its climax in the freeing of markets for financial services and insurance and in lifting the barriers between commercial and investment banking. At that point, there were simply no significant economic sectors left in which government regulation impeded the free interaction of market forces.

Market deregulation was always at the heart of a united Europe. At the same time, Europe had to tread carefully. Lengthy transition periods were always part of the deal and, where necessary, compensation was offered.

After more than 40 years of hard work, markets for goods and many services have been set free throughout the European Union. However, other important markets such as financial services, insurance, postal services and energy are by no means free and increasingly bitter political and legal battles have to be fought to achieve small steps forward. The same holds for labour markets. All the citizens of member states are free to seek employment or to set up a business anywhere in the EU. Yet taxation, pensions, insurance and the problem of EU-wide recognition of professional qualifications still act as barriers to the mobility of workers and entrepreneurs. It appears that each dossier that comes before the EU commissioner for the internal market has a long and unhappy history. Many are still waiting for breakthroughs that depend on deal making among the highest political echelons. Ideology is nowhere to be seen, either in the form of emulation of the great US example or in the form of the pursuit of European ideals. National interests increasingly guide member states.

## Supporting free trade

The fourth political priority that is embraced by Americans is the furthering of international competition and trade. US interests are there for everybody to see. Strong and highly sophisticated companies, not forgetting banks, need market access around the world and should not be hampered by artificial barriers. Building on talks to stimulate world trade, the Uruguay Round (from 1995 to 2000) led to a reduction of import tariffs levied by the developed countries from 6.3 to 3.8 per cent. In 1997, the package was further improved by an agreement among 40 countries to eliminate import duties on information technology products. As a result of these and many more measures, international trade flourished and grew 75 per cent between 1990 and 2001.

The Doha Round of trade talks set even more ambitious targets: improved protection of foreign investments and intellectual property and the removal of barriers to the trade of agricultural products. Agreement was far from guaranteed. Bigger subsidies for US farmers, a modest reform of support for EU farmers and sky-high Japanese import levies on agricultural products proved formidable obstacles. In December 2002, a failed attempt to reconcile the financial interests of large pharmaceutical companies and the protection of their patent rights with the needs of AIDS sufferers in Africa was seen as a bad omen and produced a hardening of negotiating positions by all participants in the Doha Round. The subsequent failure of the talks in Cancun as a result of US intransigence and the desire of developing countries to change the balance of power in the WTO was the most serious disruption in the development of free trade since the Second World War.[5] Repair work is ongoing, the framework agreement of the United States and the EU on the phasing out of export subsidies for agricultural products is helping, but final negotiations still have to be started. Europe remains a strong supporter of the multinational framework; the United States puts increasing emphasis on bilateral agreements.[6]

## Reducing union power

During the 1980s, US president Ronald Reagan and UK prime minister Margaret Thatcher successfully concluded crusades against, respectively, air traffic controllers and mineworkers. The power base of the trade unions was eroded as a result of new legislation and a gradual but persistent reduction in union membership.

The days of fiery anti-labour proclamations seem to be over. The Bush administration is now resorting to a strategy that could be even more effective, made up as it is of a broad range of initiatives. Nothing is too big or too small to escape government attention. The administration is trying to put up barriers to overtime payments. It wants to allow employers to pay below minimum wages to workers on welfare and is trying to ban labour agreements on all federally funded construction projects. It also denies workers a say in the drafting of industry-specific guidelines for health and safety. And so the list goes on.[7]

In the UK, the 1990s were a period in which unions regrouped. They regained confidence and found more and more support in their criticism of government policies, in particular the implementation of changes in health care and education.

The Netherlands used the 1990s to turn its long history of amenable union–employer–government relations into a competitive advantage. Restraint in wage demands, tax cuts to increase net income and labour market reforms such as the facilitation of part-time work, proved to be a powerful mixture. Against this background it was possible to make a meaningful start in restructuring social security in the interest of long-term sustainability.

At the same time, the development of industrial relations in Germany and France lagged behind. Contrary to the smaller nations in Europe, both of these countries postponed confrontation with the unions when it came to reforming social security and pensions in the 1990s. However, during the summer of 2003, social unrest in France and Germany failed to prevent government proposals in these areas from going ahead and this could herald the start of modernization for the trade union movement in these countries.

This thumbnail sketch of the United States and European economic and socio-political agenda illustrates two propositions. (1) The US world-view is very much intact and, where President Clinton was inclined to smooth the roughest edges of policies pursued by a Republican House of Representatives, a Republican president with control of Congress unashamedly rejuvenates the Reagan era. (2) European politicians, regulators and the general public are becoming increasingly sceptical of the effectiveness of US-style economic policies.

## THE CORPORATE GLOSS LOSES ITS SHINE

Over the past decades, most corporations have embraced the notion that survival and the improvement of their position in relation to competitors depended primarily on access to capital markets at reasonable, or at least competitive, conditions. An increase in shareholder value, as reflected in a persistent rise of the share price over an extended period, was seen as the best means to that end. A high share price was also essential if a company wanted to be involved in the consolidation process that all economic sectors underwent. This was true whether the company was paying in shares to take over a competitor or as protection against a hostile takeover. And the belief was that the way to a higher share price was a persistent increase in corporate profit per share. Confidence that stock markets would reward such virtuous behaviour seemed limitless.[8] Markets were considered tough but knowledgeable; they passed fair judgements on corporate performance and even had the gift of clairvoyance.

A choice for profit per share determined that corporate management would concentrate on five broad areas for improvement as the surest and quickest way to satisfy shareholders: financial restructuring, corporate redesign, mergers and acquisitions, staff reduction and improvement of margins via market leadership. Each is increasingly ineffective.

There was much less time for research, a gradual building of market positions, engagement in alliances, development of personal and organizational competencies, adjustment of corporate cultures, or any other programme that could not be seen as contributing to profitability in a direct and unequivocal way.

## Financial restructuring

In restructuring their finances, companies relied on a finite number of possibilities, each with a built-in limit.

Hidden financial reserves and a large investment portfolio are very useful in smoothing profits over the years. Insurers such as ING and particularly Aegon have been masters in this form of profit taking used to report a gradual increase in profit. Reserves for reorganizations can for example be made very generous. Funds that are not used return as profits at the management's convenience. Information technology companies that sell hardware at a loss in combination with profitable services, which they will deliver over a number of years, are tempted to spread the total net profits of this strategy evenly over the duration of the contract. Yet hidden reserves can only be unveiled once and new bookkeeping rules make concealment of new reserves during good times for use in bad times increasingly difficult.

Another way to make the company more attractive to shareholders is a reduction in the amount of capital tied up in corporate operations. Capital at that point could be returned to its rightful owner. The 1990s saw a wave of financial arrangements whereby companies sold and leased back offices and other tradable assets. It is obvious that the stock of such assets is finite.

Lowering stocks is another tried and tested method to reduce working capital. Much can be freed up by streamlining supply, production and distribution. However at a certain point down this road, the risk of disruption increases because buffers in the supply, production, sales and distribution chain that could help to cope with fluctuations in demand or with operational problems have become too small. For example in the United States supply and demand for petroleum products is finely tuned. In this very mature industry where every cent counts, production and distribution were optimized over decades and as a result product stocks could be brought down to absolute minima. It is now apparent that the slightest disturbance causes shortages with occasional interruption of deliveries and, at a minimum, greater volatility in the price of gasoline and heating oil.

Furthermore, the squeezing of receivables and the relaxation of conditions of payment are still on the agenda. At the risk of seriously disturbing the relationship with their customers and suppliers, companies continuously seek to reduce the number of credit days they allow. At the same time they postpone the payment of their own bills, deliberately testing contractual limits. A unilateral decision by supermarket chain Albert Heijn, the flagship subsidiary of global retailer Ahold, to change its conditions of payment caused a brawl with Unilever and other suppliers and the sanctity of contracts is now at stake. Such desperate actions are a sure sign that the low-hanging fruit has been plucked and consumed.

Large improvements in the ratio of 'profit per share' can be achieved by reducing the denominator, ie the number of outstanding shares. US companies bought their own shares on a grand scale during the 1990s. As outlined in Chapter 2, they borrowed heavily to finance their acquisition programmes, encouraged by low interest rates and benevolent fiscal treatment of interest payments. Naturally, at some point the financial resilience of the company is undermined, with all the risk this entails.

The most extreme form of manipulation is the leveraged buy-out, whereby existing shareholders are bought out with a small initial investment and a large loan, secured by the company's own assets. After the takeover, the corporate cash flow is used to service the debt on the high-risk loan – the illustrious junk bonds. Sales of corporate assets are then used to pay off some of the debt. In this way, return on equity can be pushed to dazzling heights. Equally impressive risk limits the applicability of this approach.

Finally, a number of tricks to improve profit per share, legal in the 1990s, are no longer available. The cost of option programmes can no longer be accounted for in a footnote in the annual report, corporate contributions to pension funds can no longer be dodged and the use of offshore constructions to reduce corporate tax bills is attracting increasing attention.

There are only so many tools in the toolbox. The wide-scale use of illegal practices during the late 1990s testifies to the fact that many tools had become blunt while calls for increased shareholder returns of investment sounded louder and louder.

At the end of the day, even the cleverest financial engineer runs out of effective tricks to prop up profit per share.

## Corporate redesign

Corporate profit receives a big boost when profit-making activities are acquired and goodwill (the difference between actual price paid and the book value of the acquired unit) can be put on the balance sheet and gradually depreciated. The same applies to the sale of loss-making activities above book value.

Concentration on core activities became one of the mantras of the 1990s. In this context, the division of corporate activities into business units had a number of advantages. It provided insight into the performance and value of the units. Moreover, business units were viable organizational entities and could be traded without too much disruption. Strategy consultants and investment banks were at hand to assist corporate management through such restructuring.

Of particular interest was the identification of the so-called 'bleeders'. These are activities that booked losses year after year, often despite costly restructuring efforts. In many cases much energy had to be devoted to the disclosing of hidden internal subsidies as a stepping-stone for their disposal. The high premium attached to the focus on core activities compelled companies to sell perfectly respectable and profitable activities that appeared out of line with the rest of the portfolio. It was assumed that these units would do even better under different wings and the profits on these deals benefited the shareholders.

A master in this area was Cor Boonstra, CEO of Philips Electronics during the late 1990s, who purged company units such as the loss-making Grundig and the highly profitable PolyGram. Engineering conglomerate Stork is an extreme example of the effect that streamlining can have on the perceptions of the financial markets. Stork is involved in six very different activities, from building poultry processing units to aircraft maintenance. A simple announcement that the company would divest three of these units, without identifying which, was enough to see the corporate share price rise.[9]

Buying and selling business units is, of course, a permanent feature of corporate life, but by the end of the 1990s most companies had been reconstructed and any remaining moves were finishing touches. The stock of 'bleeders' had been exhausted in most companies at any rate, and firms had also learnt to intervene earlier and harder when units start to drift. Corporate overheads and other fixed costs can be cut to the bone, but this can only be done once. Savings on research and development cannot be repeated. Unprofitable partnerships can only be abolished once.

The organization of the company can be made simpler, but the introduction of business units is a one-time benefit. The web of company committees can be sanitized, but the need for coordination is irrepressible and the limit is clearly reached when committees start to return under a different name. The number of organizational layers can be reduced but so-called 'spans of control' cannot be made too wide. Many managers now have around 10 people reporting to them where five or six was the norm in the not-too-distant past. The CEO can be burdened with more and more proposals but, at a certain point, his physical limits become apparent and the quality of his decisions starts to deteriorate. In Chapter 4 much more will be said about these and other unintended consequences and unaccounted costs of a US-style organizational structure.

Outsourcing, generally based on the reduction of labour costs by moving to low-wage countries and on economies of scale enjoyed by the supplier, has been and will remain popular for some time. Yet with every step, risk increases. The logistics chain becomes more vulnerable. The flexibility required to respond to changes in market demand and changes in product specifications decreases. More outsourcing means more partners, a larger geographical arena and more ICT systems that need to be connected or integrated; the result is that transaction and operational costs for outsourcing go up. Other economic but less tangible limits to outsourcing are the need to preserve minimum levels of expertise, and eventually the need to preserve the corporate identity.

The first broadly based evaluations of outsourcing are now in and are highly disappointing. A survey by Gartner consultants reveals that 50 per cent of all projects end in failure. Advisors DiamondCluster point out that contracts for the outsourcing of the management of ICT systems are ended prematurely in 79 per cent of the investigated cases. Bain & Company joins the chorus by finding that cost reductions, the prime objective of most efforts, are a disappointment and finally Significant, a Dutch spin-off of accountancy firm PricewaterhouseCoopers, cannot find in a sample of 110 companies out of the Forbes Global 2000 any evidence whatsoever of improvement in operating profit.

Finally, the performance and behaviour of partners hardly ever work to the benefit of the outsourcing company. An extreme example of outsourcing is sportswear company Nike that does not own one single factory but relies on 700 partners in 50 countries for the production of its goods. Most of these partners are in Third World countries and in 1996 Nike was accused of exploiting child labour when *Life* magazine published a picture of a

12-year-old Pakistani boy who received 60 cents for sewing together one football. The damage to Nike's reputation was considerable, and falling sales forced the company to guarantee that all its products would be produced in a child-friendly manner in the future. Interestingly, Nike decided to outsource control over the compliance of suppliers with this strict condition – and was subsequently confronted with three more cases of child labour in as many years with more adverse consequences.

## Mergers and acquisitions

Many companies submerged themselves in a world of restructuring and consolidation in pursuit of shareholder return on investment. In the first quarter of 1995, the value of worldwide mergers and acquisitions amounted to $180 billion. Activity reached its zenith during the first quarter of 2000 during which transactions were agreed for a total of $1,150 billion. Over the same period, the number of transactions per quarter rose from 200 to 900.[10] There were four supposedly well-founded justifications for this.

Firstly, the belief was that a company or business unit needed to be number one or two in its worldwide markets to obtain price leadership on its way to sustained profitability. Secondly, it was taken as given that, in mature markets, growth could only be achieved by acquisition. Thirdly, it was vital to capitalize on potential cost savings by streamlining the operations of the partners. Fourthly, mergers were necessary to gain sufficient scale to spread the spiralling cost of research and development and ICT and to share the risk of large investments in general.

In addition, fear and greed played their parts. Fear of being taken over pushed many companies to acquire competitors in an attempt to become a less attractive or simply too large takeover target themselves. In doing so, many companies started to live beyond their financial and managerial means. Companies that were quick off the mark could be greedy and string a number of acquisitions together. Once a first purchase is received well and the share price goes up, a flywheel is set into motion. A high stock price makes many takeover targets seem cheap. Takeovers, financed with the company stock, were also seen as helping to spread risk and to lock in increases in shareholder return on investment that resulted from previous takeovers.

Ahold, the Dutch retail giant, is one of many examples. Geerhard Bolteh[11] and Jeroen Smit have both provided compelling accounts of its rise and fall. Ahold's buying started in earnest in 1996 with the purchase of

Stop & Shop in the United States and several supermarket chains in South America. The favourable response by the financial community enabled the company to issue 900 million euros of fresh stock in 1998, the biggest issue ever in the Netherlands at the time. With the help of this war chest, the pace quickened. Disco, with stores in a number of South American countries, is the next target, followed by Giant Food in the United States. In 1999, Ahold acquired interests in the Netherlands, Spain, Poland, Sweden, Argentina, Brazil, Guatemala, El Salvador and Honduras. CEO Cees van der Hoeven was now one of the most respected managers in the world. Rapid expansion and the worldwide number three position within reach plus sustained profit growth and a consistently rising share price were an astonishing achievement by any standards. In March 2000, Ahold spent 3.6 billion euros to obtain control over US food distributor Foodservice and a number of small supermarket chains were added to the portfolio.

In 2001, long before the Foodservice scandal broke, the story started to unravel. Integration of supermarket chains in Spain failed. The fall of the Argentinian peso caused havoc. Fraud committed by Ahold's partner in Argentina forced the concern to spend 500 million euros on two unstable supermarket chains. For the first time, van der Hoeven had to give a profit warning, but the spell was not yet broken. In 2002 he was still Holland's Manager of the Year overseeing a company with an annual turnover of 72.7 billion euros. A second profit warning late in 2002 was the beginning of the end. After one more acquisition in the United States, the curtain dropped in February 2003 when van der Hoeven had to make a public announcement of fraud at Foodservice. After his departure, new accountants found evidence of the illegal boosting of reported turnover and evidence that Ahold had claimed management control of subsidiaries where there was none. The reputation of Cees van der Hoeven disintegrated and the Netherlands had its own financial scandal.

Acquisitions and mergers as a fast road to higher shareholder returns destroy value on a grand scale but continue to be seen as a sign of economic vitality. Their popularity is undiminished despite overwhelming evidence that mergers fail to deliver shareholder value (see Chapter 4 for some of the explanations for this phenomenon).

In the autumn of 2002, *BusinessWeek* reported the results of a sample survey of 302 major mergers between 1995 and 2001. This concluded that 61 per cent of acquiring companies had destroyed their own shareholders' wealth.[12] This is a highly flattering assessment because the study, conducted by the Boston Consulting Group (BCG), excluded cases where a merger was followed by another within a year. It is common knowledge, but not reported by BCG, that serial acquirers are the greatest sinners, among them Dennis Kozlowski of Tyco and Bernie Ebbers of WorldCom.

The study also ignored the fact that, in the majority of cases, the health of acquired companies deteriorates. Several other studies indicate that between 17 and 47 per cent of these companies are resold at a considerable loss 10 years (on average) after acquisition.[13]

Even more interesting are the conclusions drawn by Hans Schenk, professor of economics at Utrecht University, from his own extensive research and a meta-analysis of the multitude of merger studies in industries as diverse as manufacturing, advertising and banking.[14]

Schenk notes that productivity either does not improve as a result of a merger or improves less than would have been the case without the merger.[15] Furthermore, mergers appear to have a detrimental impact on market share growth, investment in research and development, and research and development output.[16] Worst hit are the innovative small and medium-sized enterprises (SMEs) whose performance deteriorates dramatically as a result of a takeover. They can only recover (if not dismantled or fully absorbed into the buyer's organization) after having been spun off again.[17]

Pharmaceutical multinationals appear to be particularly prone to making this type of mistake. Roche acquired Syntac in 1998 and three years later the people and the intellectual property – let alone the commercial opportunity the company once embodied – had disappeared without a trace.

## Staff reduction

If market circumstances deteriorate, lay-offs help to mitigate the impact on the corporate profit per share. Nobody appears to be interested in the cost of rehiring once the market returns to normal. Reducing the workforce to structurally lower levels carries a penalty in the form of reduced capacity to grow in the future. The direct cost of staff reductions is considerable and by no means limited to severance payments. There is other less visible restructuring expenditure, such as regrouping and relocating activities, the adaptation of management information and ICT systems and the renegotiation of supply and sales contracts. Logic dictates that even more employees have to be laid off to make the restructuring worthwhile.

The real cost dwarfs the direct cost. The process by which staff reductions are achieved is particularly harmful. Rumours fly long before a rationalization programme is announced. No announcement can address all concerns and this is the start rather than the end of an arduous process. More often than not, consultants get into the fray. Objectives are fixed, constraints identified, tools explained, scores of interviews conducted, detailed analyses of corporate studies undertaken and more studies commissioned. Under considerable pressure, individuals, business units and corporate departments defend their corner with all possible means. Delays are inevitable and individual employees are informed of their fate only after a protracted period of uncertainty.

During this episode, the best and the brightest, those who stand a good chance on the labour market, leave. There is an irrepressible tendency to distribute the pain as evenly as possible over the organization. The good, the bad and the ugly all suffer, with the proviso that managers suffer less than ordinary folk. In most companies seniority counts. Senior staff enjoy a degree of social protection and union membership helps too. Newcomers and ethnic minorities pay the price.

In such a whirlpool, any management effort to save necessary skills and expertise for the company and to build an organization for the future is bound to fail. Worse still, the need for confidentiality and the understandable desire to escape the wrath of redundant employees contribute to the isolation of management, and the quality of decision making suffers accordingly.

Given the virtually random character of lay-offs, valuable informal relationships cease to exist or fail to come to fruition. This also applies to relationships with suppliers, customers and all other corporate stakeholders.

Once a rationalization is formally concluded, a painful process of adjustment follows. According to Manfred Kets de Vries, both the executives that implemented the programme and the surviving employees pay a heavy psychological price.

Inevitably executives lose credibility, even in their own eyes. They cannot escape the conclusion that they did not anticipate the forces that led to the rationalization or that their strategy was flawed. In addition they carry direct responsibility for all the failings of the ad hoc organization that was created to design and implement the rationalization programme.

Surviving employees go through denial, anger, anxiety, guilt and relief. In the immediate aftermath they face an increased workload and have to take up unfamiliar assignments. With many colleagues gone and many in new positions, the collective corporate memory needs to be rebuilt.[18] Old lessons need to be learnt anew; lost relationships need to be re-established and new lines of demarcation established.

With each round of restructuring and rationalization it becomes more difficult to identify savings. With each round of restructuring, the stakes go up because more and more activities will have to be abolished altogether. With each round of restructuring and rationalization, the tangible and intangible costs go up and risks increase.[19] The resulting organizational fatigue becomes a chronic ailment.

The most extreme example of a company that was willing to pay any price as long as lay-offs contributed to profit growth was General Electric (GE) under the regime of CEO Jack Welch. This firm and its CEO were at the receiving end of total and unqualified admiration from the United States and Europe throughout the 1990s. Staff reduction was part and parcel of the remit of any GE manager at all times, irrespective of the financial performance of the unit or division. In the mid-1990s, the company stated publicly that GE's Power Systems realized profits to the tune of $1 billion pre-tax. Yet 1,800 employees were dismissed in a year during which sales rose by 7 per cent and profits by 21 per cent. A new collective labour agreement was signed for 2,800 workers at a plant in Indiana – only to be followed by an announcement that the plant would be closed.

Then there was the travel conglomerate Montgomery Ward that was acquired by GE in the latter's quest for diversity. A much older firm than GE itself, Montgomery Ward was put out of business overnight due to a disappointing holiday season, leaving 28,000 employees in 50 states in the cold. GE was a company that lived by the principle that the least productive 20 per cent of any workforce drags down the company's profitability and should be dismissed. Yet even at GE, awareness has grown that it cannot afford such practices any longer. The corporate spin-doctors now check for banana skins and Welch's successor Jeffrey Immelt has now let it be known that people are his first priority.

In light of the picture sketched above it is hardly surprising that the results of downsizing have been very disappointing. Share prices receive a boost when the announcement is made, but positive medium-term effects are indiscernible. Contrary to popular – and particularly management's – belief, the long-term impact of downsizing on productivity has never been proven and there is not even conclusive evidence that costs actually go down over time.[20]

A 1995 study by Watson Wyatt Worldwide found that only 46 per cent of companies surveyed met their expense-reduction goals. A 1997 study conducted by the Business School of the University of Colorado, which analysed downsizing trends at Standard & Poor's 500 firms over a 12-year period, found companies that downsize are generally no more profitable than those that do not. A 1997 Wharton School of Business analysis of 52 studies involving thousands of companies found that corporate restructuring had little if any positive impact on earnings or stock performance. To top it all, the American Management Association, in its 1998 Staffing and Structure Survey, concluded that firms that showed a workforce decrease in the 1990s are far more likely to report long-term decline in worker quality, product quality and operating profits.

Despite all this evidence, lay-offs remain one of the most important tools in the hands of US managers. From when the recession started in early 2000 to 2003, some 3.2 million jobs were shed to improve profitability and regain shareholder confidence.

## Market leadership

As far as marketing is concerned, financial markets and corporate management became attached to the vigorous pursuit of one, and only one, commercial objective: achievement of market leadership. The following logic seemed inescapable: the company with the highest production and sales enjoys the lowest cost per unit. This company will set prices and many competitors will be keen to seek protection under this umbrella. Companies that try to compete on price can be disciplined by temporary deep discounts. The margin advantage of the market leader enables it to invest more than its rivals, strengthening its position and securing profits.

The logic described above applied to both companies and business units. A worldwide position as number one was essential and abandonment of an activity was inevitable if there was no realistic prospect that such a position could be obtained quickly and in a 'cost-effective' way.

This explains why the drive for market share in the new communication and internet sectors was so brutal and why products and services were more or less given away. It was all done in pursuit of market leadership and in the mistaken belief that, after a shake-out, the remaining firms would enjoy economies of scale, bring costs under control, and push up and maintain prices at satisfactory levels.

In more developed sectors, companies bought and sold units to achieve dominant and sustainable market positions. In mature industries such as food and personal care, a reduction in the number of brands and concentration on leading brands became the fashionable route to market leadership. Increasing the marketing and sales budgets for the winners and abolishing or selling weaker brands seemed to make sense. In the late 1990s, Unilever embarked on a major five-year programme to reduce thousands of its brands to a mere 400 in an attempt to bring revenue growth to a structurally higher level. In the first three years, the 400 brands grew at the desired annual 5 to 6 per cent, but at the expense of higher advertising cost. However in the fourth year the growth rate started to drop and in the end objectives were not met.[21] More aggressive advertising was seen as the appropriate response and costs were projected to go up further.

These hardly exciting results from the best and the brightest in marketing and sales are one sign among many that marketing is reaching a dead end when it comes to achieving market leadership.

Dutch professors Theo Poiesz and Fred van Raaij[22] draw attention to the commodity trap, situations in which market parties are continuously adding comparable features to their products, increasing their costs but not customer appeal. As a result market parties have to compete on price.

Looking more closely the following mechanisms can be discerned. With quality no longer a distinguishing feature, market leadership requires innovation. The number of innovations is increasing but the number of truly new products is small because investments are considerable and risk unaffordable.

Therefore the emphasis is on the redesign of, and adding functions to, existing products. These are innovations that are notoriously difficult to protect by patents. They confuse rather than entice the public and the more sophisticated consumers become weary and critical. The result is that distinction from the competition, if perceived at all, gets a lukewarm response most of the time. In the case of a positive response, the new feature will quickly be copied by the competition. These responses add more pressure to continually renewed products.

Another route to market leadership is to reduce the time it takes to put an innovation on the market to get as much of a head start on competitors as possible. However at a certain point the costs of doing this rise exponentially. The key to success or failure is often not the time and expense that are required to design and test prototypes. More damaging to profit margins are high marketing budgets and the cost of rapid increases in production capacity that come with aggressive campaigns. New products can only be allowed a limited period to prove their success before they have to make way for their successors. Consequently the number of outright failures increases.

Looking at market communication, the creation of brand loyalty becomes increasingly important when customers are unable to appreciate the technical features of a product. Communication of a brand in all its dimensions adds to an already substantial information overload. In response, consumers become more and more skilful in ignoring commercial messages, which in turn sows the seeds for even more determined efforts to get across information that differentiates a product from its rival. The simple purchase of a book, an insurance policy or a car is generally a starting point for an avalanche of marketing and sales efforts. It is not surprising that the trade in customer databases is flourishing.

All these vicious circles contribute to the commodity trap. If innovations are confined to improvements, if the number of product features increases and comparisons between products becomes difficult to make, consumers become confused. If, at the same time, consumers do not pay attention to communication intended to inform them about distinguishing features and can avoid direct contact, it becomes virtually impossible to charge for a product's added value. As a result, return on investments in innovation comes under pressure, products become more and more alike and they eventually become commodities. At that point, price is the only remaining marketing weapon and the trap has closed.

Many examples present themselves. The production and sales of computers, consumer electronics, cars and white goods are a massive race to an unattractive future. The same holds for services provided by airlines, banks, insurers, hotels and the media. In all cases the products and services become increasingly indistinguishable and discounting is rampant.

The escape routes reflect despair. Managers that seek the solution by further and further customer segmentation and identifying and discarding unprofitable segments provide a first example. This is a highly delicate operation that can easily backfire. Companies that simply inform customers that their business is no longer appreciated do very little for their reputation. The standard route is to chase customers away by reducing service and making terms and conditions less attractive. Retail banks are continuously struggling with what they kindly call the lower end of the market. Airlines have their cattle class and big retailers have their sales fodder. Antagonism between companies and their customers is on the rise, a topic that we will return to in Chapter 4.

In rationalizing a customer base, the first 5 or 10 per cent of customers – those that do not make a contribution to overheads, let alone profitability – can be easily identified, but subsequent segments contain customers with more value to the company and the picture soon becomes blurred. This process cannot continue forever; at some point the contribution customers make to overheads and other fixed costs starts to be missed.

Selling off batches of customers only works if the buyer can produce and deliver a comparable product at much lower costs and if he can expect to retain a sufficient number of customers.

A second example is the seeking out of soft targets. The market for food products is highly saturated from whatever perspective one cares to take. In 2000, more than half of all US adults and 13 per cent of US children were considered overweight or obese. The number of Americans who are overweight remains constant, but obesity is on the increase. The number of obese adults has almost doubled from approximately 15 per cent in 1980 to an estimated 27 per cent in 1999.

In such a market, consumers have to be lured to buy products in a variety of ways and through a number of channels. They can be tempted by convenience food, by the inclusion of service elements, by more attractive packaging and by increasingly sophisticated advertising. The number of distribution channels for food has also risen enormously. The total US food bill has exploded from $450 billion in 1990 to $585 billion in 1998. The so-called farm value only increased from $106 billion to $119 billion over the same period. However, despite all the creativity in the world, the price weapon has become more important and price wars rage unabated.

Trying to escape the commodity trap, the food industry increasingly targets children, minorities and the poor, all market segments where knowledge about market prices and healthy eating habits are in short supply. The budget for marketing targeted at children rose from $6.9 billion in 1992 to $12.7 billion in 1997. Coca-Cola and Pepsi-Cola for example have extensive programmes to reach children via television advertising, school and the internet (12 million children between the ages of 2 and 12 have access to the internet, representing 25 per cent of all children in this age group). Many companies get their message through to kids via logos on toys and clothing, discount cards, telephone cards, product placement on TV and at the movies, celebrity endorsements and fast food tie-ins. At school, there are logos on vending machines, sport facilities and clothing. There are free samples, coupons for fast food, club and activity sponsorships and even advertisements in teaching materials.

The third escape route is the relaxation of laws and regulations. This calls for an increase in the lobbying of politicians and regulatory agencies. The food industry is permanently engaged in keeping government initiatives to improve public health in check. It seeks permission to put health-promoting benefits on the labels of products and tries to counter government attempts to have unjustified claims removed. The makers and sellers of dietary supplements managed to convince Congress that its products did not need to be regulated according to the strict standards applied to conventional foods. The sugar lobby has been very successful in keeping prices high for domestic sugar cane growers. And so it goes on.

Senators and members of Congress from states whose interests overlap those of the industry are encouraged to support local industries. Hard and soft campaign contributions are made and the 'revolving door' of former congressmen who become lobbyists (by 1998, 12 per cent of elected politicians who had left office since 1970) keeps turning.

In conclusion, it is revealing to note that even top managers of blue-chip companies like Unilever and Procter & Gamble have openly expressed doubts about the effectiveness of marketing. Unilever Chairman Niall FitzGerald pointed to the madness of spending around 45 billion euros to make the company's products and another 45 billion to sell them. He believes that 90 per cent rather than 50 per cent, which used to be the industry's rule of thumb, of advertising and promotion budgets are now wasted.

## Solving the wrong problems

The consensus is virtually complete. The purpose of the company is to provide their shareholders with an ever-increasing return on investment. Growing profits per share are at least a necessary condition for achieving this. Only a limited number of policies can achieve this at sufficient pace.

However a small and shrinking corporate repertoire makes it tempting to define corporate problems in terms of available solutions. Solving the wrong problems is of course extraordinarily costly and the American Enterprise Model leads the world down this path. It is chilling to note that the favoured policies become increasingly ineffective even in pursuit of shareholder return on investment. More determined action would increase cost further.

The final and most damaging conclusion is that all popular policies are followed at the expense of future cash flows and therefore at the expense of the economic value of the company.

## CAN THE FRANCHISE BE RENEWED?

If the most popular corporate policies of the 1990s have lost their lustre, the question is: why do they not give way to new approaches?

In Chapter 1, the point was made that the American Enterprise Model functions increasingly as a conceptual and operational straitjacket. Financial markets continue to push for quick and substantial improvements in corporate performance and this limits the action companies can take. A second reason for the lack of new approaches is the fact that US companies encouraged their mavericks and independent thinkers to leave throughout the 1990s, replacing them with MBA graduates. As a result, many firms became far too homogeneous for their own good, both in terms of ideology and in terms of professional backgrounds. The search for innovative ways to improve the business suffered.

The 1990s were also an era in which consultants lost much of their independence. A source of new thinking since time immemorial, adding prestige to their profession, consultants could no longer step aside because they had become part of the revolution (see Chapter 4). They pushed the financial performance of their own firms as never before. Like their clients, they too hired MBA graduates, the foot soldiers of the shareholder revolution, and sacrificed diversity. Some broadened their services to include financial advice, as in the case of McKinsey. Many, such as Bain & Company, tied their remuneration to the improvement of the financial results of their client or even directly to its share price.

The recession played a role, as did increased competition from specialized firms in information technology and human resources. Since the economic peak in 2001, top consultancy firms shed 30 per cent of their workforce, still leaving an overcapacity of perhaps another 30 per cent: not an environment in which many conceptual breakthroughs or lavish funds for product development can be expected to survive. Their wage and bonus bills were high, competition was fierce and they could ill afford to lose too many 'beauty contests'. Expressing deviating views, let alone views that challenged a client's belief, would have been a commercial risk.

When the bubble burst it was too late to point to different directions. Some of the best consultants had lost credibility through their association with spectacular corporate disasters. McKinsey was hurt by revelations about its role in the Enron, Global Crossing and Swissair disasters. Others, such as Boston Consulting Group, Bain, and Booz Allen & Hamilton had supported the dot.com revolution that produced equally horrendous results. Arthur D. Little disappeared altogether.

## Measures of last resort

Bain & Company acknowledged the lack of fresh thinking in its 2001 survey of 25 existing and new management tools.[23] The well-tested tools, the fads of the past, are all there, from 'supply chain integration' to 'scenario planning' and from 'data mining' to 'dynamic pricing'. It is revealing that only corporate venturing and customer relations management (CRM) could be added to the list of well-trodden paths, albeit with the qualification that neither was completely new.

Corporate venturing refers to the spinning-off of business ideas in various stages of development that for a variety of reasons have no future in the company. Generally the managers that were engaged in the project and believed in it take the plunge and receive corporate support that can take many different shapes and forms, from equity to purchase commitments and from equipment to intellectual property. Given the uniqueness of each new company, arrangements have to be tailor-made and are likely to be retailored several times before the new company settles. Flexibility and mutual trust are of the essence and it is for that reason that such risky ventures will do much better in the context of the European Enterprise Model (see Chapter 6).

The approach that comes closest to a new and widely applicable technique close to the bone of the American Enterprise Model is CRM. The focus of CRM is on the realization of the potential monetary value that an individual customer represents to the company. In plain language: how much will a customer buy of the company's products, when, and at what margin? His net present value is equal to the sum of the discounted total annual margin on these sales for each year of the customer's life.

CRM combines a variety of tools and in many ways represents the ultimate that the 1990s had to offer. It takes 'market segmentation' to its extreme as it focuses on the individual customer. It leans on 'total quality management' in its drive to match changing customer requirements. It draws on the 'core capabilities' of the company 'at the moments of truth' when company and customer meet. The approach is a child of its time with its orientation on the bottom line and close control of costs. It is also a child of its time by pushing the limits of information technology.

The design of a commercial approach to win over and to retain these valuable customers is based on an in-depth analysis of so-called contact points between the company and its customer. In the airline industry for example, contact is made at the reservation desk, at check-in, in the departure lounge, at boarding, during the flight, during transfers to connecting flights and at luggage collection. At each contact point, part of the service is delivered. More or less service can be provided at lower or higher costs at each contact point. The name of the game is to provide additional service based on customers' personal preferences. Some customers have pets that require special attention. Others always travel with children and will be interested in discounts. Yet others have tight connections and so want to sit in the front of the aircraft. A database is built for each customer with a history of his and his family's flights, a profile of preferences and specific requirements. The database also contains the net price paid by the customer for each flight, the pro rata cost of the basic service and the extra cost of additional service at each contact point. Based on this data, the margin that is realized per customer can be calculated and can be projected into the future. These projections become more dependable as the travel pattern of the customer unfolds over time. If the travel pattern changes, incentives and service can be cut or added. Airlines structure all this in the context of their increasingly sophisticated customer loyalty programmes. Needless to say, all these insights also help to target the customers of the competition.

Sceptics have argued that loyal customers are not necessarily the most profitable. Furthermore the expense of costing all the different incentives provided to millions of clients in various parts of the world at different times in diverse currencies has to be recouped.

Another weak point is that many of the targeted clients, mostly businessmen, are not the decision makers when it comes to choosing an airline, hotel chain, telephone company or rental company. Cost cutting dictates that travel managers buy services in bulk on the sharpest possible conditions. Under these circumstances, the loyalty of individual customers is not relevant. It also remains to be seen whether more personalized service, based on extensive customer records that need to be accessible to many, will not be considered as an intrusion of privacy in the future. It is questionable whether customers fail to distinguish between spontaneously delivered service and so-called scripts: programmed communication per event.

Furthermore, the information technology needed for customer relations management is stupendous and the costs considerable. Market research by US consultants Gartner Group and the Mesa Group suggests that the necessary software performs to standard in only 20 to 30 per cent of cases.

Finally, CRM has an Achilles heel. All things being equal, younger customers are more important than older ones. It is cynical, but young customers have more years ahead of them during which they can buy the company's products and contribute to its cash flow. At the same time, older people need and expect a higher level of service. The commercial need to focus on the young runs counter to the basic social values of service staff that have been selected for their traditional attitudes and demeanour. It is unlikely that instruction and training can fill this void.

The conclusion has to be that, by the end of the 1990s and beyond, the best the consultancy industry had to offer is found wanting.

## False dawn

Believers in the US economy and the American Enterprise Model have to believe in the future of the largest and best-performing sectors of the 1990s: ICT, retail and wholesale.

Communication technology will continue to advance for some time. But the growth rate of the sector will depend on the development of demand for mobile information services and customer demand for more calculating power in mobile phones and improved mobility of PCs.[24]

An article titled 'IT doesn't matter' by Nicholas Carr in the *Harvard Business Review* has triggered a major debate about the future of information technology.[25] The majority of industry analysts, not to mention CEOs of IT companies, are predicting a return to growth rates of the 1990s in the demand for computer hardware, software and services. The underlying assumption appears to be that business will continue to see investment in information technology as the preferred weapon in the battle for productivity and competitive edge. It is this assumption that Carr calls into question, drawing comparisons with the railways, electricity and the internal combustion engine which all became 'commodity inputs' in a short period of time. The underlying economic forces leading to standardization are irresistible. The coupling of railway, electricity and ICT networks produces enormous cost reductions while at the same time the product becomes so much better that it takes on new dimensions.

Carr asserts that, after demand for computing and communications hardware has caught up with supply, demand will grow in line with GNP or slightly higher to reflect a gradual change to a more service-oriented society. The consequences of having reached saturation in demand for infrastructure is that production increases will level off and that the associated high productivity increases of the late 1990s in the production of ICT hardware will not return.

The future of the retail and wholesale sectors is shrouded. In 2003 and 2004 the two sectors that comprise 70 per cent of the US economy continued to advance, supported by the continual rise in income of a small proportion of the population, very low interest rates, house price inflation, the refinancing of mortgages (which produced a hefty $300 billion in additional spending during 2003 alone) and sizeable government hand-outs in the form of two tax rebates.

It has been well established that consumers react to improvements in spendable income and far less to absolute levels. The impact of most of the stimuli mentioned above is now ebbing away. Tax cuts are out of the question, interest rates are already rising and the threat of lay-offs prevents wages from increasing. Savings have reached both a historic and an absolute low and have to rise to repair pensions and to cope with the rapidly rising cost of health care and university education (traditionally important reasons for Americans to save). Credit card debt is close to an all-time high, as is households' total debt service as a proportion of disposable income. The stock market is improving but price–earning ratios are far ahead of the levels experienced at the start of the previous recovery, and the crash of March 2000 to October 2002 that more than halved the quoted value lingers on in people's memory. Finally, a jobless recovery (or a recovery that does not produce more than the 100,000 jobs per month that are required to keep up with the growth of the working population) does not do much for consumer spending.[26]

Only house price inflation remains as a source of continued growth in consumer spending, but mortgage refinancing in 2004 was, compared with 2003, already down 80 per cent due to a small increase in mortgage rates.

All in all, income and wealth effects will be modest for some time. This is particularly important in light of the fact that new economic powerhouses are not yet in sight. Much-heralded advances in genetics and nanotechnology have a long way to go before new products reach the market in meaningful numbers. Much earlier breakthroughs in biological research are only now translating into a large biotechnology sector, but this sector is by no means large enough to draw the US economy out of recession. The revenues of all US publicly traded biotechnology companies rose from $8.1 billion in 1992 to $28.5 billion in 2001. Despite its success, this remains a modest contribution in a $10,000 billion economy.[27]

Looking at the state of the union, the US economy is not likely to come to the rescue of the American Enterprise Model. To the contrary, a break in optimistic expectations for the decade, for example by a dollar crisis and the ensuing deep US recession, will open many European eyes.

## IN SUMMARY

During the 1990s, both the United States and Europe made great strides in deregulating markets, privatizing state companies and removing trade barriers. At the end of the decade they parted ways. The Bush administration, showing its true colours and facing a recession, rejuvenated the Reagan revolution. At the same time, European governments – having shed much of the ideological ballast taken on during the 1990s – started to become more cautious and pragmatic.

Prospects for the American Enterprise Model are unfavourable. The financial community dictates concentration on shareholder return of investment and a limited number of corporate policies: corporate and financial restructuring, industry consolidation, cost cutting and achieving market leadership. It turns out that these policies are reaching their limits, that they are becoming increasingly costly and less and less effective. Marketing tools in particular have lost their sharpness and there is increasing reliance on crude forms of market communication and discounting.

There are no new recipes on the horizon. Strategy consultants, with a vested interest in creating and selling renewal, became ensnared by the ideology and priorities of the 1990s and could not play their traditional role as innovators.

The American Enterprise Model is also under threat as a result of the less-than-bright prospects of the US economy in the medium term.

Looking at the economic sectors that made the largest contributions to productivity increases and economic growth – retail and ICT – the prospects of individual companies vary, but far too much hinges on the capacity and willingness of the US consumer to continuously increase spending.

The policy options open to the Federal Reserve Bank and federal government that were available during the 1990s and during the ensuing recession to keep consumption going are now exhausted. If the US consumer is forced to keep spending constant (not to mention the possibility of lowering spending), the United States will have to take a different route. Economic growth will then have to depend on a cheaper dollar to ignite exports, on investment and on increased employment. The substantial decline in the dollar has so far done very little for the competitiveness of the United States in world markets.

Many believed that the formula for sustained corporate and economic development had been found at the end of the 1990s: the American Enterprise Model. But at the end of the day, it proved impossible to break the age-old pattern: new technology produces initially modest and then accelerated growth followed by deceleration and finally stagnation.

The true believer in the American Enterprise Model is of course not discouraged; he stays the course and increases his efforts. He can point at an increase in corporate profitability, but the world has become a riskier place (Chapter 2) and he cannot escape the law of diminishing returns.

Moreover companies that are forced to stick to the corporate policies of the 1990s increasingly face unintended consequences and incur more and more unaccounted costs, the topic of the next chapter.

# 4

# Unintended consequences and unaccounted costs

The 1990s were the decade of technological and political revolution, shareholder activism and the restructuring of organizational and commercial life.

The previous chapter concentrated on the resistance to once-popular government policies, on fashionable corporate policies that ran out of steam, on market saturation and on the increasing bluntness of classical marketing instruments.

In this chapter, the focus is on the unintended consequences and the unaccounted costs of the organizational and cultural changes companies introduced to facilitate the pursuit of shareholder return on investment. These are important aspects of the American Enterprise Model as first described in Chapter 1.

The most visible change was the establishment of the CEO as an institution. The CEO was elevated to star status both on a personal level and as a function. The belief was that inspirational leadership is required to make the big leaps forward demanded by shareholders.

Secondly, the need for major change in the way companies operated enhanced the role of financial advisors and strategy consultants in corporate decision making. These professionals were required to identify the big opportunities. And the best brains were needed to help firms through their inevitable transition.

A third crucial shift was driven by a strongly felt need to focus on the customer. This required the grouping of operations and commercial activities in small so-called business units that could operate close to customers and react swiftly to their changing preferences. Decentralization of decision making had of course to be accompanied by the strengthening of financial planning and control systems. Corporate head offices became a thing of the past as costs were reduced and any overlap between corporate and business unit activities avoided.

Then there was a complete overhaul of performance planning, evaluation and remuneration. All business units received unequivocal (preferably financial) targets and the responsible manager was judged against these. Companies started to rely heavily on financial incentives to guarantee vigorous pursuit of the units' objectives and compliance with shareholder interests. Managers who believed in financial incentives for themselves and their employees rose to prominence. Tensions rose because of sharp increases in total remuneration, in the differences between the ranks and in the variable component of the package.[1]

Finally, management selection and development changed in a fundamental way. The 1990s saw the emergence of the 'change agent', a new type of manager who was mentally prepared for major reform and operated with ideological zeal. He believed targets existed to be surpassed. To this end all available means had to be mobilized. Sacrifice was inevitable. Competition created value and an internal labour market was the most effective way to allocate scarce management resources.

# THE HERO OF THE 1990s

With the private sector as the engine for economic growth, entrepreneurship as the major driving force behind corporate well-being, and personal responsibility and accountability as the basis for corporate management, the chief executive officer was bound to dominate the 1990s.

## A new public figure

Many helped to raise the CEO (and in 70 per cent of the US companies he was also chairman) onto a pedestal.

Financial analysts for example had a predilection for strong and assertive CEOs who were capable of simplifying a complex world and brave enough to commit themselves to ambitious financial targets. One man had to be held accountable in the event that expectations were not met. Only unity in command could guarantee decisive action, and a transparent management structure made it easier for analysts to read corporate intentions.

The press played an important role. Both the position of chief executive and the personality of the man in the job made good copy. The United States was a nation of shareholders with 85 million by the end of the decade, and they needed heroes. Creating heroes was profitable for the CEO himself, his company and the media. Appearing on the cover of *Forbes* or *Business-Week* signalled that a CEO had arrived.

Politicians became involved in promoting the cult. Many sought to associate themselves with corporate America as the embodiment of everything that was good about the country. The business backgrounds of President George W. Bush and Vice-President Dick Cheney, who had been involved in the management of the Texas Rangers baseball franchise and construction and services company Halliburton respectively, were presented as great assets. Other, possibly more sceptical, politicians had little choice but to cosset business leaders to raise funds to cover the exploding cost of political campaigns.

Forces inside companies that reinforced the position of the CEO were also at play. The chief executive, faced with growing accountability and goaded by ever-increasing financial incentives, had every reason to pull as many strings as possible. At the same time, many managers were only too happy to abdicate responsibility and to hold fire until the CEO had expressed his preference.

Corporate culture required that the modern CEO stayed close to his rank and file. Appearances on the shop floor were not a duty but a privilege; there were phone-ins; and e-mails to bring an idea to his attention were much appreciated. What he said, to whom and on what occasion spread like wildfire. Those who exchanged a few words with him basked in glory. Internal publications and well-chosen public appearances put the finishing touches to an image that in many companies was professionally designed and maintained. Being allowed to send the CEO a memo, attending meetings at which he was present, getting an appointment with him and building a relationship were all rungs on the ladder of corporate success. The CEO figured prominently even in meetings that he did not attend. His ambitious followers suggested closeness to the boss by referring to him frequently – by his first name – while making liberal use of his buzz words.

The boards of US companies really believed that super-CEOs existed, and went out of their way to find one. They relied heavily on the help of head-hunters who had no interest in reducing expectations and who seemed to be able to produce the goods. Observers such as management gurus Warren Bennis and James O'Toole note that boards went for the hard facts about candidates' achievements, such as increases in stock price, higher market shares and big decreases in expenses.[2] With the pursuit of share value as the prime concern, CEOs had to be deeply embedded in the world of finance. Knowledge of a particular industry was of secondary, if any, importance. The 1990s were the heyday of the general manager and omnipotence.

## Illusions of control

The underlying premises were that a CEO made better decisions than his underlings, that he had the time and energy to do this, and that he exercised sufficient control to see that their rapid implementation was in line with his original intentions. Consequently he could and should be held accountable for corporate performance.

In reality, corporate performance is determined by a plethora of decisions taken in the recent and distant past.

A CEO inherits a company with all its strengths and weaknesses. He inherits its corporate reputation, commercial positions and an extraordinary number of commitments both internally and to third parties. He takes over an existing management team that has often worked together for years and whose dynamics are initially difficult to read. He has to build a relationship with his board members and to familiarize himself with many procedures and customs. He is confronted with a range of complicated plans in various stages of development and decision making. Not surprisingly, any new CEO needs time to determine what he wants to do and what can be done. Therefore he has to create the conditions for change before he can put his stamp on the company. He has to identify who is with him and who is not. And he feels compelled to bring in new managers. Very few newly appointed CEOs refrain from reorganization in one form or another. Only then does he feel able to make his first moves, often annulling minor decisions made by his predecessor.

Before making his first major moves, he needs to build support for a new direction and to shepherd the formal decision through the system. Once a decision has been taken, implementation proves to be more complicated than anticipated, resistance has to be overcome and invariably plans have to be adjusted. It is clear that it will be years before the hand of a CEO becomes visible, if at all. Rather than being almighty, he is perpetually struggling, dependent as he is on outside help and the cooperation of so many throughout his organization.

Belief in the CEO's capacity to control is further undermined by the very tenuous link between his decisions and improved corporate performance. His actions drown in a sea of initiatives both by his own organization and by competitors. Even in the rare situations in which such a link is unequivocal, it is difficult to pass fair judgement. Decisions applauded today appear to have been blunders in a subsequent era, only to turn into epitomes of foresight years later. The former chief executive of Unilever, Floris Maljers, speaks from experience when he characterizes the role of the CEO as the guardian of a largely autonomous evolution.

At a very practical and personal level, it is physically impossible for CEOs to exercise control in any real meaning of the word. Popular ideas such as the reduction of management layers and the decrease of overheads have lumbered him with a wide span of control (10 so-called direct reports is not unusual) and deprived him of staff support. Even 18-hour days, seven days a week, are far from enough to allow him to attend all meetings, carry out all formal duties, function as the company's number one public relations officer, stay close to financial markets and keep the board and senior managers up to date on developments. This leaves no time to think and lead the company. The chief executive officer is not even in charge of his own agenda and is simply dragged from commitment to commitment and from crisis to crisis.

Embracing the fallacy of the almighty CEO was costly in a number of respects.

## Destabilization of the company

The emergence of the dominant CEO changed the balance of power in terms of corporate governance and management structure. In a long US tradition, many were also company chairmen, but even where this was not the case, as in many companies on the European continent, boards lost control. When the board of Philips Electronics appointed Cor Boonstra as CEO in the mid-1990s, it was well aware of the trail of dismissals he had left behind him in all the companies he had worked for. It was therefore hardly a surprise when Boonstra, against the wishes of the supervisory board chairman (ex-Unilever CEO Floris Maljers), forced the resignation of Doug Dunn, who was head of consumer electronics and the company's crown prince at the time. Having pushed the value of Philips's share from 6 to 20 euros within the first two years of his tenure, Boonstra was unassailable and, four months later, Maljers resigned.[3]

Harvard professor Margarethe Wiersema asserts that many US boards are not even engaged in planning for CEO succession.[4] This is the fiefdom of the American CEO himself. The board lacks essential knowledge about the quality of possible internal candidates. Furthermore few board members fully understand the business they supposedly oversee and the issues that drive performance. They are poorly equipped to give headhunters specific criteria for finding a new CEO. Investors' interests drive the selection process. There is a strong bias towards an outsider to signal a break from the past, and those who promise a quick turnaround. The bias is against insiders who might have scruples and lingering loyalties to employees. This was the case with Toys R Us. This retailer of traditional toys never came to grips with competition from large discount stores and the rise of computer games. Ferocious cost cutting by a new CEO, Robert Nakasone, was clearly not the answer to the problem as the company continued to suffer and its stock price declined by 45 per cent during his 18-month tenure.

While CEOs were supposed to serve shareholders, some became so powerful that they were difficult to dislodge even when the writing had been on the wall for some time. Steve Case of AOL Time Warner is a prime example. A number of reorganizations and a number of dismissals of former AOL managers led to the emergence of Time Warner as the leading company and the relegation of AOL to division status. Only then was the time ripe for Case's departure. Such a dismissal battle, stretched over two years, distracts from the business at hand and cannot be fought without considerable collateral damage.[5]

Internally, the distance between the CEO and his management team grew in the 1990s. Many chief executives negotiated far-reaching mandates with their boards. This, in combination with the personality traits deemed necessary for a modern CEO, reduced dialogue, discussion and dissent. As a result the quality of decision making suffered, risks increased and implementation of far-reaching or controversial decisions suffered.

With a lack of professional supervision and no internal checks and balances, performance of CEO decision making suffered.

## Personal style and preferences

The myth of the almighty CEO attracted potential successors with the corresponding personality and self-image. As pointed out by Manfred Kets de Vries, professor of human resource management at France's INSEAD, and others, there is a thin line between healthy ambition and sense of duty on the one hand, and megalomania and narcissism on the other. His overview of healthy character traits for competent managers sets standards that were totally ignored in the heady and frenetic atmosphere of the 1990s. The scandals of the decade have revealed that many companies had been trusted to CEOs with serious personality disorders. .

Since the company's way of doing business and the personality of the CEO became more and more intertwined, his personal likes and dislikes, friendships and rivalries left significant marks. CEOs, much more than other corporate officials, were extended an implicit right to be guided by personal considerations in matters of considerable corporate interest.

Personal preferences played a role in appointing and dismissing senior managers. Professional qualifications were necessary but by no means sufficient. It was considered permissible and even desirable that there was a rapport between the chief executive officer and his appointee. It was even accepted that a personal dislike by the CEO, possibly dressed up in some other form, was sufficient grounds for dismissal. It was not at all unusual that loyalty to the company was equated to loyalty to the man in charge. In *At Any Costs* (which chronicles the rise of General Electric and the damage the company left in its wake) Thomas F. O'Boyle reports a number of brutal dismissals by CEO Jack Welch.[6] These were often executed without warning and without explanation.

Personal preferences also play a major part in the realm of mergers, acquisitions and alliances. Firstly, there is a bias towards takeovers at the expense of mergers and alliances. CEOs are selected to lead and to dominate. The sharing of responsibilities implies loss of power and is therefore considered risky. Consequently, attractive opportunities to merge or to cooperate are passed over at unknown expense to the future of both potential partners. Even when the commercial and operational logic to merge or to cooperate stares everybody in the face, bad blood between the protagonists is an acceptable reason to dismiss the opportunity. This unrealized potential does not show up in the corporate accounts but represents real damage to the company.

Conversely, nobody can estimate how much value CEOs destroy when they are determined to forge a deal despite the lack of business logic. Certain companies never recover from a forced marriage. Dutch distiller Bols and food group Wessanen were brought together in the 1980s by their CEOs on the basis of very little more than the fact that some customers eat cheese with their drinks. After the inevitable separation, Bols disappeared without leaving much of a trace and Wessanen went through numerous strategy changes, ending up as a US distributor and retailer of food supplements, a fickle and risky business that requires constant restructuring.

The profile of the CEO and the personality traits that he apparently required acted as a deterrent for many highly talented managers with knowledge about the real world. Moreover exposure to the media, the dominance of form over content and the relentlessness of corporate infighting were not particularly enticing to clever and balanced personalities. Many, like Rob Pieterse of Dutch publisher Wolters Kluwer, yielded to pressure and accepted an offer to become CEO out of duty and against their better judgement, only to regret their decision. The business community as a whole paid an unknown price for a shrinking pool of potential CEOs.

## The expectation game

Financial analysts and journalists occupy the high ground in a world in which the need to concentrate on the pursuit of shareholder return on investment is considered self-evident. They operate under the banner of shareholders' justified interest in the need for, and right to, transparency and predictability. As a result, CEOs are under continuous pressure to be clear about the direction of their company and to be specific about its future financial performance. Even occasional vagueness carries a penalty. Inability to be specific over an extended period reflects lack of control and leadership. There is also a high premium on action over reflection. As described in the previous chapter, the options are all there: financial engineering, corporate restructuring, acquisitions, cost cutting and outsourcing. Difficult but wise decisions to prevent damage to the company by dumping poor plans cannot be traced and are therefore ignored.

It is not surprising that many CEOs were lured into detailed and quantified projections for the short and medium term. This was particularly true of those who were given to illusions of control, whose confidence was boosted by rising stock prices and whose vanity needed to be fed by favourable press coverage.

The result was a soothing but false sense of security for both the CEO and the professionals responsible for following company performances with a critical eye. When over time the projections proved to be untenable, the CEO was challenged by the same analysts and journalists who extracted excessively optimistic forecasts in the first place and converted these into client recommendations and articles.

Companies paid a considerable price in their dealings with the outside world. The authoritative CEO, the darling of the financial community and the financial press, distracted attention from company performance. When he was rated highly, the firm was more likely to be overrated. If the CEO, for whatever reasons, had fallen from grace, the rating of the company suffered unduly. The European example par excellence is the rise and fall of Messier and the value of the Vivendi stock.

A costly paradox presents itself. The prevailing world-view – which stresses the need to deregulate, open markets and privatize – may have pros and cons but inevitably produces a great deal of uncertainty for the business community. All this was at a time in which the average company was prepared to be shackled by increasingly specific projections.

The pursuit of return on shareholder investment was a priority shared by CEOs, financial analysts and journalists. The irony is that the quest for certainty where there is none causes considerable tension between CEOs and analysts which undermines the credibility of the company at the expense of the shareholder.

## Paradise lost

Companies internally paid a price for their unrealistic expectations of CEO performance.[7] Long before business leaders abused their positions, disillusion among the company's rank and file had set in. According to a study of employee attitudes and opinions by Washington-based human resource consultants Watson Wyatt in 2000, only 50 per cent of US employees expressed confidence in senior managers. A similar survey in 2002 revealed substantial doubts about management's capabilities of leading a company through major transformations, one of the hallmarks of the truly outstanding CEO. Only 43 per cent of all employees said that their companies effectively managed restructuring, downsizing, mergers, expansion and growth. In addition, there was much uncertainty about 'the line of sight', the causal link between the employee's tasks and performance and corporate objectives. Unrealistic expectations were bound to produce disillusionment and subsequently to lead to the erosion of authority.[8]

The credibility of CEOs was further undermined by the cynical way in which many violated the very principles they publicly espoused. CEOs cushioned themselves on a grand scale against the gyrations of the stock market by having their remuneration packages adapted if and when required. John Snow, chairman and CEO of transport conglomerate CSX (he later became secretary of the Treasury under President George W. Bush), saw the basis of his remuneration change every single year from 1993 to 2001 – and always for the better. At some point the link between the award of stock options and performance was severed, additional options were awarded to compensate for options that had become worthless, performance measures for annual bonus schemes were changed and a performance share scheme was replaced by a long-term cash scheme.[9]

CEOs were also capable of negotiating substantial golden parachutes. This was again in clear violation of the spirit of the 1990s. Golden parachutes undermined the credibility of many chief executives from the very start of their tenure, particularly of those who felt they had to steer their companies down risky paths.

In these cases, the idea of high rewards for genuine risk taking and subsequent success – a defendable and laudable principle established at the outset of the US economic revolution – was treated with contempt. CEOs with power but without authority are a danger to the company.

## Knock-on effects

The pressure is intense, expectations are sky high and shareholders feel entitled to changes for the better sooner rather than later. There is a high premium on action but the CEO is very much restricted. He is pushed towards whatever he can do to improve corporate performance quickly. As it happens, his options are the favourite recipes of the financial community: financial restructuring, corporate reorganization, takeovers and mass layoffs. These are exactly the arenas in which the application of the American Enterprise Model is becoming less effective, as indicated in Chapter 3.

All in all, it is not surprising that, despite the problems involved in dismissing a CEO, more and more were asked to leave. Sources disagree as to the precise numbers and the criteria used in different studies vary. Booz

Allen & Hamilton reports that, among the 2,500 largest companies in the world, merger and performance-related dismissals of CEOs increased from 1.8 per cent in 1995 to 6.4 per cent in 2000, falling to 4.8 per cent in 2001. US sociologist Michael Beer presents evidence that the average tenure of the US chief executive officer declined from 10.5 years in 1990 to 4.2 years in 2000.[10] Rakesh Khurana, professor at the MIT Sloan School in Massachusetts, shows that chief executives appointed after 1985 are three times more likely to be fired than those appointed before that year.

The general picture is clear: more CEOs were dismissed during the 1990s than before or after, despite the considerable cost to the company in terms of fighting and paralysis before the dismissal and in terms of the time that is required to find a new leader and the time he needs before he can operate effectively. All of this is compounded by the fact that a falling CEO drags an average of five managers down with him. The benefits of such secondary dismissals are highly dubious.[11]

In an article in the *Harvard Business Review*, Margarethe Wiersema presents the case of the AT&T board. In 1997 the board dismissed Robert Allen, a company veteran of 40 years, and brought in a celebrated outsider, former Hughes Electronics executive Michael Armstrong. The market responded and AT&T stock rose from $47 to $90. But this success was short-lived because Armstrong could not find a way to tackle increased competition in the crucially important long-distance market and his attempts to generate earnings growth in other markets failed. Earnings per share went down from $2.44 in 1997 to $0.89 in 2001.

Often the upheaval of replacing the CEO was futile and the associated invisible costs were wasted. Wiersema analysed the selection process of 83 new CEOs within the 500 largest American companies in 1997 and 1998. Of these, 37 per cent were the result of dismissals. Comparing corporate performance two years before their appointment with two years after, it appears that the firing of the CEO did not make a difference in operating earnings or return on assets and had a negative impact on stock return.[12]

## CORPORATE HEAD OFFICE

As highlighted in previous chapters, the pursuit of shareholder value was considered good economics and morally just. Companies appointed financially oriented top management and enforced the position of the CFO and the corporate controller. In general, financial management gained considerable prestige and power throughout the period and could greatly extend their influence in strategic corporate decision making.

In pursuing a higher share price, companies invested heavily in communication with the financial community, bankers and analysts. They beefed up their investor relations departments. They paid more attention to their reporting and strengthened relationships with financial journalists. 'Roadshows' (visits by the CEO and CFO to the world's financial centres to report on corporate performance and prospects) became a fixed item on the management agenda. A flow of press releases had to keep the company in full public view.

At the same time, head offices lost considerable commercial and techno-logical expertise. Some was shifted to the business units but mostly exper-tise was simply lost in cost-saving drives. Moreover CEOs had to prove their mettle by cutting their own support staff. The savings were modest, the potential damage to future cash flows considerable. A 30 per cent cost reduction in Shell's geological department in the late 1990s contributed years later to problems in assessing reserves and the capacity of Shell to secure oil reserves. It is a spectacular example of how a negligible contri-bution to the profit per share was achieved at the expense of extensive damage to future cash flows. Companies made their experts redundant and became more dependent on external advisors frequently at higher expense.

On top of this, investment bankers, business analysts and strategy advi-sors needed, for commercial reasons, to develop footholds in large corpo-rations. The inevitable result was mutual dependence between financially oriented corporate management and the financial and consultancy communities.

If one adds a common educational background (accountancy, business economics and management), the comparability of careers and the social homogeneity of professionals on both sides of the corporate fence, the con-tours of an informal but powerful group straddling the corporate boundary become visible.

Once well and truly on board, the guardians of the American Enterprise Model – the financial and consultancy communities – took charge and started to skew strategic decision making.

## The investment banker as guardian angel

During the 1990s, investment banking became dominated by US interests. Merrill Lynch, Goldman Sachs, Morgan Stanley and J P Morgan became household names. They operated on a very large home market and conquered Europe with ease. European commercial banks, such as Deutsche Bank, Dresdner Bank and ING, tried to turn the tide by buying English rivals and US niche-players but to no avail, with an exception to the rule in the form of Credit Suisse which took over First Boston. US investment banks never disguised their roots and were instrumental in spreading the American Enterprise Model. No questions needed to be asked about the purity of their thinking and their determination to succeed.

Investment banks scrutinize industries for untapped shareholder value. They are a dynamic force, investing considerable creativity, tenacity and analytical power in identifying potentially beneficial transactions. They offer companies access to the stock market and other sources of finance. They look in particular for potential mergers and acquisitions, either to represent one of the parties or to defend one party against the other.

The financial community was preoccupied with the selection of takeover candidates. Diversification needed to be avoided at all cost. Pure takeovers were far better than fuzzy mergers, let alone alliances. Acquisitions justified by cost savings were preferred over deals designed to capture technological synergies or revenue growth. Scale was held in high regard and a top position among the industry leaders in any particular sector was considered necessary. And speed was of the essence.

In scrutinizing the market, the investment banks excluded many possible transactions that did not fit the strategy concepts of the day and did not meet specific financial criteria. Potential mergers and acquisitions that did not contribute to short-term corporate profitability, that would on announcement have a negative impact on the share price of the acquiring company or that would lead to a reduction of income per share were rejected out of hand. By excluding these opportunities, investment banks acted as the custodians of short-term shareholder interests. Throughout the 1990s, the merger of British Airways (BA) and KLM was depicted as 'a deal made in heaven'. Substantial value could be added by turning Amsterdam's Schiphol Airport into Heathrow's terminal 5, KLM could provide BA with a defendable position on the Continent and the intercontinental networks and partnerships of both airlines were complementary.

BA's investment banks proved incapable of appreciating the very significant additional cash flow the integrated company would generate. They concentrated on the market capitalization (outstanding shares times share price) of both companies as a basis for the distribution of future profits and were obsessed by the need to fully control KLM. Both conditions could not be met. Four serious attempts over a period of 10 years that would have made BA the world leader in commercial aviation and would have created substantial value came to nothing.

While mergers that fail for the wrong reason attract considerable attention, and damage is traceable and tangible for a long time, they only represent one kind of error. Opportunities that are not even explored because of a financial form of self-censorship leave no record. Value that is not created is lost for ever.

When corporations engage investment banks to explore a specific merger or a takeover, the way these banks are paid poses a serious risk to independent decision making. There are a number of incentives at work that weigh in favour of completing a potential deal even if issues come to light during the course of negotiations that would warrant withdrawal by one or both parties.

A typical contract between a company and an investment bank includes a modest monthly retainer, one-off rewards when certain milestones are reached and, most importantly, a success fee which is usually expressed as a percentage of the total value of the transaction. Such percentages range between 1 per cent and 3 per cent, or $5 to $15 million for a modest $500 million transaction. Much larger sums are at stake when, as part of a transaction, shares have to be placed with institutional investors or with the public. Underwriting such placements is risky but highly rewarding when the shares are taken up. Investment banks might be forgiven for putting such a possibility in a favourable light. Bringing companies to the market is, and remains, the most prestigious of all banking activities.

During the 1990s competition among investment banks was already fierce, and financial talent scarce and therefore expensive. Investment banks often felt forced to accept assignments at conditions below their profitability criteria in the hope that a long-term relationship could be forged and that follow-up business would be more profitable. As a result, transactions took on additional importance. No transaction, no follow-up business.

Another very powerful incentive was built into the remuneration of the individual investment bankers. A very large part of their income was variable and could amount to between 40 and 100 per cent of total income in any given year. The variable part is almost always linked to turnover or margin. No transaction, no turnover. No turnover, no bonus or options.

On top of this, the investment banker was under significant pressure from his own management. Many deals take a long time to reach closure with collapse looming around every corner, and a high percentage of negotiations do not produce an agreement. A banker can only keep his expensive team on the case for so long. Progress is essential if he is to fend off calls on resources from colleagues with more promising prospects.

Finally, the banker's reputation is on the line, each and every time, adding to his burden to succeed. The uncomfortable truth is that an investment banker is as good as his last transaction. No transaction, no last transaction. Investment banks, the standard-bearers in the pursuit of shareholder return, restructure on an ongoing basis. The pace only accelerates when the market for mergers and acquisitions is weak.

All of the above would not matter so much if the role of the investment banker was confined to market and technical advice and to negotiating, but this is only so in a minority of cases. Given the need to succeed, investment bankers have every reason to control as many aspects of the corporate decision-making process as possible, and they have the experience, weight and assertiveness to follow through. Investment bankers can quickly build positions of considerable authority within the client company. This is based on unrivalled knowledge of financial markets, highly specialized negotiating expertise (whereas many corporate officials are facing a situation that is completely alien to them), solid intelligence about the other parties involved in the game, determination and sheer hard work. Their network of contacts among strategy consultants, lawyers, accountants and public relations experts is highly valuable and increases the banker's leverage. A final and crucial source of authority is the close relationship between the banker and corporate top management, the CEO in particular. The more personal the relationship becomes, the better it is. Charm is an indispensable attribute of the investment banker. Pressure, loneliness at the top, the need for strict confidentiality and the division of the world into friend and foe should do the rest and make the investment banker the confidant of the CEO. Trust and total confidentiality are so important that even players on the same side of a potential deal employ different investment banks. In the early 1990s, Lord King and Colin Marshall (respectively British Airways chairman and CEO at the time) hired different investment banks when dealing with potential partners.

Obviously, the fee structure and position of the financial advisor on the side of the potential partner or takeover target is comparable if not identical. As a result two investment bankers, each strongly motivated to close the deal and working in deep secrecy, become an independent and hidden force that may or may not work in the best interest of both clients or may or may not generate most economic value. Their common interest might lead both bankers to mould the perceptions and ambitions of their respective clients to increase the likelihood of an agreement.

## The strategy consultant as guardian angel

Every revolution needs an intellectual elite who will translate general prin-ciples into practical proposals for specific enterprises. It is by no means simple to convert new technology to marketable products. Restructuring needs to be done in the most professional manner. Justification for a major upheaval requires sophisticated arguments. Throughout the 1990s these and many other tasks fell to the management consultancy community with McKinsey, Bain and the Boston Consulting Group (BCG) as the most pres-tigious firms.

These were already well positioned at the start of the 1990s. Internal training and international assignments had already built an international core of partners, and most local offices were managed by professionals who grew up with the business elite of their country. They had also built a closely knit corporate culture: there was always too much work and impossible deadlines but working for these consultancies was also intellectually excit-ing and socially interesting. Morale was always high and total dedication was a minimum demand.

A comparison with the Jesuit Order in the days of a rapidly expanding Catholic Church is difficult to avoid: soldiers for God, fighting important battles, strong enough to have a significant impact on the policies of the Church, smart enough to move with the tide, never losing sight of the interests of their order.

Like investment bankers, strategy consultants combined position, opportunity and drive. This produced impressive results. Total revenues in this sector in the United States increased from $34 billion in 1994 to $102 billion in 1999.[13] Supply of services became more diversified. The large accounting firms such as KPMG, PricewaterhouseCoopers and Deloitte & Touche entered the market in a big way, as did specialized information technology, e-commerce and human resource consultants. A significant degree of concentration in a once highly fragmented industry was achieved. In 1999 the 10 largest consulting firms generated over one-third of the industry's revenues. Finally, and for the arguments put forward in this book a highly relevant shift, US consultants came to dominate the industry worldwide, but particularly in Europe.

As stressed in Chapter 3, the 1990s were also the decade during which strategy consultants lost their independence. They too were the children of Reagan and Thatcher; they too focused first and foremost on the financial performance of their firms. Their offerings became more and more comparable.

Focus on so-called core activities went hand in hand with the application of best operational and commercial practices. The help of consultants proved indispensable in identifying and implementing these practices. Consultants had the databases to compare the corporate performances against competitors. 'Benchmarking' became the name of a highly popular game. This well-sold product narrowed and distorted the corporate agenda in three different ways. Firstly, corporate activities for which no industry data was available to measure performance were less likely to be tackled. Secondly, comparisons could only be made in fields in which performance could be quantified. As always, quantification came at the price of a distorted view of the real world: sales cost per unit can hide differences in service levels. Employee turnover says nothing about the reasons for leaving. And stock levels only provide useful insights in combination with a record of missed sales opportunities. Thirdly, once it is demonstrated that a unit is weak in certain respects, the problem cannot be left unattended and action has to be taken. In this way management time and resources are drawn to a limited number of fields that might or might not be of crucial importance. Of course only consultants were able to transfer new concepts and the methods for implementation. Approaches that worked in one or two companies were generalized and became a crucial contribution to the next project with a new client. In this way consultants not only identified but also defined best practice.

While many investment bankers remained in the airy sphere of high finance, strategy consultants got their hands dirty and could, if invited, cover all aspects of corporate operations. Like the commercial tactics of investment bankers, an initially small project could serve as a loss leader for things to come. Companies in distress were of course prime targets. The consultants looked for firms with the sort of problems that would suit their own methods, solutions and track record. And it was the consultants that gave potential clients a little help in defining their problems. Once inside a company, consultants were avid learners, collecting data, improving their insight and refining their methods. All this was with an eye to acquiring new clients.

Senior partners in consultancy firms were very much engaged during the acquisition phase but left the work to more junior colleagues once contracts were signed, reappearing only at crucial meetings, particularly those during which follow-up business might be discussed. Once a project was started, middle managers were initially less than impressed with these consultants, but hard work, good-looking software, superb presentations and the capacity to learn quickly often helped to build credibility. In Europe, good command of English played a major part in conveying an air of sophistication, with consultants enjoying their advantage at all organizational levels, including the top echelons.

Throughout the 1990s, corporate restructuring and cost cutting in its many shapes remained the best-selling articles in the shop window.

Even more damaging was the convergence of corporate strategies that resulted from benchmarking by strategy consultants. The airline industry provides a spectacular example. If the number of city couplings (connections between two cities) that airlines can offer is seen as essential to build competitive advantages, every airline will introduce a hub-and-spoke system – ie concentration of arrivals and departures within limited time frames to increase the number of connections, and therefore city couplings – even airlines that stand no chance of making such a system successful for straightforward reasons (such as geography and size of the home market). If market share on the North Atlantic routes is defined as the key to success, all European airlines will engage in alliances with US partners and will obtain anti-trust immunity in exchange for open-sky treaties between their own and the US government. They all introduced expensive entertainment systems, on-line booking service and increasingly sophisticated frequent-flyer programmes. For years they added cost only to see that the competition followed suit before too long – at lower expense. In the end there were only two strategies left: restructuring and cost savings.

Strategy consultants were there when the CEO had to demonstrate his value at short notice. Most were still present when decisions were announced. Some of them were there when new plans were implemented. But all had left by the time projected structural improvement in the company's competitive position failed to materialize.

The convergence of strategies is one of the major unintended consequences of the American Enterprise Model. Instead of encouraging innovation and risk taking, the model confines competition to small playing fields with a limited number of players. It plays into the hands of the many shareholders, boards and managers that hate exposure. Signing off on a consultancy report is an efficient way to spread the responsibility in case of failure.

When the bubble burst, the reputation of industry leaders in the consultancy sector suffered because of their close association with corporate catastrophes. McKinsey was instrumental in the demise of Enron, Global Crossing and Swissair. Other firms such as BCG, Bain and Booz Allen had supported the dot.com revolution. Arthur D. Little disappeared altogether.

Strategy consultants take strategic options away from their clients. They encourage investments that are justified on the basis of a presumed or projected gap with the competition. Offering standard solutions to postpone an inevitable demise means that valuable resources are tied up for far too long and gradually waste away. Unfortunately many companies that eventually conclude they are heading towards the abyss also discover that the point of no return is long past.

The trail becomes narrower and narrower. Far too much energy is devoted to the milking of exhaustible sources of value. The end is predictable but strategy consultants have already moved on to different pastures. It is the principle of slash-and-burn economics.

## BATTLEGROUNDS

As already stressed, the single most important organizational change companies introduced in the 1980s and 1990s was the business unit. This was a response to the many problems of managing corporations that had grown organically and to the inefficient matrix organizations (split responsibilities for sales and product management) that were fashionable in the 1980s. As outlined in Chapter 1, the reasoning behind the introduction of the business unit was solid: there was a need to reduce complexity, a desire to create focus and transparency and a wish to step up accountability. Delegation of responsibility was considered essential to react quickly to changing market circumstances. Business units also helped to foster entrepreneurship, the most cherished quality of the modern manager. Finally, the introduction of business units helped companies to restructure their business portfolios by trading in and trading out organizationally and economically viable units.

There is no doubt that the benefits of this organizational revolution were considerable, albeit that many of the benefits were only one-time gains, as pointed out in Chapter 3. The majority of corporations learnt to serve their customers better, open up new markets, reduce the time for new products to get to market and improve production efficiency.

But at what price? What were the organizational costs of this approach which dictated that business units were split up into sub-business units which in turn were divided into product-market combinations?

The choice for business units had to go hand in hand with the introduction of more sophisticated budgeting and planning systems, coupled with performance planning and remuneration systems for individual managers. The more decision making is decentralized, the greater the need for control by those at the top, the bigger the emphasis on simple and comparable financial parameters and the greater the need for a direct link between the unit's performance and the remuneration of its manager.

The American Enterprise Model comes with built-in fault lines. Because of the incompatibility of their objectives, there is one fault line between the financially oriented head office and the business unit. A second one runs between the CEO and the business unit manager, caused by overlapping roles. The third is among business units themselves, set up as they are to compete for scarce resources. In all these cases, the constant tension that is built up is released in the form of conflicts that damage the company and its prospects.

## Us and them

As indicated, the first fault line runs between the corporate head office and business units. Financial expertise and the perceived need to improve shareholders' return on investment are heavily concentrated in the head office. The pressure from financial institutions is felt continuously, as is peer pressure from advisors and analysts. Corporate head office follows its brief by pointing continuously at the discipline required by the financial markets. At the same time, vigorous cost cutting has deprived head offices of most of their commercial and technical know-how and contacts.

Business units are the masters of their universe. They create the value and the cash flows that keep the company going. They are of the opinion that nobody in head office understands or is even remotely interested in their business. What they perceive as meddling by head office is therefore unacceptable. Raising doubts about the corporate strategy is a favourite pastime of the business units. Management's hold over the business unit controller is a constantly moving feast. Is his first loyalty to the business unit and its manager or to the CFO back at headquarters?

Discussions that used to take place with a degree of peace and discretion within head office now take place across clear demarcation lines between corporate representatives and business unit experts. Diverging interests and different cultures colour analysis, policy preparation and decision making. The number of damaging conflicts increases.

In the past, the division of roles between corporate head office and commercial units was simple. 'Corporate' looked after long-term issues; business units handled day-to-day struggles. In an interesting reversal of roles, the importance of the quarterly report, ongoing restructuring, mergers and acquisitions and corporate exposure in the press have significantly shortened the time horizon of corporate head offices. Business unit managements on the other hand are painfully aware of what it takes to build a market position, reorganize a unit or forge a partnership – and how long it takes.

Head office's preoccupation with shareholder return on investment and the focus of business units on value creation manifests itself particularly when one side depends on the other. One struggle concerns head office approval of business units' investment proposals. Others relate to business unit support required for centralization of ICT and other services, for new activities and for mergers and acquisitions.

## Two captains

The second fault line runs between the CEO and the business unit manager. They both need a high profile but are catering to different constituencies with different requirements. As discussed, the financial markets hold the chief executive officer accountable for the corporate results, the financial press has a predilection to report on the performance of the top man and, within the corporation, the CEO is pushed into the limelight for a variety of reasons. His mandate is so all-encompassing that he is bound to exercise maximum control over his business units.

At the same time, delegation of commercial responsibility to the business unit manager is an intrinsic part of the American Enterprise Model with 'closeness to the market' as its mantra. The very concept implies a continuous focus on a product-market combination and everything is geared to improving the unit's market position and lowering cost levels vis-à-vis the competition.

The business unit manager has to demonstrate leadership in his unit's operational activities. He needs to give his unit an identity and becomes the personification of that identity. He is expected to gear everything – the organizational structure, procedures, culture, management information systems and ICT – to satisfy his customers' needs. His unit expects him to secure the flexibility and resources to do this. The unit's monopoly in dealing with one or more category of clients is its power base. The need to occupy a unique place under the sun is enforced by a natural tendency of all organizations to mark boundaries and to differentiate for the sake of differentiation.

The visibility of managers and CEOs, the diverging demands of their respective positions and their personality profiles make the relationship between them strained. These tensions are compounded by the semi-public statements they are encouraged to make by their respective entourages. These reduce room for manoeuvre and therefore increase the risk of conflict.

What is said by whom and about which issue is, irrespective of the confidentiality of the meeting, taken up by warring factions, amended and distorted. The CEO and business unit managers spend a lot of time issuing clarifying statements.

Tensions also arise from the composition of the business unit portfolio. The profitability and size of a unit determines its relative influence in dealing with corporate management and other business units. The relationship between a CEO and a clearly dominant business unit manager is particularly difficult to manage.

Much of this came to the fore in the public row between Jurgen Schrempp, CEO of Daimler-Benz, and Helmut Werner, chairman of Mercedes-Benz. Schrempp presided over a conglomerate including electronics company AEG, aircraft builder DASA, financial service unit Debis and car maker Mercedes-Benz. Werner enjoyed a very strong position as he led a unit that provided 70 per cent of Daimler's turnover and virtually all its profits. Werner booked success after success. Sales and profits went up. Mercedes even lost its stodgy reputation by introducing smart new cars. Werner was the personification of the brand. He considered his employees as the true inheritors of the legacy of Gottlieb Daimler and Karl Benz and commanded deep loyalty throughout the Mercedes-Benz organization. His independence from Daimler was partially based on the dedication of his finance and personnel staff, his own information systems and his own PR, legal and even public affairs departments. Mercedes had a strong and diverse culture and its managers kept the largest possible distance from the Daimler head office. Schrempp had minimal control over his most prized asset and this violated his pride and frustrated his ambitions. He knew that he had to control Mercedes to take Daimler further. After a well-designed campaign which combined rational argument for the streamlining of the cumbersome Daimler and Mercedes bureaucracies with some dirty fighting (including leaks to the press and the promise of choice jobs to members of Werner's team in the new set-up) Schrempp prevailed. Mercedes was integrated into Daimler and Werner resigned.[14]

There is an obvious commercial need to appoint assertive and decisive CEOs and business unit managers. They also have to be very competitive to cope with ever-increasing pressures. But the same traits turn against the company when their opinions and interests start to diverge and resources become scarce. A high profile very quickly makes conflicts personal and the last vestiges of restraint disappear. Corporate resources are mobilized to pursue personal objectives. The direct cost of this type of guerrilla warfare is considerable, but nobody can quantify the damage done to the reputation of the protagonists or the company as a whole. Worse still, the damage to future cash flows which comes from a mixture of corporate paralysis, inferior investment decisions and lost savings and market opportunities is a dirty secret that nobody cares to expose.

## Among colleagues

The third fault line runs between the various business units themselves. It has been stressed that business units need to develop different modes of operation to serve their respective markets, and this leads to tensions. When units are comparable in size there is the struggle for supremacy. If they are different in size, the smaller units are continuously under pressure to adapt to the standards of the largest unit. In the absence of market prices for intermediate products, intra-company trading of products and services is a minefield. Common use of plant and equipment produces endless discussions about the allocation of costs and revenues.

The cargo divisions of airlines for example face a continuous and uphill battle with the much larger passenger units. Their customers could hardly be more different and their markets only partially overlap geographically. Destinations and the frequency of flights are usually determined by the passenger division's larger contribution to corporate results. But while the reliability of cargo deliveries and passenger arrival times are both adversely affected by technical difficulties and problems with airport operations, passengers enjoy priority over cargo when delays have to be made up. For example, when planes exceed their weight restrictions, passengers remain in their seats and cargo is offloaded. All this makes it difficult for cargo divisions to break into the high end of the market where punctuality is essential. In addition, the profitability of a cargo division exists only on paper, as it depends largely on the assessment of the market value of the aircraft's belly space, a source of endless arguments. Finally both divisions lock horns over investment in aircraft that are more or less attractive to one or the other. Freight planes are the solution but there is much resistance to such investment in a structurally unprofitable branch of the aviation industry.

Large and small business units compete for investments and the finances required for restructuring, for the best managers the company has to offer and for the attention of the CEO. Shifts in corporate strategy affect them in very different ways and lead to intense internal lobbying. This is particularly true in the case of mergers and acquisitions. In a disconcerting number of cases, business units have more to gain by the successful outcome of an internal fight than by facing the competition, and act accordingly.

Given the emphasis on individual responsibility, accountability, transparency and the commercial need to split the market into smaller and smaller segments, the tendency is to create more and more business units. However, more business units mean more demarcation lines. More demarcation lines cause more feuding between units and corporate head office as well as among business units themselves.

## The perils of performance planning

With the rise of financially oriented management, the need to create transparency for the outside world and commitment to tough targets, financial control became corporate management's most important tool.

Most companies set their objectives for the short and medium term on an annual basis, taking projected macroeconomic, exchange rate and market developments into account. These objectives are translated into financial targets for divisions and business units. Business units have to distribute the targets over their different operational or product-market combinations and in this process a wide range of production, cost, sales and margin targets gets fixed. This cascade of targets is neatly divided over the year, taking seasonal effects into account. Close and frequent monitoring of the difference between targeted and actual results enables companies to take remedial action at the earliest possible moment.

It is up to the business unit manager to carve out a route to achieve his targets, for example the net margin at which a particular product sells. He estimates the sales volume on the basis of his knowledge of the market and figures out his purchase price, marketing and sales costs. He is the only expert in this field and of course he makes sure that his projections are achievable. More often than not, the integration of business unit projections by the corporate controller does not add up to the corporate objectives. Business unit managers clash with senior managers, there are negotiations and the business units are requested to revise their homework. Numbers are consolidated, problem areas are reduced, top management exercises more pressure and eventually the budget and medium-term plan are agreed and approved by the company's directors.

Even under the best of circumstances, the budget and planning cycle amounts to an operational and managerial nightmare for everybody. In the first place, the disciplined application of common definitions throughout the company takes years to achieve, if ever. Making numbers of different origin square takes away time and energy from discussions about the business itself. Secondly, true understanding of the myriad cause-and-effect links throughout the organization is an illusion. Improvements in one area produce costs in unexpected places or require resources that cannot be missed elsewhere. Thirdly, economic and commercial circumstances change throughout the planning cycle and adjustments have to be made from day one after formal approval.

This exercise is not conducive to concentration on value creation in any business model, but the American Enterprise Model involves additional pressure and complications, and therefore cost.[15]

The problems described above increase exponentially with the number of business units. Moreover while the world becomes more uncertain, shareholders and the media demand more accurate budgets and plans.

As discussed, many CEOs are lured by analysts and the media into making commitments that are unachievable. The resulting pressure on business units is formidable and the positive impact of these so-called 'challenging objectives' on motivation and creativity is an illusion. When corporate objectives are not met, companies are tempted to change the rules of the game, switch strategies, replace the CEO, appoint new senior management or any combination of these remedies. Furthermore, fashions change and advice from the financial community on how to improve shareholder return is consistently inconsistent.

For all these reasons, business units' targets and the indicators to track performance change frequently. The rise in costs associated with all this (management time, running and adjusting of information systems) remained unaccounted for in the 1990s. Even more important is that, with each change, historical perspective is destroyed and with it an important perspective for the evaluation of new policies.

An example in case is the Dutch ABN AMRO bank which changed strategy twice in two years. The concept of a US-style CEO was first introduced by the bank in 2000 with the appointment of Rijkman Groenink. This marked the end of the company's collegial form of management which was abolished. He grouped the bank's activities into a number of divisions at the expense of the country organizations and positioned the bank as a world player offering corporate clients all over the world a full range of banking services. The objectives were unequivocal. In the medium term ABN AMRO aimed to be in the top five of its peer group of 21 banks (using shareholder return on investment as its key objective), profit growth was projected at 17 per cent annually and share price was to double. The retail business provided the cash for this strategy.

As early as August 2001, ABN AMRO had fallen to the bottom position on its self-selected ranking list and management decided to change their performance criteria. Its 'wholesale' business (providing credit to large clients and investment banking) was still important but the bank decided it would concentrate on 2,000 rather than 4,000 clients, with the emphasis on Europe.[16] With results dropping, the bank subsequently embarked on a major cost-cutting programme in the Netherlands whereby one-third of the workforce were told they had a future with the bank and the remaining two-thirds simply had to wait to hear whether or not they would be made redundant.[17]

In 2003 Groenink completed his *volte face*. Pointing to the good results in the bank's three home markets (the United States, Brazil and the Netherlands), the retail business was reinstated as the bank's core business. The provision of a full range of services was restricted to existing European corporate clients. It was acknowledged that the bank could no longer hope to attract new customers with worldwide operations.[18]

A new man at the helm, fulfilling a new role as CEO, the pursuit of an unrealistic target, two new strategies, a new organizational structure and a major cost-cutting operation – any company would feel the strain of any one of these, let alone the combination of all of them within a three-year period. Meaningful budgeting and planning under such circumstances are a tall order indeed.

## Carrots and sticks

With tensions and conflicts played out in the open, the damage caused by the closer and closer coupling of the business units' targets to those of their managers was even more insidious.

In the heady atmosphere of corporate budgeting and planning, division and business unit managers have every reason to commit only to a limited number of attainable, internally consistent and quantified targets. This is the safest route to the ever-increasing bonuses and options that are part of the remuneration package. It is also a matter of self-protection in a world in which even meeting targets does not guarantee job security.

Companies pay a high price for this rational behaviour on the part of their managers. The functioning of large and complex organizations is reduced to the optimization of a few parameters whose origins lie in the facilitation of book keeping. A gap between the world of management and the real world opens up. The greater this is, the greater the likelihood of poor decisions.

Resistance to unrealistic, but also realistic, targets increases. Managers are bound to resist targets that depend on exogenous variables such as the cost of labour, energy prices and currency fluctuations – despite the fact that these are normal business risks that any entrepreneur faces. Furthermore, targets without the necessary and properly secured resources to achieve them are poisonous. This adds fuel to the struggle for corporate resources.

Managers also resist targets that require help from, or cooperation with, other business units or corporate departments. They do not want to be held accountable for the action, or lack of action, of colleagues. Moreover cooperation requires an investment with an uncertain return and, even if things run smoothly and both units gain, there is always the chance that their priorities will start to deviate if circumstances change. So even established and well-functioning forms of cooperation come under pressure and potentially beneficial forms of cooperation are not explored.

Once more it has to be kept in mind that these negotiations are conducted by highly visible managers, selected, among other skills, for their capacity to negotiate and to fight to the last man. It is also relevant to note that the true disciples of the Reagan revolution strongly believe in financial incentives for others, but also for themselves.

These tensions are somewhat mitigated by a common interest between the subordinate and his superior. The subordinate has an interest in a limited number of internally consistent and quantified targets, as has the superior, because such an outcome produces a sense of control and can be easily explained to the next person up in the command chain. Ultimately, concentration on a limited number of quantitative targets takes the sting out of the performance evaluation to be undergone by the subordinate. The numbers do the talking and judgement is not required. This removes a source of unhappiness and potential conflict which could put the working relationship under strain. However the company pays a price for all this convenience. A true exchange of views, insights and knowledge should be part of a performance review, and nurtured. But it has become nothing more than a mechanical exercise that does not trigger ideas for the next phase. It has merely become the basis for negotiations for the next planning cycle.

Finally, the close link between business unit targets and the personal targets of the responsible manager has a detrimental impact on corporate flexibility. A budget and corresponding individual targets are agreed and approved after considerable effort and a delicate balance is achieved. Any change in the plan as a result of unexpected competitive action, market disruptions or any other good reason also affects the achievement of personal targets. The greater the variable part of a manager's income, the greater the concerns of the manager involved and the greater the distraction, while the focus should be on making the necessary adaptations to the plan. Precious senior management time has to be devoted to the soothing of nerves, but, in the hyped-up atmosphere of the 1990s and with trust in short supply, general assurances that changes in the business plan would not affect the outcome of the performance evaluation were often not sufficient. Fresh negotiations ensued to fix new personal targets.

Some of these mechanisms can be traced in the first remuneration package of Anders Moberg, the former IKEA executive who succeeded Cees van der Hoeven as CEO of retailer Ahold in 2003. His original contract included a maximum bonus of 2.5 times the base salary with an annual 1.5 million euro guarantee for the first two years.[19] After unprecedented criticism from shareholders and customers, Moberg agreed to make this bonus dependent on performance. After weeks of renegotiations between Moberg and the supervisory board, Ahold announced that 70 per cent of the bonus would be payable when specific targets for cash flow, investment in material assets and stocks were reached. Another 24 per cent would be made available when Moberg designed new company and financial strategies acceptable to the supervisory board, shareholders and financial community.[20]

In the aftermath of a corporate crisis and 11 months into the year, the scope of this massively complicated company is narrowed to three quantifiable targets and two assignments that are part and parcel of the job of any CEO. Also, the explicit reference to the financial community is totally out of line. Under Dutch law, the supervisory board must take the interests of all stakeholders into account. To add insult to injury, at the end of 2003 Ahold also announced that the performance criteria for 2004 were still the subject of discussion.

## The convert

The 1990s were unique in that the world-views of individual managers became a distinguishing factor. The right attitude to the pursuit of shareholder return on investment, to performance, to change and to accountability were required to move up in corporate life. Put more strongly, companies had every right to expect that their managers were ardent believers in the creation of shareholder value, ruthless when it came to improving performance and passionate agents for change, and that they would give and take when the day of reckoning arrived. Sensitivity to financial incentives was a plus; sensitivity to the needs of colleagues was a distraction from the task at hand.

For sitting executives who did not embrace the new ideology there was a clear choice to be made: adapt or leave. While any technological revolution comes at a price in terms of the depreciation of existing human capital, the revolution of the 1990s incurred considerable additional cost in its pursuit of ideological purity and homogeneity. Some of this was achieved by natural attrition. Managers and experts saw their company move away from them and felt unable to follow. Modest reformers were inclined to stay and fight for the soul of the company. But those who had seen the revolutionary light considered them as a threat and steps to purge them were taken without delay. The idea was that the holes they left could easily be filled by promoting the right people – which was also a very potent way of showing personnel which style of management was appreciated. In an expanding economic universe, revolutionary change could be further accelerated by capitalizing on the availability of an abundance of new soldiers, fresh from business school, with the right ideological zeal and keen to join the fray.

While the loss of human capital was considerable, the real price was paid in the form of an erosion of the informal checks and balances any sound company should nurture. Organizations need their sceptics and mavericks. The law of requisite variety can only be ignored at considerable cost. Organizations embody the capacity to cope with unforeseen developments but this is only possible when they employ people with different outlooks who flourish under different circumstances. It is not far-fetched to postulate that many of the outrageous and doomed investments during the latter part of the 1990s would not have occurred without the preceding sanitation of corporate thinking.

Of course, CEOs paid extensive lip-service to the value embodied by their managers and employees. Equally obvious was that the highest standards needed to be applied but well-functioning labour markets helped to get the right person for the right job.

The reality was different. In this new world, it was self-evident that lifetime employment was no longer on offer and no longer expected. Employees became a production factor and were labelled 'human resources': ie not as important as capital, but still valuable. Part of the American Enterprise Model is a hardly disguised return to a form of 19th-century capitalism that combines capital and labour as creatively as possible. An impressive amount of money was spent on the concept of human resource development. This became all the more vital as human resources became an increasingly important ingredient in the production of services. Of course these 'human resources' had to meet the highest standards, good people were in short supply and the battle for talent raged. Fortunately markets for managers and experts were well developed, headhunters flourished as no other professional service, and the availability of a range of financial incentives guaranteed the right allocation of management talent throughout the economy.

With belief in markets so deeply engrained, it was only natural that companies introduced internal markets to allocate their human resources. Vacancies were advertised; qualified candidates were encouraged to apply. Again ideology played a role. It was up to the individual to try to advance with appropriate awards for the most ambitious and best qualified. All this played very much into the hands of the reinvented manager, coolly calculating his chances, always on the look-out for opportunities both inside and outside the company. The new manager has no qualms, his sole concern is to optimize his personal market value and he will jump ship at the moment he has acquired the right set of skills and experience.

This situation also suited the needs of the business units that could recruit from a broad base and select those who could make an immediate contribution to their results. Managers who failed to attract and retain key personnel had something to answer for.

The powerful management development units in corporate head offices became a thing of the past. The role of personnel officers changed from allocating management resources and building the skill base of the company to counselling senior management regarding their human resources needs, to facilitating transfers that others had decided on and to removing redundant managers from the payroll. Companies benefited from the substantial advantages offered by all this flexibility, but they also incurred considerable hidden cost.

Companies sacrificed the benefit that had been available from the judgement of seasoned senior managers who had knowledge of past conflicts, personal preferences and family circumstances when it came to appointments. These managers could often select a particular manager for a specific assignment based on first-hand experience of the candidate's work.

Moreover companies also gave up the benefits that come from the optimization of transfer chains: the planning of individual careers and the filling of unattractive but crucial vacancies with the promise of better positions in the future. Senior managers had not only been familiar with the qualities of candidates but also had a clear picture of the company's current and future staffing needs.

The reduction of organizational layers and the corresponding decimation of the ranks of middle management also had a negative impact on the introduction of newcomers. There were simply fewer people available to provide genuine on-the-job training, to transfer corporate values and to initiate young recruits in the subtleties and intricacies of operating in a large organization. Moreover the middle managers that were still around had less opportunity and were less motivated to play a role in management development, bound as they were by their performance targets and increased accountability.

The overall effect is that new recruits often had a scrappy start to corporate life. Those who decided to stay did so with less enthusiasm and for reasons that differed from the reasons for which they joined the company.

With the concept of the corporate career abandoned, the prospect of interesting future career moves as an enticement for remaining with a firm is no longer there. Key managers have to be retained by contract or by tailor-made financial incentives. In many instances the financial stakes of these managers act as golden chains. Motivation, pleasure, the knowledge that one is making a genuine contribution, all of these become subservient to the negative financial consequences of an early departure. In fact managers become less suited for their jobs but disguise this at the expense of the company.

The chance to obtain a position high in the corporate pecking order has always motivated managers and will continue to do so. However in the highly strung world of the American Enterprise Model, promotion counts for much more than a better remuneration package and membership of prestigious committees. It means more control and resources to do battle with the internal enemy. A promotion, and particularly a series of upward moves, is a very important signal that leads to shifts in loyalty and realignment of coalitions. Even more significant is the missed promotion. Wounded managers carry on, but their authority will never fully recover and many feel forced to leave. With so much at stake, promotion battles take on new dimensions. Nomination procedures are there to be circumvented or at least used to the best possible advantage. Colleagues are reminded of past favours and undermining rivals is part of the game.

Tensions also surface in the ranking of management positions as the basis of a remuneration policy. Many companies bought complete systems, including procedures to give points for operational, commercial and managerial responsibilities, for doing this from specialist firms such as Hay Consultants. Such systems make seemingly incomparable positions inside and outside the company comparable in terms of demands on the manager, and allow companies to base remuneration on the market price for comparable functions. In companies that do not expand, these systems are in essence distribution rules for dividing a fixed number of points over a number of managerial positions. Gaining sufficient points brings a position into a higher category with a more attractive remuneration package, but always at the expense of a colleague. For the sake of transparency and fairness, the system focuses on individual tasks and responsibilities, on quantifiable characteristics and on corporate activities over which full control is exercised. Important intangibles such as an ability to cooperate with other units or maintain relationships with partners cannot be taken into account. Once again, the world of management and the real world are driven apart.

This mechanism for weighing functions plays an important role at any moment that changes in the organizational structure are contemplated and division of responsibilities comes under scrutiny. Seemingly rational debates about organizational changes to improve efficiency and enhance customer services are, in fact, loaded. Corporate and individual interests are intertwined at the expense of the best solution.

A market approach to the allocation of management talent and experience is supposed to be transparent and fair with proper job descriptions set against the qualifications of the candidates. The credibility of such a system very much depends on open communication for all vacancies and access for all. The reality is much more ugly.

Halfway through the 1990s, Cor Herkströter, who was head of the Royal Dutch Shell Group at the time, embarked on a major programme to change the structure and the culture of the company and introduce the American Enterprise Model. Up until that point, Shell had been built around strong local organizations that were increasingly managed by local residents with deep and long-term commitments to the host countries in which Shell operated. Herkströter created global business units such as Exploration and Production, Oil Products (marketing and sales) and Chemicals, each headed by a member from the Committee of Managing Directors (CMD), a function that was effectively the same as that of a CEO. Herkströter was the CMD's chairman. The focus was on profitability and return on investment (a target of no less than 15 per cent) and these were presented as the best way to serve the shareholder, a gallant attempt in an industry where share prices are largely determined by energy prices. For all intents and purposes, Shell introduced the American Enterprise Model. Herkströter's new organization was simple, costs were cut, 10,000 members of staff were asked to leave and research and development was made dependent on the commercial priorities of the businesses.

It was in this context that Herkströter also introduced a market-based system to allocate management resources. Prior to this, Shell's approach to recruitment and management development had been the envy of the sector and was also emulated by many companies outside the oil industry. The CMD devoted a whole meeting every month to appointments. The top brass was directly involved in the selection and appointment of the best and the brightest. Traditionally, management recruits at Shell had a mentor and their careers were carefully planned to exploit their potential. Competition between managers was muted because they were all aware of their estimated potential – the management level that they were expected to reach in their late forties (assuming a satisfactory performance along the way). All this changed when the marketplace concept was introduced. In principle, all managers were entitled to apply for all management jobs. Whereas in the past the group's human resource department kept a close eye on careers and future corporate needs, it was now a free-for-all and there was much managerial manoeuvring to ensure favourites were brought on board. At times of reorganization, layer after layer of management jobs are open to applicants from all over the world. The many that are rejected for senior positions join those who have set their sights at the next level down – all the way to the middle management ranks. Long-term employees have to go through the humiliation of applying for mediocre jobs together with hundreds and sometimes thousands of colleagues. Many feel forced to apply for unappealing jobs in unattractive countries.

# THE GULAG ARCHIPELAGO

Under the American Enterprise Model, access to equity markets is crucial, as is strong leadership. Large head offices do not add sufficient value. To operate according to best industry practice, it is wise to involve external consultants. Commercial responsibility has to be delegated to independent units and, as a consequence, financial controls need to be enforced. Accountability and remuneration have to go hand in hand, and personal sacrifices need to be rewarded. Transparency in appointing managers is desirable and, with competition increasing all the time, managers who can stand the heat are required.

All this sounds reasonable enough. Yet by the end of the decade, the large corporation had become a very threatening place. Manfred Kets de Vries, professor at INSEAD, called it the Gulag Archipelago.

The combination of what were in isolation reasonable changes created fault lines in the form of tensions that made modern office politics a permanent distraction for all managers. Disagreements about how to solve problems are never what they seem. Different ways of settling an issue have different consequences for the balance of power and the capacity of quarrelling parties to engage in future battles. The distinctions between personal and business conflicts become increasingly blurred. Loyalties shift all the time, feelings of insecurity spread, motivation and commitment to the company suffer, there is constant anxiety about losing one's reputation and, in the end, fear rules.

These tensions are all too noticeable at lower levels. Projects can run into problems at every step of the way. Early signs could be that management starts to postpone decisions, meetings are cancelled and team members are given different assignments. In many cases it is unclear why initial enthusiasm evaporates and resistance – believed to have been overcome – returns. Projects drag on. Problems are apparently so large that rejuvenation of a project is too risky, but cancelling carries a price too in that it could run counter to the interest of unknown senior managers. Meanwhile the team is rudderless and unproductive. Its morale and confidence suffer.

It is obvious that conflicts are costly, but the daily grind of coping with tensions is worse. Preventing – and at the same time preparing for – conflict, engaging in conflict either overtly or behind the scenes, and coping with the aftermath of conflicts takes attention away from the business. Managers are forced to spend much of their time protecting their positions by currying favour with the CEO and senior management, creating a loyal following and building coalitions with like-minded colleagues. They have to be an active player in the internal market for favours. They have to keep their ear to the ground to make sure they hear the latest gossip: the foreboding of things to come. Some feel compelled to strike pre-emptively. Many feel the need to take revenge. The American Enterprise Model has pushed office politics to record depths.

Companies pay a heavy price in the form of slower decision making and poor implementation, offsetting part or all of the efficiency improvements they achieved. The number of erroneous decisions on investments, marketing initiatives and partnerships increases when they are influenced by the need to protect and strengthen positions of power. Economic value is destroyed at every turn

However the greatest damage remains invisible. Where there is discord, creativity suffers, support for new initiatives is difficult to mobilize and cooperation is in short supply. As a result many potentially promising ventures simply do not see the light of day. Potential economic value is not realized.

That eventually the unintended consequences and unaccounted cost of the American Enterprise Model are passed on to shareholders, employees and customers, belongs to one of the best-kept and darkest secrets of the defenders of the faith.

# 5

# A European Enterprise Model

The recovery of the US economy which started in 2001 can be attributed to an unprecedented increase in government spending, a historical decrease of interest rates and an artificially strong dollar that helped to keep inflation low. Such a combination is unique and was only possible for a nation that felt beleaguered. Even US Federal Reserve chairman Alan Greenspan now believes that these policies have reached the end of the line. US economic and productivity growth in late 2004 was falling to European levels and the medium-term prospects do not look bright.

Meanwhile Europe is not yet living up to its potential. Germany and France await the effects of modest but painful reforms, consumers refuse to spend and economic recovery is still dependent on increasing exports. The prognosis for the medium term is more uncertain than ever.

## THE FOUNDATIONS OF GROWTH

The question is what can Europe and European companies do to accelerate renewal and growth?

The 1990s were not what they seemed and can no longer serve as a source of inspiration. Radical government policies are yielding less and less, and the restructuring of the corporate world has destroyed value at an astonishing rate. More and more markets are saturated and marketing tools are becoming increasingly less effective. The net result of cost-cutting operations and other tried and tested approaches is dwindling and fresh management ideas to improve productivity and profitability are in short supply.

The simultaneous push for shareholder return and the strengthening of market positions is causing significant friction. The heavy emphasis on financial incentives has backfired and the new-style managers have left a lot of debris in their wake.

The standard answer to the question comes in three parts. Firstly, scientific and technological breakthroughs will lay the foundation for a new generation of products that will gradually meet evolving and expanding market demand. Secondly, the availability of a proper legal framework, an independent judiciary and deregulated markets will make it possible for entrepreneurs to invest. And thirdly, efficient financial markets will secure the right allocation of capital for the production and marketing of new products.

But a very different reply is that at this juncture neither technology, regulation nor the functioning of financial markets is the factor constraining corporate and economic development. All the traditional conditions for long-term economic expansion are in place. There is a host of technological breakthroughs waiting to be exploited. Governments are bending over backwards to entice companies to invest and there is pent-up demand, particularly for good-quality services. On top of this there is also an abundance of capital chasing a limited number of original and viable business ideas. The answer has to be sought in a different direction.

## Breaking away

The fundamental difference to the 1990s is that the quality of people and the quality of their cooperation have become the limiting factors that hold companies and economies back.

Technology dictates ever-increasing specialization, but real-life problems and opportunities, for example in haematology, can only be dealt with in joint efforts by haematologists, immunologists, cell biologists, geneticists and computer scientists. The capacity to teach and to learn, the capacity to be scientific and problem oriented, the capacity to compromise and to deal are all new and taxing requirements that are beyond the reach of many.

In the corporate world recruits have to meet ever-increasing standards. They have to be productive almost immediately, and they need to be on top of new technologies while maintaining a broad view.

At the same time the backgrounds and outlook of recruits become more homogeneous as business schools continue to proliferate. Demands on managers increase continuously and the number that fail to meet these higher standards rises too. Talented managers are pushed out for ideological reasons and a growing percentage of them are not prepared to sacrifice everything to survive in the corporate jungle. The combination of these factors produces a tight market for true talent. Companies that are consistently more successful than their competitors in the battle for talent enjoy a structural advantage.

The second fundamental difference with the 1990s is that the creation of value has come to depend on the quality of cooperation between top management, experts and battle-hardened middle management. This applies to value creation within a single company, alliances between companies, and cooperation between companies and government, regulators and other institutions.

Anyone who is familiar with the launch of innovation projects knows that the majority have a low life expectancy as a result of human inaptitude, lack of communication and office politics. Many partnerships do not break up for financial or commercial reasons but because irritations accumulate and reach a point from where there is no return.

The world of information technology is full of examples whereby technological breakthroughs were not translated into profitable products purely for lack of cooperation among and between the ranks. The failure of the Xerox Corporation to exploit breakthroughs in computer technology from its Palo Alto research centre is legendary. Digital Equipment Corporation squandered a head start over IBM in the field of PCs. Teams of talented engineers and marketing people at Apple Computers understood the need for lower-cost products but were hindered by senior management for a very long time.

Focus on cooperation is part of a deceptively simple management concept that can be summarized as follows. Management secures and distributes the resources required for corporate continuity and development, but the company will only have a permanent call on resources if, now and in the future, sufficient value can be added.

It falls to management to develop and express a vision about present and future sources of value. In other words, management creates or identifies the business concepts that underpin value creation. Management becomes, at least in part, entrepreneurship.[1]

Managers choose the team experts and commercial and operational middle managers that have to work together to develop and test these ideas. Cooperation can either be on an ongoing basis embedded in the company structure or on an ad hoc basis in project teams.[2]

Management turns viable business ideas into businesses run by business units. It supports business unit managers in their quest for growth and continuity.

Finally, if business ideas cease to be viable and business units no longer create value, management has to wind up such units in as orderly a fashion as possible and free up resources for use elsewhere.

In short, a company is its people and the next round of corporate and economic development depends on new forms of cooperation, on social innovation.

## Corporate objectives

The first and only objective of such a company is to create economic value, the net present value of all future free cash flows: future revenues minus all future costs including the cost of capital. In order to capture its full economic potential the company has to strive for continuity as many promising investments and initiatives will take time to come to fruition and will then generate a free cash flow for many years.

This chapter presents the contours, or preliminary design, of a competitive European Enterprise Model for large corporations. Its goals contrast sharply with the key objectives of the American Enterprise Model: shareholders' return on investment spurred on by increases in profit per share. Not surprisingly its structure and culture are very different indeed. It is not the other side of the same coin. This European Enterprise Model represents a fresh look at economic life. Those who attempt to combine attractive features of both models are ill advised. Both models are internally consistent and firmly embedded in the US and European contexts. Considerable confusion reigns in companies that try to develop hybrids.

This enterprise model is not only more efficient and effective than the American Enterprise Model, but also has the edge on the Rhineland Model which was so effective from after the Second World War until recently, but is now found wanting.

The Rhineland Model, based on the simultaneous pursuit of capital and labour interests, knows a few variations but these share a number of characteristics: a government that sets the country's economic goals and that makes full use of its instruments to guide economic life; powerful unions that protect their members' financial interest and employment and that represent their members in co-determining corporate strategic decisions; employers' associations that seek to protect corporate profitability and continuity and to defend the shareholders' interest. Each party fulfils its role in full recognition of the rightful place of all three parties at national and at corporate level.

The Rhineland Model is now suffering because the conditions for its functioning that prevailed in the economic build-up after the Second World War are no longer there. Governments stood back, their authority undermined by the increasing ineffectiveness of their subsidies and fiscal policies to steer economic life. Unions saw their membership dwindling and ageing. They never achieved a position in the new service sectors and their right to represent is increasingly questioned. Employers' associations fell victim to a rapidly diversifying economy, and as a consequence the diverging interest of their members. Most importantly, the model came under pressure because more and more companies required tailor-made government support and labour agreements to deal with their specific market circumstances.

Defence of entrenched positions and conflicts about substantive issues became more and more intertwined, which further eroded the model. The emphasis on the great variety of European Enterprise Models is an answer to an irresistible need for decentralization and is destined to undermine the Rhineland Model further. Where practical, labour agreements need to be struck between individual companies and their employees. A form of co-determination should be agreed on a company-by-company basis.

## A developing model

The new European Enterprise Model for large companies still has to be fully tested, but many non-listed European companies have already embraced a number of its features. Some of these firms have expressed confidence in this comprehensive new approach and will embark on a full implementation programme.

Of course enterprise models are not designed; they develop. Looking at the rise of the American Enterprise Model, the concept of shareholder value was a breakthrough but was blended with other emerging ideas such as individual rights and obligations and competition. Furthermore political and business leaders moulded the new principles to fit their own interests (for example replacing shareholder value with stock price). Day-to-day encounters with employees, suppliers and customers did the rest. It was during the implementation of the principles of the American Enterprise Model that limits became apparent and individual and corporate interests were defined and aligned. Businesses in which the application of these principles proved to be practical and beneficial came to the fore. In retrospect it would seem that the American Enterprise Model and the rapidly expanding ICT sector were made for each other.

A European Enterprise Model will go down the same road. It will initially consist of relatively few basic principles that will be amended and supplemented over time. It is a thorny path and the rate of change will be modest at first, but, as with any major turnaround, change feeds change and once the acceleration becomes visible the new model will take off, unleashing considerable potential economic value. This will guide the way business is conducted. It will facilitate organizational change and assist in socializing corporate recruits. A European Enterprise Model will be a product of its time and will suit the requirements for the production and marketing of new products and services.

Two familiar approaches to corporate growth and development can be revived and expanded in a new way. One is internal growth, the stepchild of the 1990s. As described in Chapter 3, managers occupied themselves with everything except increasing value by developing business ideas based on new technology. They were neither interested nor equipped for the task.

The second is the building of corporate and business unit partnerships. In the 1990s, financially driven mergers and acquisitions dominated the scene at the expense of building a wide range of flexible commercial and technical partnerships with a broad spectrum of partners.

Both approaches define a vast arena in which companies can achieve expanding and lasting advantage over their competitors.

If the new areas for growth are to be exploited, new ground will have to be broken simultaneously in all of the following areas, that in combination define the European Enterprise Model:

- ownership, control and distribution of economic benefits;

- governance;

- organizational management and structure;

■ the strategic agenda;

■ organizational development;

■ performance planning, evaluation and remuneration.

Publicly listed European companies are so embedded in the American Enterprise Model that very few can make such a transition. Only companies that face extinction but have a sound business idea may find the time for a total overhaul. This happened to telephone equipment supplier Cisco which changed course completely when faced with the prospect of bankruptcy. There are also publicly traded companies with a long history and deep roots, such as IBM, that can turn themselves round. Recently privatized state companies such as Air France too can reject the American Enterprise Model and design their own enterprise concept. Most private companies were created by strong-willed founders with very explicit views about people and the way they should cooperate. Many of these already show a number of the characteristics required for the proposed European Enterprise Model.

# OWNERSHIP, CONTROL AND ECONOMIC BENEFITS

The core propositions of the American Enterprise Model are as follows. Shareholders own companies and therefore have the legal and moral right to the value that companies create. Shareholders appoint managers. Shareholders make sure that their interests and those of the management are aligned through a tight bond of remuneration and share price. If managers implement policies that shareholders cannot support, they vote with their feet.

## Ownership where it belongs

A radically different view is the following. As a matter of principle, the ownership of a company lies with those who have conceived, developed and implemented its underlying business idea: a combination of people, equipment and resources that can add value on a sustainable basis. JCDecaux for example is a service company that exploits advertising space on bus shelters. The business idea entails the simultaneous satisfaction of different demands by very different parties. Marketing companies want eye-catching and top-quality advertisements in prime locations. Municipalities and public transport companies are under pressure from voters and customers to lower prices and improve services, including the provision of good-quality bus shelters. JCDecaux meets all their requirements by placing well-designed bus shelters as well as by cleaning them regularly and repairing them at very short notice.[3]

There is no fundamental difference between this sort of innovative business idea and scientific findings, works of art or books. They are all forms of intellectual property and inalienable rights are established at the moment of creation.

Business ideas differ from other forms of intellectual property in only two, non-essential, respects. One is that entrepreneurial ideas as such cannot be legally protected. At best, certain elements of the business idea can be protected such as a finding that can be patented or a brand that can be registered. Most companies have to rely on scale, distinctive competences, innovation and other means to defend themselves against infringement of their concept. The second difference is that many people make creative and practical contributions to the development of a business idea and its implementation. As a result the ownership of a concept, again as a matter of principle, does not rest with an individual inventor or designer but with the organization as a whole.

It is therefore right and proper that in a number of European countries the interest and continuity of the company are the sole concern of its governing body. It also follows that neither the shareholders, labour representatives nor any other stakeholder can a priori lay any claim to ownership.

The sharing of economic benefits and abdication of partial control over corporate decision making in return for finance or labour is secondary and does not affect the basic principle. At any rate, it defies both logic and morality that, under the American Enterprise Model, public company shareholders whose commitment lasts no longer than the next trading day can exercise substantial control over its board and management.

## Finance and the distribution of control

Some companies can finance their operations and expansion from their cash flow. In such instances, all future value accrues to the company and directors and managers retain full control. If a company sees opportunities for faster growth than cash flow allows, additional investments can be financed by a bank. From that point onwards, the company shares economic value with the bank in the form of interest payments. Conditions attached to the loans provide the bank with a degree of control over the company. Such conditions can range from the standard repayment schedule for the principal via the transfer of ownership of plant and equipment in case of default, to the right to appoint directors. It is important to note that this is a two-way street. If and when a company redeems debt, less economic value has to be sacrificed and a proportional degree of control can be regained.

Companies can also call on the capital of private investors in exchange for shares and control. Shares represent a call on economic value that the company will generate in the future. In this context control has many different guises, for example the right to appoint and dismiss management or the right to preferential treatment when new shares are issued.

Public companies pay a different price in the form of dividends as part of a wider obligation to optimize shareholder return. In the United States, companies give up ownership and a considerable amount of control when they obtain a stock exchange listing. Shareholders have rights by law and derive influence from stock market rules and regulations.

In Europe pressure to extend existing shareholder rights is building. The European Commission, institutional investors and individual shareholders as well as their lobby groups are becoming increasingly vocal. Takeover protection is being eroded, stock certificates that entitle the holder to share in the economic progress of the company but lack voting rights are looking decidedly old-fashioned, and better governance becomes synonymous with extended shareholder rights.

Again there is a way back. Companies can refinance themselves and withdraw from the stock market, returning ownership and control to the original owner, private investors or a combination of both.

Whoever puts up capital, the longer the duration of the commitment and the higher the risk inherent to the business, the higher the price. The more qualified the management, the lower the price. The more unique the business concept, the more secure the future commercial success, the lower the risk and the higher the value of the company. The higher the value of the company, the less future benefits and control will have to be sacrificed for the same amount of capital. It falls to management to trade on a huge market where money, the form and duration of commitment, exposure to risk, future economic benefits and control over the company are exchanged. This approach is far more flexible and therefore superior to the congruency of ownership and control in the American Enterprise Model. Of special interest is the corporate solvency that management has to protect against lazy and unimaginative investors who want to run with the corporate cash.

Management can call on the stock market but the terms are unattractive, both in economic terms and increasingly in terms of control. Corporate prospects are difficult to assess, the track records of financial analysts are poor and independent advice is hardly available. As a result the market demands a higher risk premium which is reflected in the price of equity.

Moreover stock market regulations are increasing rapidly. Most importantly, management is finding itself caught up in a web of expectations from which it is difficult, but not impossible, to escape (as described in Chapters 3 and 4).

Listed European companies that for historic and other reasons cannot withdraw from the stock market, and companies that find the demands of the private equity houses in their sector unreasonable, could take a different route. They could develop a common standard of corporate objectives, governance, management and organization along the lines suggested in this chapter. Such a standard would appeal to institutional and private investors that are interested in above-average returns over the medium and long term. The companies that adhere to the standard could be admitted to a separate 'European Enterprise' stock market index. Such an approach, but not the focus, would be comparable with the 'Sustainability Index' of the NYSE and other specialized indexes. It would help the large institutional investors whose funds can only to a limited extent be absorbed by private equity houses and who also face liquidity requirements from their regulators.

## The private investor as modern saviour

Calls on private equity remain the most attractive alternative for small and medium-sized companies – 99 per cent of all European companies – for the following reasons.

Firstly, the repertoire of financial arrangements is infinite and can be made to measure for every company. Financing, governance, management, strategy and the corporate organization can be comprehensively tackled. Tailor-made solutions based on a deep understanding of the business ideas can be laid down in loan and shareholder agreements.

Secondly, private equity allows partners to alter agreements when circumstances change and/or the position and priorities of the partners change. Some financiers will leave; new ones will commit themselves.

Thirdly, the professionalism of the financiers on the one hand and the quality of the management and its experts on the other hand can be assessed by the protagonists directly.

Fourthly, the interests of financiers and companies involved in private equity agreements are much better aligned than in the case of a stock market listing. Increase in economic value is the common interest. For investors it measures the sought-after increase in the value of the company. Banks want to see a high interest coverage (ie the number of times that a company can cover its interest obligations from cash flow). Management and employees have an interest in continuity that self-evidently depends on the creation of a surplus.

Investors reduce risk not by desk research and careful monitoring of companies, but by building experience in specific sectors, due diligence and putting their considerable weight behind the company once the agreement is closed. All this is a far cry from the inherently superficial relationship between public companies and their shareholders.

Finally, the management of the company becomes far simpler under equity capital financing. Managers can concentrate on their real duty: caring for the continuity and growth of the companies entrusted to them. They save the rapidly increasing cost of a stock market listing.

This view on ownership, control and economic benefits liberates companies. Owners, banks and private investors can support projects with short and long lead times; adding value to the company is the only criterion for decision making. As a result, the risk of the portfolio is far easier to manage. Companies can take the time that is required to build the skills of their employees and the expertise of the organizational units. They can deviate from the converging strategies of competitors and, if they face difficult times, they have the option to persevere.

It is important to point out that the European Enterprise Model developed in this chapter presupposes a moderate negotiating hand for the providers of capital. For companies that depend on a conventional stock market listing or have performed so poorly that private investors call the shots, the model will remain elusive.

On the other hand, the Brenninkmeijer family provides one example out of many where independence of financial markets was crucial in developing and maintaining a very distinct and very successful enterprise model.

The family built C&A, a clothing retail chain, from very humble beginnings and turned it into a major success with trendsetting shops in most Western European countries. During the 1990s, they were left behind by the competition. They endured massive losses for many years but decided to persist. Finally, in 2002, they returned to a modern version of their original concept and are once again booking success. Meanwhile the acquisition of commercial property to house their stores has propelled them in a completely new direction and their real estate business is now much bigger than their retailing activities. A third division was created in the form of a private equity fund with investments in a variety of companies, including a major and high-risk investment in solar energy based on a technology that is fundamentally different from that of the competition.

All this comes with a distinct governance structure, management philosophy, management development system and remuneration that depends on the achievement of financial and social goals.

Finally, it should be noted that both the European Enterprise Model and the American Enterprise Model are internally consistent and fit the political and social context in which they are applied. Investors and managers that try to integrate appealing features of both models will not succeed. Chances are that the disadvantages of features of the American model will continue to be felt while the advantages of European features will never materialize.

# GOVERNANCE

Governance can be defined as the division of supervisory and executive powers and responsibilities among top company officials.

The relative merits of continental Europe's two-tier system (a supervisory and an executive board) and the Anglo-Saxon single-tier system are subject to debate. The new European Enterprise Model currently developed builds on the advantages of the two-tier board.

Under this, the CEO retains the independence he needs to lead the company but is embedded in a structure composed of a supervisory board and a management team. The structure is geared to support the CEO but at the same time provides checks and balances at crucial stages of corporate decision making. There are different roles to play and clarity on responsibilities helps open an informed debate and prevents boardroom scheming.

The present mandate of most governing boards on the European continent gives them the following responsibilities: the appointment and supervision of the CEO and senior management; determination of executive remuneration; evaluation of company performance; signing off of management accounts; approval of investments, partnerships and other major decisions; approval of changes in the financing of the company and in the articles of association; the giving of advice. In principle such a mandate is sufficiently broad and flexible to exercise any required degree of control.

This approach is superior to the situation in the United States where the wisdom of the all-American combination of chairman/CEO is called into question but the practice changes only gradually. The approach is also better than the non-executive chairman and CEO as members of a one-tier board whereby the CEO continues to enjoy major advantages over his chairman. His insights into the limits and capabilities of the organization, his views on the industry, his industry contacts and his personal acquaintance with all corporate managers that matter constitute an unassailable power base. The chairman is inevitably drawn into corporate decision making and loses his independence far too soon – a problem that is augmented by the social bonding that flows from proximity.

## How to steer the company

In judging corporate performance, three broad areas need to be considered. The first area is the functioning and integrity of the organization as a whole and of the business units. Have legal, regulatory and corporate standards been met? Have agreed investment, planning and budgeting procedures been followed? Have investment decisions been implemented in accordance with original intentions? Have contractual obligations to suppliers, customers and partners been honoured? Has the corporate culture been upheld?

Only a well-functioning organization can hope to realize its potential cash flow, given its market position and its assets, people and organization. The quantitative measure of performance in this area is the actual and projected cash flow. Where is it generated, what is its quality and is it sufficient to sustain and develop the company?

In the second area, the key questions concern the structural enhancement of the value the company is creating given its present portfolio of activities. Are past investments, appointments and agreements with partners, all designed to bring the free cash flow to a higher plane, paying off? Which adjustments should be made to increase their economic value? Which programmes need to be abolished? Moving to the present: which new initiatives have been taken to strengthen the asset base of the company in the broadest possible meaning of the word? In isolation, investments in plant, equipment and ICT are hardly exciting. More interesting, for example, is how much economic value will a specific investment in information technology yield in combination with which organizational change programme? Which training programme will increase productivity and by how much? Which new partnerships will strengthen the corporate market position, in what ways and by how much? Which management team has what type of mandate to restructure a business unit?

Given the lead times involved, the size and the quality of the pool of ideas, initiatives, plans and programmes that could improve the free cash flow of business units structurally at some point in the future become very important. This pool contains initiatives in various stages of development and decision making – all the way from a proposal to study ways of integrating newcomers into the organization faster, to an investment proposal for building a new production line.

It is the area of the corporate balance sheet, not only in financial terms including the value of the so-called 'real options', but in the broadest possible sense everything that is required to develop existing corporate activities that add economic value.

The third area of performance evaluation concerns the effects of efforts to add value by changes in the portfolio of corporate businesses. Which activities have been abandoned and which have been added, and at what cost? What is the impact on the capacity of the company to generate economic value?

The lead times here are even longer and boards have to make sure that the company creates and defends the freedom to manoeuvre. Questions here include: which activities are under pressure? Which business ideas that lead an anaemic life elsewhere could thrive under the wings of the company? Which partnership could help enter new and promising territories?

Some of these options present themselves, others can be acquired and yet others can be traded in and out. And some expire quickly while others can be kept in the portfolio for years. Sometimes the lifetime of an option can be extended, generally at a price, while others simply run out. A combination of options could be worth more than the sum of isolated options. This is the world of 'real options' where proper management can generate real value. Like share options, the value of this form of option – say the opportunity to acquire a company – goes up when the price for exercising it (in this example the capital outlay for the investment) comes down. The value is also influenced by the lifetime of the option. For a biotech company, the value of an option in the form of a patent depends on the period for which it is granted. The more volatile the market, the more valuable the option. Drilling rights for oil become more valuable when oil prices fluctuate frequently and with increasing amplitude. It is the world of strategic management, the quest for options, the trading of options, the extension of options and eventually the exercise of a few of the options: the strategic investments of the company.

Sustainability by constantly focusing on the creation of economic value is demonstrated in the history of many large private companies. One example is the Dutch conglomerate SHV which is controlled by the Fentener van Vlissingen family. According to one of the prominent family members, SHV had to reinvent itself several times. The company started out by trading in coal. When coal for heating and electricity generation was largely replaced by oil and natural gas in the Netherlands, the firm changed course completely and became one of the biggest European players in LPG trading and propane and butane retailing. At the same time it invested on a grand scale in a new concept of wholesale stores on three continents. Later the European interests in this latter business were sold and a private equity company was established with small stakes in many companies.[4]

Such a success would not have been possible without genuine interest in and care for operational management, a willingness to invest and a preparedness to change.

One overarching corporate objective supported by continuous improvement in the three distinct areas has major advantages. Each and every company should identify the factors that matter in each of the three areas. This should help companies to distinguish themselves from their competitors. Moreover the premium on change, so typical for the American Enterprise Model, disappears. Sustainability requires very good care of the existing activities.

Secondly, it makes visible the most crucial dilemmas that companies face. Time, talent and financial resources have to be distributed over the three areas in a way that optimizes the chance that the company survives. Very uncomfortable trade-offs have to be faced.

Thirdly, the approach binds all constituent parts of the company. The supervisory board, managers and staff carry responsibility for all three areas albeit in different roles and with different relative weights. Supervisors carry a special responsibility for the renewal of the company, management for all three areas and only business unit managers can directly influence the integrity of the company. The relevant questions vary for each role. The examples provided in this section are particularly relevant for the supervisory board. Typical questions for business unit managers will be asked in the section that deals with performance planning and remuneration.

## Composition and mode of operation of the board

The European Enterprise Model envisages the company as an independent organization pursuing continuity by value creation. The quality of management, employees and organization determines success. This has to have repercussions in the way supervisory board members are nominated and appointed.

As already suggested, the shareholders or any other stakeholders (for example the trade unions) that are not committed to the company in any real sense should not have the right to nominate, let alone appoint or dismiss, board members. The appointment of new board members is a matter for the company itself, as is any change in its articles of association.

New board members are nominated by the chairman of the supervisory board and appointed by a committee composed of a cross-section of employees, including middle management and experts, but excluding the CEO and senior management. The members of this committee are elected by all employees with long-term contracts. This procedure does not affect in any way the obligation of the board to pursue continuity of the company and to take all necessary decisions to that end including changes in the organization and cessation of activities. Board members are not employee representatives and act without any consultation of the aforementioned committee, but receiving a mandate from the committee would add significantly to their legitimacy and authority.

The supervisory board, independently or on the basis of the advice of the CEO and the senior management team, can propose changes in the articles of association of the company including the governance structure. It falls to the committee of employees to approve such proposals. At no point can the committee withhold its approval from changes that are required to add economic value, for example in the case of mergers or acquisitions. It is important that board members are appointed for one term only and that this is of a reasonable length.

This situation resembles the governance of Roland Berger Strategy Consultants, the only non-US advisory firm that operates worldwide. Its supervisory board is chaired by the company's founder Roland Berger who built the firm from scratch to 2,000 professionals. He is accompanied by a number of senior partners of the firm. Together they supervise an executive committee made up of three other company partners. It also resembles the procedures that are followed in electing the supervisory board of a Dutch 'Structuur NV' where the works council can nominate three members of the supervisory board for approval by the shareholders' meeting. In this system the board is required to pursue continuity of the company.

In a world in which companies' competitive success is to a large extent based on the quality of their executives and their decision making, there is every incentive to appoint the best candidates as board members and to design the best possible governance structure. In this context there is ample reason to deviate strongly from the way most boards of large European companies operate.

The following criteria should apply when it comes to appointing board members and deciding on governance operation. Companies should have small, hands-on and professional supervisory boards. The chairmanship of the supervisory board should be a full-time assignment and the other three or four members should not sit on any more than two other boards. The board will have professional support and its own budget to obtain second opinions if and when required.

A small, committed and therefore well-informed supervisory board can be a real asset to the CEO. It can meet with relative ease at fixed intervals and on an ad hoc basis, and decision making can be fast. Frequent meetings unburden the agenda overload that exists at present and difficult decisions can be done justice by allowing sufficient time for discussion. Proposals that do not meet the grade can be sent back for improvement and resubmitted at short notice. Both the speed and the quality of decision making will improve.

Some of the board's members should be able to assess management proposals on the basis of sound knowledge in the fields in which the company is active. They should be able to evaluate the skill base of the company and should have well-founded ideas on its management requirements. Personal acquaintance with candidates for senior management positions is of great value. All of this points to the need to promote some outstanding corporate managers, capable of fulfilling a totally new role, to the supervisory board. The CEO is not necessarily one of them, and if he is chosen he cannot become its chairman.

An additional advantage of this approach is that a wealth of experience remains available to the company and a valuable network of personal relationships, inside and outside the company, is preserved. This enhances the board's advisory capacity. Even more importantly, appointing former managers goes a long way in restoring the balance of power between the CEO and the board. The wide gap in knowledge between the CEO and his board is largely closed and the board's scrutiny of implicit and explicit assumptions that underpin major management proposals gains credibility.

A second category of board members is required to provide an external perspective. The members of this group are acquainted with the fields in which the company operates but their real expertise lies elsewhere. They are well placed to evaluate the company's organizational culture and structure, decision-making procedures and financial controls. They pay particular attention to the company's rules of engagement, both inside the company and in its dealings with the outside world. More specific tasks include taking a fresh look at the candidates for senior management positions and challenging the opinions held by past and present executives.

Both categories of board members fulfil different roles but work together and take joint responsibility for the well-being of the company.

All this is a major departure from prevailing European practice whereby board members who sit on the boards and executive committees of other companies are selected along with a sprinkling of former politicians and university professors. Most members are not familiar with the markets in which the company operates and individual members are interchangeable. The size of boards is impressive; 10 or more members are about the standard with considerable consequences for the quality of the discussion and decision making. Boards rely on a limited number of meetings during the year to meet their responsibilities, often slowing down corporate decision making. No board member can expect to exercise any discernible influence via the standard 10 meetings a year. A CEO is simply too far ahead on any issue and his will prevails.

# THE EUROPEAN MANAGER

The statutory responsibility for day-to-day decision making on all commercial and operational matters as well as the charting of the company's future rests with the CEO. He is supported by a management team that embodies all the relevant commercial and operational expertise and external contacts. Management tasks could be divided in many different ways but there are three team members that, in addition to their other duties, must carry special responsibility for the identified three performance areas: corporate integrity, corporate development and corporate renewal. The difficult trade-offs between the three areas can only be made at the top. A fourth team member supports the CEO by representing the company to the outside world. He needs his rank to gain access to the highest echelons of government and regulatory agencies.

Finance, financial control, financial auditing, legal services, public affairs, public relations and human resources are support functions. Given the great variety of decisions the CEO and the management team have to make, the call on functional support will vary considerably and will require different teams on different occasions. As a result the support functions need not be represented in the management team.

The CEO can only take decisions after consulting his management team. This team can also take the initiative and advise the CEO regarding any issue. In this way checks and balances are built into the system and much of the informal organizational pressures can be channelled and brought into the open in the interest of an informed debate.

The business unit remains the workhorse of the company. Its manager is responsible for the unit's free cash flow, structural improvement of its position and contributing to corporate renewal. This will be discussed further in the section 'Performance planning, evaluation and remuneration' later in this chapter.

## The perfect leader

The CEO and the members of the management team need many qualities. It is obvious that perfect managers do not exist, but it is important to identify the areas in which individual managers are weak and seek compensation among other members of the team.

The perfect manager understands the world in which he lives. He holds realistic expectations of people and is mild in his judgements. He is very much aware of the intricacies of corporate life and how they affect his managers and employees. He knows that people and organizations can only change at a measured pace and he does not play cards that he does not have.

He feels that he is the custodian of a precious entity, a complicated apparatus that needs protection. At the same time he has an entrepreneurial and team spirit. He is well aware of his dependence on the cooperation of many. Cooperation depends on trust. The building of trust throughout the organization starts with managers who adhere to the social virtues: openness, honesty and authenticity. True leadership can only be exercised by real people, warts and all, who do not hide behind their public relations officials and other spin doctors.

While managers value trust, they know that at times trust will be broken. They can set all the right conditions for cooperation but certain teams will fail. Real-life managers are also aware that breaches of trust create deep rifts and that, although there will be fewer conflicts to manage in comparison to the American Enterprise Model, the conflicts that do arise will be more personal and might fester.

Corporate leaders set standards and must maintain them both privately and in business. Trading in the shares of their own company provides an interesting test case. In the American Enterprise Model executives have no qualms about trading in the stocks or stock options of their companies. They have to stay within the bounds of complicated rules designed to prevent insider trading, but loopholes and different interpretations of the law are there to be explored. Some cross the line, and some cross the line and are caught.

The prevailing practice that prohibits trading during fixed periods before the publication of results and in the run-up to major announcements (such as mergers and takeovers) is a very odd arrangement. It means that outside these periods trading based on exclusive knowledge of many developments that have an impact on corporate share price is allowed – and as such can be nothing else but insider trading. The problem is that a large and complicated issue is narrowed down to the availability of corporate results and the access of corporate officials to this information ahead of publication. In a world in which managers look forward and concentrate on the cash the company will generate in the future, intimate knowledge of the projects that will make the difference should disqualify managers from trading in the shares of their own company at any time.

Not all defining moments are positive. Knowledge of impending disasters provides even better trading opportunities, as in the case of ImClone where problems started when a few insiders became aware that the US Food and Drug Administration (FDA) would withhold the approval of a new drug.

To avoid even the slightest whiff of impropriety, managers must also never trade in the stock of partners or competitors – let alone potential takeover targets.

By the time they have reached the top of their companies, managers should have earned a reputation for competence, fairness and collegiality and be held in high esteem by their colleagues and, equally important, by the managers of their business partners and competitors. They are knowledgeable in the commercial and technical fields in which their companies operate. They have participated in and have championed major organizational, commercial and technical innovations. This is the new source of authority and one that is very different from the capacity to improve corporate financial results.

The new manager has been a member of, and has built, effective management teams. He knows many people throughout this organization and has a fair assessment of their strengths and weaknesses.

The CEO of IBM, Sam Palmisano, is a man who meets a number of these requirements. He brought years of practical experience to the top position and is widely respected for his technical insight and team-building qualities. His initial moves included replacing the 12-member corporate executive committee with three management teams responsible for operations, strategy and technology. This reorganization helped him to engage directly in corporate innovation. He wants his company to set the agenda via a new, inspiring and all-encompassing concept: e-business on demand. This requires all hands on deck. The concept entails the building of computing grids and data-centre networks for companies with different equipment. Such grids will help improve the reliability of data processing, reduce idle computing capacity and bring information processing costs down by 50 per cent. The aim is for information processing to become a utility. In an attempt to change IBM culture, Palmisano set aside part of his bonus for the stimulation of teamwork among the top 20 executives of the company and embarked on a $100 million programme to teach 30,000 employees how to lead and not how to control.[5]

## A man of the world

The independence of US companies from a government that wants to set markets free is simply folklore. The new European manager takes a genuine interest in regulatory and political issues and sees all layers of government as potential partners and not adversaries. This opens the way to innovative corporate relationships with governments and regulators.

One example is the opportunity that arose from the construction of Malpensa Airport outside Milan with the help of the Italian government, the European Commission and the European Investment Bank (EIB). Once KLM and Alitalia launched their plans for a unique dual-hub system (Malpensa and Amsterdam's Schiphol Airport), the public and the private sector in both countries worked closely together in the interest of Italian economic development, the value of the Italian government's share in Alitalia, stronger European competition, return on the Malpensa investment and the common future of KLM and Alitalia.

True innovation threatens competitors. The American Enterprise Model primes companies to use all legal and regulatory means to increase competitors' costs and to delay or, better still, prevent the introduction of innovations. It is up to management to lead the counter-attack. US and European airlines challenged the plans of the Italian government and the EC for many years. They aligned themselves with the Milan business community to fight against the closure of Milan's city centre airport, Linate. The authorities wanted to shift air traffic from Linate to Malpensa for environmental and economic reasons. A lack of public transport between Malpensa and Milan provided KLM and Alitalia's competitors with a useful argument for opposing the move. After a lengthy and costly delay, KLM and Alitalia had to make do with a cap on the number of Linate flights – enabling Lufthansa and Air France to siphon off local traffic for intercontinental connections via Frankfurt and Paris. Nevertheless, counterpressure along the way by Alitalia and its CEO Dominico Cempella helped to fix the cap low enough to keep the damage to the KLM–Alitalia merger within reasonable bounds. The viability of the business idea was preserved and merger negotiations could proceed. Eventually, the merger fell through for different reasons.

Innovation leads both companies and regulators into uncharted waters. The new corporate manager is sensitive to the legal constraints and pressures facing regulators. The rhetoric of American managers is always punctuated with 'the profound desire to work with regulators'. The clash between General Electric's Jack Welch and Mario Monti, the European commissioner in 2002, about the company's intended takeover of Honeywell illustrated Welch's total ignorance of European law and of Monti's mandate. Different views on the future of the IT industry also played an important role in the heated exchanges between GE and the EC. In the end, the deal was blocked by Monti.

Finally, business leaders must be both realists and idealists. Corporate performance is the beginning and the end, but the way in which these results are achieved matters. Their instincts must drive them to decision making by consensus, their professionalism to speed and action.

In dealing with the outside world, business leaders are under no illusions about the competitive and other pressures the defenders of the American Enterprise Model can exercise. Unlike their US counterparts, European business leaders have to be masters of two games: those based on both the European and the US world-view. They are true Europeans in believing in the power of reason but they have to be equally well versed in the skills of power play.

# THE MANAGEMENT AGENDA

As emphasized management must strike a balance between running the business, expanding and strengthening existing businesses, and building new ones.

The CEO and his management team can greatly enhance their leverage by guiding decision making in its very early stages. Management must lead from the front. It must steer discussions on macroeconomic premises for budgeting and planning. It falls to top management not only to express views on the future composition of the portfolio of businesses, but also to lead the charge forward.

## Management by setting standards and by designing rules

No matter how big the temptation, managers should resist taking the same sort of decisions – now on a bigger scale – that they have always done. For example managers with a commercial background are most comfortable with commercial decisions. Managers that have a good track record for small acquisitions have a predilection for large takeovers when they reach the top.

Unlike their predecessors, today's managers must lead by setting standards and not by applying rules. They have to lead by evaluating the use and possible abuse of existing rules, by making adjustments and by abolishing non-functional rules altogether. They design few new regulations and ensure they are properly implemented and respected. Managers should not lead by taking decisions that could be left to lower echelons. Attention to standard setting, risky and controversial as it may be, is an investment with a high rate of return.

It is very important to have a set of business principles at corporate level to guide managers and employees alike. These standards should provide practical advice for dealings with colleagues, suppliers, customers and shareholders. Solid statements setting out corporate values in plain language are very powerful tools when drafted by respected managers who do not hesitate to live up to them even when doing so becomes costly. If they do not, adverse reactions could be considerable. Politically correct and high-minded corporate principles were of course ludicrous in the hands of Enron's leaders. A more recent example is Deutsche Bank, which according to its business principles values customer focus, teamwork, innovation and performance, and was seen to ignore those principles when a major lay-off programme was announced.

In addition to a general set of principles, the CEO and his team have ample scope to design more specific sets of principles in areas such as the hiring and dismissal of managers and employees, innovation and the termination of corporate activities.

The CEO and his team head companies that seem well integrated to the outside world but are in fact responsible for a large, diverse and forever evolving network of operational and commercial entities. These include companies over which they exercise various degrees of control and a rapidly increasing number of alliances. The reputation of the company as a partner is part of its assets and its protection and enhancement should be pursued vigorously. The CEO and his team provide guidelines for the selection of partners and set the criteria for the evaluation of existing partnerships in line with the corporate objectives. In financial terms, partnerships could contribute to the corporate cash flow, help to put cash generation at a structurally higher level, or help develop new sources of cash. Alliances are based on three indispensable elements. The first is a legal agreement. The second is a joint management team to deal with the many unforeseeable turns and twists of business life. And the third is a commitment to build a trusting relationship. The CEO and his team must design new rules for new forms of cooperation. Gerard Kleisterlee, CEO of Philips Electronics, travels the world to promote pre-competitive research (such as the joint lab of Motorola, Thomson and Philips in Grenoble in France) and new industry standards. The latter is designed to prevent bruising battles between rival standards so that companies can focus on product development, marketing and sales.

The budget and the medium-term plan remain indispensable instruments to guide the company towards its new objectives. They form a comprehensive overview of all the marketing, sales and operational decisions that build economic value in the following year and in the medium term. Even more important is the way the plan is arrived at. The questions that need to be addressed by the CEO and his team are: Who throughout the company sets which objectives on what grounds? Who decides on the distribution of the available resources in pursuit of which objective? And also: How can plans be adapted more quickly? How can spending stay in tune with original objectives? How can savings on approved capital outlays be stimulated?

Investment decisions constitute a separate category of decisions, and the CEO and his team have to devote much time to the formal approval of proposals that reach them as the outcome of sometimes convoluted bureaucratic processes. Again, they are far more effective by focusing on direction, criteria, processes and procedures.

Based on their vision for the company as a whole, management must select areas and issue guidelines on the types of investment proposals they would like to see developed. Hurdle rates (the minimum required return on investment) and other decision criteria need to be evaluated frequently. The most up-to-date methods are needed to assess the comparative merits of alternative investments in terms of their contribution to value creation. Processes must be put in place to implement and evaluate investment decisions. And management must design tailor-made decision-making processes for ad hoc cases, such as major investment in plant and equipment, mergers and acquisitions, or corporate restructuring.

Another crucial area of decision making is the hiring, development and dismissal of employees. Creating sound recruitment criteria and procedures, fixing the design criteria for the corporate management development programme, and guidance for dismissals are more valuable than deciding on individual cases. In the area of performance evaluation and remuneration systems, management defines the design principles, makes sure that implementation is in line with original intentions and is directly involved in the evaluation of the system.

Given the all-important contribution of people, management is directly involved in the positioning of the company on the labour market.

In evaluating criteria and procedures, management must be particularly interested in the unintended consequences of rules and counterproductive effects of rewards. On the positive side, it is necessary to build in incentives that build trust among colleagues and partners. Management must also be on the look-out for rules that can be abolished if they no longer serve a purpose or, worse, only serve the interests of individual departments and business units.

## Management of innovation

The top echelon of a company is well advised to support the day-to-day management team and strengthen existing activities by focusing on setting and evaluating principles. But when it comes to innovation of existing businesses and/or changes in the portfolio of activities, the CEO and his team must be personally and permanently involved at all stages of decision making. They must lead the search for new business ideas or more efficient ways to produce. And they must draft the terms of reference for the project teams that develop the most promising ideas. The CEO and his team must also appoint the project leader and make sure that the team has the right expertise. They must secure the team's independence and specify the contributions that are expected from corporate departments and business units. Management have no choice but to stand shoulder to shoulder with their experts to gain a deep understanding of the value that is being conceived. The conditions for change and the necessary resources have to be identified if the proposed innovation is to be successful. If the team is successful, management must shepherd the idea through the formal decision-making processes. The CEO remains in charge during implementation to make sure that the original idea is not lost along the way as an increasing number of employees become involved in the venture. This process turns the manager into an entrepreneur.

Bernd Pischetsrieder, the CEO of Volkswagen AG and German manager of the year in 2004, showed many of these traits in supporting his negotiator Josef-Fidelis Senn in achieving a landmark collective labour agreement that made Volkswagen production processes far more flexible and therefore more efficient.

One advantage of early involvement by top management is the strengthening of the so-called 'line of sight', the causal link between corporate objectives, new initiatives, the mandates of different teams and the contributions of individual team members. It is also a form of inoculation against power play and double mandates: the involvement of the CEO right at the beginning makes it clear that the mandate comes directly from the top and business unit management will have to concur. Corporate constraints can be made clear at the outset – rather than surfacing along the way, as is often the case in conventional decision-making processes – which greatly improves efficiency.

This deviates significantly from present practice whereby management is brought into play only in the final and formal stages of decision making – just in time to conclude that it has been deprived of potentially interesting options or, even worse, that an excellent solution has been proposed for the wrong problem.

This form of management engagement is not for the faint-hearted: some of managers' early assumptions will prove wrong, and differences in emphasis or even disagreement among top managers will be difficult to conceal.

In the American Enterprise Model CEOs stay away from guiding innovations and partnerships. They have learnt the hard way that even the slightest show of their hand reverberates throughout the organization, that even the most careful statements are abused for personal and bureaucratic reasons, and that any hint of the direction in which the CEO is leaning gets greatly amplified. This is one of the more insidious by-products of the strong CEO heading an organization in which office politics is a way of life.

In all this, management have a keen eye for the behavioural and organizational consequences of rules. Management form an opinion about the proportionality of incentives in relation to the tasks. They also check the consistency of incentives across the organization. They do away with informal veto rights and prevent these and other forms of abuse from creeping in. Management protect consistency of corporate values.

## Management of financing

Under the European Enterprise Model more emphasis is put on long-term partnerships with investors when it comes to financing the company and its expansion.

In the American Enterprise Model the relationship between a public company and its shareholders is basically antagonistic. Despite public endorsement of the shareholder, companies want to attract equity as cheaply as possible. Public placements are sold with all the marketing and spinning power that investment banks and their clients can mobilize. The keys to success are the packaging of optimism in neutral terms and the mixing of claims and disclaimers to convey the impression of a bright future while avoiding future litigation. Shareholders' distrust of corporate management has apparently reached such depths that they are approving very costly option packages as the only way to guarantee that management focuses on the company's share price.

As stressed, equity markets only cover the capital requirements of European companies for 25 per cent. There is therefore a strong basis for partnerships with banks, private investors and specialized investment funds. This base should be enforced and expanded.[6]

A number of developments play into the hands of truly European companies. Pension funds and other institutional investors were severely hit by the stock market crash. Many operate perilously close to, or even beyond, the solvency requirements set by regulators. There must be a reduction in exposure to stock market volatility, while at the same time return on investment has to be increased. Study after study shows that the yield of equity investments in existing companies is significantly higher than the yield of investment in publicly traded stock over the medium term. Pension funds are moving slowly in that direction. The number of specialized investment funds, each with its own network of advisors, is increasing. Corporate treasurers and private equity fund managers are developing a healthy degree of mutual dependence.

Competition among European banks will heat up in the future and their offerings are bound to become more attractive. The expected consolidation of European commercial banks will help to strengthen balance sheets, and as a result credit can flow more easily. Moreover a number of European banks will be allowed to increase their equity holdings based on the quality of their loan portfolio, which will broaden their product range. The European Investment Bank will become a major supporter of innovative small and medium-sized companies.

On top of this, the chance is that financial markets will become more transparent. Whereas only stock markets could bring parties together in the past, banks are now trying to couple smaller investors with investment funds and individual companies. Experiments with the help of the internet are ongoing and could open up new channels.

Financial markets are forbidding places where mercy is neither asked for nor given and all providers of capital have justified interests to defend. However the big difference between equity finance and other sources of capital is that the former is based on professional decision making including sound knowledge of the client's business and its risks and the quality of its management. Banks build industry expertise and can make a contribution to the client's plans. They have separate credit committees that assess the risk and rewards for each loan and provide second opinions. No stock market analyst can come close to this.

## Organizational development

Many exponents of the American Enterprise Model confuse the innocent observer by stressing the importance of human resources for the well-being of the company. Fred Hassan, chairman and CEO of pharmaceutical conglomerate Schering-Plough, sees himself as the chief developer of talent and claims to value 'open minded behaviour, including shared accountability, transparency and cooperation'.[7] But this is only meaningful if his shareholders allow him the time to demonstrate the benefits of this approach in financial terms, and if means are found to integrate these new demands into financial target setting and performance evaluation. The company culture of Schering-Plough, not known for its benign working environment, has to change too. Jeffrey Immelt, chairman and CEO of General Electric, gives the game away by claiming that he travels the world to build up a personal network and by boasting that he personally reviews 5,000 to 6,000 CVs per year. He turns into the very caricature of the all-American CEO when he instructs his human resources manager to hand 'a double dip of stock options' to people that impress him.[8]

If a company is first and foremost a community of workers who create an economic surplus, managers and employees cannot be considered 'human resources' comparable to other means of production such as capital or intellectual property. Stressing the importance of 'labour' is a spruced-up version of the 19th-century concept of labour and capital. Under the European Enterprise Model only people add value, and that potential can only be realized by well-structured forms of cooperation. All the rest is of secondary importance.

The CEO and his senior managers should spend all the time that is required to build and evaluate their organization, and decide on the division of tasks and responsibilities and the rules of engagement between units and departments. Organizational forms must be fluid and the overlap of responsibilities must no longer be a deadly sin in companies where collegiality has been reintroduced and financial incentives no longer drive people apart.

The new-style manager must consciously build a corporate culture and provide role models both for individuals and for teams, nurturing attitudes that are conducive to cooperation. Management must use the promotion of well-respected colleagues to communicate the sort of attitudes and behaviour that is appreciated. It should visibly intervene if and when there are serious breaches of the desired behaviour.

Nowhere is the building of a structure and culture more important and more visible than in corporate decision making. Developing and discarding alternatives and eventually committing the company is where everything comes together: creativity, cooperation, risk taking, persistence and discipline. No management course and no intervention by consultants can hold a candle to a successful decision-making process.

European managers avoid the pitfalls associated with ever-increasing specification of tasks and responsibilities, accountability and tight control. They do not want to work for a company where trust is neither given nor required, a company that gives employees no reason to believe that their individual contribution is appreciated. They do not want to work for organizations where everybody is painfully and continuously aware that careers can end abruptly, in a world in which job descriptions and CVs have become increasingly standardized to facilitate quick firing and hiring. And finally, they do not want to work for companies where employees have ceased to express their concerns and alienation is the norm. The human price is simply too high and the economics are awful.

Even in companies that avoid these pitfalls, European managers need to be aware that defensive routines are deeply embedded in organizations. The whole truth hardly ever comes to the surface as employees and managers are fearful of threatening or embarrassing their superiors, peers, subordinates and, last but not least, themselves. People do not speak up because they lack psychological confidence. They fear for their acceptance as individuals and for their careers. They also question the point of honest feedback when experience tells them that their suggestions will be ignored.[9]

Conversely, because trust and communication can be restored, errors can be corrected earlier, more ideas reach the right managers and employees put more into their jobs. Companies that get this right enjoy an impressive competitive advantage.

Organizational and management development go hand in hand. European managers are recruiting managers for today and tomorrow and continuously (re)positioning them to match available skills with immediate and future corporate requirements. They are fully aware that the early social and organizational integration of newcomers contributes significantly to corporate efficiency, and intervene directly when this threatens to fail.

Rather than filling vacancies, corporate leaders must build and evaluate management teams throughout the organization. They must ensure that all the essential fields of expertise are covered for each unit and that teams have a strong external orientation. If a group ceases to operate as a team, it must be dismantled as soon as possible to limit the damage. Managers must also provide protection for individual team members if and when necessary.

Management teams depend on their counterparts elsewhere inside the company and on the management teams of partners. Under the European Enterprise Model, senior managers must give priority to the formation of management teams in joint ventures and alliances.

As stressed in Chapter 4, the negative impact of organizational tensions on commercial and other relations is generally underestimated. Personal conflicts are a luxury companies can ill afford and should not be allowed to linger. Interdepartmental feuding must be explicitly addressed. Joint ventures in particular are prone to personal disagreements and thus require continuous vigilance. Early interventions prevent escalation and further destruction of value.

It also falls to European managers to find solutions for those whose skill base has become obsolete and experience irrelevant. McKinsey for example makes sure that senior advisors who do not qualify for partnership find interesting and rewarding positions outside the firm. They also make sure to maintain social ties with former employees. This form of security helps consultants to take risks and many become goodwill ambassadors after leaving the firm.

To increase flexibility in filling positions and composing teams and to reduce in-fighting, European companies must decide on a partial decoupling of job level and remuneration. Given a certain level of remuneration, managers can be given assignments on, below or above par.

Where lifetime employment is neither offered nor demanded, management must seek to retain their former staff in a wider corporate orbit. It must have no qualms about re-employing past staff to capitalize on their corporate experience and the new expertise they have acquired in other organizations.

## Performance planning, evaluation and remuneration

In the European Enterprise Model, the business unit remains the workhorse of the company, but the fault lines between it and corporate head office and between business unit managers and the CEO disappear because their objectives are in alignment. This includes the management of existing activities, their enforcement and the renewal of the company. As stressed earlier, all layers of management contribute in all fields, although their input varies. For example the CEO assists the management of the business units by defining the rules of engagement with other units, but is helpless in securing compliance with accounting rules. Most business unit managers can only make a limited contribution to changes in the corporate portfolio. The latter is primarily the domain of the CEO and the supervisory board.

Like the supervisory board and the CEO and his team, business unit managers should be judged first and foremost on their capacity to secure the integrity of their organization in the broadest possible sense of the word. Are all regulations that apply to his unit correctly applied? Are corporate and business unit decisions being implemented in accordance with the letter and the spirit of the plans? Are operational procedures being honoured? Is best practice applied in all professional fields? Are the right people hired, is the full potential of employees being used and is the atmosphere conducive to cooperation? Are all contracts honoured and are all partnerships properly managed?

The quantitative measure of performance for the business unit manager is a change in the free cash flow of his unit. What use did the business unit manager make of assets made available to him, including but not confined to plant and equipment, intellectual property, sales force, back office, market positions, brands and the skill base of the unit? Such an evaluation also includes the performance of the partnerships in which a manager's unit is engaged and to which assets have been assigned. Changes in exchange rates, economic growth, energy prices and other exogenous variables are filtered out.

The second measure of performance is the value the manager is adding to his unit and organization. This covers structural improvements in the capacity of the unit or organization to generate free cash flow, income after all cost (including the cost of capital required to improve the unit's competitive position) has been taken into account. It encompasses the strengthening of the organization and the quality of decision making, the appointment of better managers and the building of the unit's culture. It covers the development and implementation of integrated programmes, such as the introduction of new ICT and associated organizational changes, investment in plant, equipment, training, intellectual property and experts as well as engagement in new partnerships.

Clearly, structural improvements also include steps that make the unit less vulnerable to external shocks, for example by hedging against undesired shifts in exchange rates or increasing its capacity to accommodate surges in demand by introducing flexible work weeks.

Given the lead times involved, the manager is judged on the basis of progress with programmes that he inherited from his predecessor, on the quality and progress of his own programmes and, at the end of his tenure, on the quality of the portfolio of projects in progress.

The third measure of performance relates to the manager's contribution to corporate innovation. This includes steps towards the foundation of new units on the basis of new business ideas. It also includes moves towards restructuring or abandoning existing businesses. Managers, together with the corporate leadership, have to judge whether their units are viable in the long run or whether skills and assets can be employed to greater effect elsewhere, either inside or outside the company. This is where the future of the industry and the strategies of competitors come into play as well as possible long-term development in exogenous variables.

Managers should also be judged on their contribution to the innovation initiatives of their colleagues. Such a contribution could take many shapes. Managers could contribute their 'intellectual property' in the form of ideas and experience. They could also make experts, facilities and equipment available to corporate project teams or teams of other units.

Once appointed, the European manager drafts a plan for the whole duration of his assignment for each of the three areas described above. It contains an evaluation of the work in progress and his initiatives. In the interest of fairness, proposals to discontinue inherited programmes need to be properly justified. The plan contains quantitative objectives: the projected cash flow of the unit and the increase in economic value that the unit will realize over the period. It also contains qualitative objectives, for example milestones to guide internal projects and collaborative efforts with third parties.

Such a plan provides a structure for an ongoing dialogue with superiors. This will not be assessed and revised at regular intervals, but at points when built-in milestones have been achieved, new insights become available, new initiatives are appropriate or external developments force a change. In this way planning becomes a living concept and there is no longer a discrepancy between the criteria for business and personal success. Mistakes or errors of judgement are identified at a very early stage but at the same time put into the context of overall progress.

The longer the managerial tenure, the more an individual's assessment is based on his record and not on temporary upswings or the positive effects of isolated decisions. This results in a more comprehensive, balanced and fair form of performance evaluation. Managers should be allowed to build something meaningful and this takes time. Therefore it is only at the end of a manager's tenure that a fair judgement can be passed. Such an approach is much closer to real executive life than artificial monthly and end-of-year cut-off points that financial accounting departments use as a basis for management control. This European model of performance evaluation can lay the foundation for management development programmes. It can also remove the need for a separate cycle of personal assessment detached from the business.

Rewards granted at the end of a manager's tenure can take different forms. A cash bonus for improvement in the functioning of the unit in all its aspects is one possibility. A percentage of the improvement in the cash flow generated by the business unit, corrected for exogenous developments, is a second one. More important is a share in the increase of the economic value of the unit that was achieved over the period. An overall judgement, including contributions to the company as a whole, could translate into a contract with a longer duration, a higher fixed income, promotion or any combination of these. Given the ongoing dialogue which takes place on the basis of the business unit plan, the final judgements of senior managers will not contain any surprises.

The European Enterprise Model also lacks pay-for-performance for the lower echelons. In Chapter 4 the unintended consequences and unaccounted costs of bonus systems were highlighted. Empirical studies, for example into the role of pay-for-performance systems in 13 Hewlett-Packard locations, do not reveal many benefits. The Hewlett-Packard study concluded that managers grossly overestimated the motivational effects of introducing a pay-for-performance system while underestimating the problems of designing and maintaining such a system. Setting targets at the right level was difficult. Adjustments caused conflicts, reduced trust and undermined the credibility of the system and supervisors. Employees came to rely on the extra income and this proved costly in a rapidly changing industry. All 13 schemes were abolished when it became apparent that alternative means, such as coaching and training, were equally effective in creating motivation.[10]

Given the many qualitative aspects that have to be taken into account when judging the health and performance of organizations, a high level of trust on the part of both the business unit manager and his superior is required. Superiors must pass judgement on the basis of measurement, experience and intuition in their role as entrepreneur, manager and colleague. The authority to judge has to be earned and leads to a preparedness to be judged. All this cannot be seen independently from the profile of the European manager.[11]

## A SENSE OF INEVITABILITY

On the surface, the situation in the US and Europe seems comparable. Listed companies take centre stage and US consultancy firms, banks, accountants, credit rating agencies and law firms each make a contribution to a European society of shareholders. It is also true that equity trading is global and that stock markets are effective conduits through which the American Enterprise Model can be exported. Yet Europe has a major card to play because, as previously pointed out, only 25 per cent of the finance requirements of European companies are met by stock markets.

Consequently there is no need to declare a counter-revolution; the world does not have to be reinvented. It is sufficient to look at the tens of thousands of enterprise models that already exist in Europe – private companies that go their own way without any form of external financing and private companies whose governance, management and organization are tailor-made to the business idea the company is pursuing and are laid down in shareholder and loan agreements. Market opportunities come and go, and the need for external finance varies; models and contracts need to be flexible to meet the new requirements of European companies and financiers. This flexibility is surely part of the explanation behind the surprisingly strong relative performance of European economies and companies reported in Chapter 2.

To summarize: when it comes to progress, governance, management, organization and people determine the competitive position of the company. Many managers know intuitively that a clear, deliberate and hard-nosed approach to so-called 'soft' issues such as emotion, behaviour and culture carries an impressive rate of return.

Attempts by the human resource community to carve out high-flying careers for themselves must be resisted with force. The place of the modern-day human resource executive is far into the background to avoid any confusion as to who has the real responsibility: the CEO and his team.

The sixth and final chapter is devoted to the competitiveness of this European model.

# 6

# The competitiveness of Europe

This battle is between people-based economics and shareholder economics and will be fought in Europe. As stressed in Chapter 1, there are too many forces in the United States pointing in the same direction to expect profound change there. There will always be exceptions like IBM, a company with a long history and a strong culture, and Cisco which suffered greatly from a total and dedicated application of the American Enterprise Model but was eventually brought back from the brink of bankruptcy. In the vast majority of US companies, profit and return on shareholder investment remain the basic concerns, the position of the CEO is left untouched and financial control remains the most essential management tool. US companies, consultants and researchers will continue to defend the American Enterprise Model. Together they will cope with changing circumstances and deal with calls for amendments.

The battle will not be fought in international markets either. Generally speaking, European companies have proved to be more capable of adapting to local circumstances. As a result Europe is a very competitive player on world markets but export markets are relatively small compared to home markets and victory abroad will not deal the American Enterprise Model a fatal blow.

The fight is between European companies operating in Europe on the basis of the American Enterprise Model, and those working on the basis of a European Enterprise Model. With the vast majority of Europe's public companies firmly putting their money on the former, it falls to Europe's liberal private enterprises, small and large, to prove that a different approach can unleash the next round of economic and corporate development.

European Enterprise Models will prevail for several reasons. Firstly there is growing awareness that the US economy and the American Enterprise Model are much less successful than generally assumed. Many European investors have already drawn their own conclusions. Ever since the recession of 2000, but also during the subsequent upturn, US bonds have been treated with suspicion. The central banks of China and Japan have filled the void to protect the favourable exchange rate of their currencies vis-à-vis the US dollar. These investments cannot be construed as an expression of great confidence in the US economy. Many Europeans shun US stocks and European direct investment in the United States has fallen spectacularly. These are some of the explanations behind the sustained drop of the US dollar against the euro in 2003 and 2004, despite favourable US and unfavourable European economic news.

Secondly, European companies, struggling to improve the profitability of recent US acquisitions, are learning about the limitations of the American Enterprise Model in the hardest possible way. The spectacular failures of some of the high-flying European CEOs who tried to emulate their American counterparts – Cees van der Hoeven of Ahold, Jean-Marie Messier of Vivendi and Thomas Middelhoff of Bertelsmann – will have a lasting impact.

Thirdly, irritation with US-style politics and the consequences for international treaties is still rising. More and more people are starting to appreciate the connection between US political philosophies, attitudes and actions on the one hand and the interests of corporate America on the other.

All this undermines the position of the American Enterprise Model and its momentum – critical for the survival of the model – will gradually be lost.

Other indications that European Enterprise Models will gain in standing come from the analyses in Chapter 3 and 4. European companies that can avoid the value destruction inherent in the American Enterprise Model enjoy a genuine and growing competitive advantage. The most compelling reason for this is that companies that are forced to concentrate on a limited number of policies geared solely to improving shareholders' return on investment (as in the American Enterprise Model) are by definition more vulnerable in a rapidly changing world.

The European Enterprise Model proposed in the previous chapter has distinct features which set it apart from its US counterpart. To start with, companies that concentrate on free cash flow to secure continuity have many more options for adapting to changing circumstances.

Moreover, the role of CEO as defined by the European model keeps corporate tensions and counterproductive conflicts within bounds. The CEO is professionally supervised by his board and is not only inclined, but also forced, to work closely with his colleagues. In this European Enterprise Model corporate head office gives greater weight to cash flow than profit. Corporate and business unit objectives are better aligned. Performance planning and remuneration are much closer to the way people work. Managers realize that large and lasting improvements take time. The conclusion is that European models can avoid some of the pitfalls of American corporate life, incur far less unaccounted cost and have to cope with fewer unintended consequences. Discussions and disagreements concern the business itself and not personal interests. Managers and employees feel secure and confident. Companies that operate in accordance with the proposed European Enterprise Model are highly attractive places to work and will compete successfully for the best and the brightest.

The most important competitive advantage of this European model concerns the capacity to identify and exploit new sources of value. The strengths of such an approach and the weaknesses of the US method in this crucial field will be highlighted in the remainder of this chapter.

Certain sources of value can be found inside the company (internal growth) while others are across corporate boundaries (partnerships). In all cases, access to these sources depends on innovative forms of cooperation and decision making. Cooperation is built on trust. Trust is the hallmark of the European Enterprise Model, while in the US system trust is systematically undermined.

## REKINDLING INTERNAL GROWTH

Internal or organic growth can be achieved by intervening in companies in distress following mergers and acquisitions, by restructuring the way innovation is organized, by improving multi-factor productivity and by following a new approach to the development and sale of services.

## Cleaning up

As stressed in Chapter 3, the 1990s left a considerable trail of failed mergers. Some were not even completed, the majority did not meet expectations and there were also outright fiascos.

An example of the last category is provided by Daimler/Chrysler and Jurgen Schrempp, the most American of all European CEOs. Announced as a merger of equals, the transaction actually deteriorated into an unfriendly (and financially inspired) $36 billion takeover. The struggle for power and major cultural clashes in the scores of teams looking for synergies culminated in the appointment of two Daimler executives to run Chrysler. The business idea – the creation of scale and the exchange, joint purchase and production of parts – took a long time to develop and, when it did finally materialize, it tarnished the Mercedes reputation for top quality and made second-tier Chrysler brands too expensive. At the same time, the competitiveness of Chrysler on a stand-alone basis was grossly overestimated. Cost slashing was one of the few remaining options and 26,000 Chrysler employees lost their jobs in a $6 billion rationalization drive. All this was not enough to prevent a $1 billion loss in the second quarter of 2003 and the announcement of more cost cutting. The $38 billion market capitalization of DaimlerChrysler is way down from the Daimler-Benz value of $46 billion before the takeover. By the end of 2003, Deutsche Bank, one of the company's major shareholders, was exercising considerable pressure on Schrempp, and his departure and the break-up of the company was a distinct possibility. In the end full operational control of Chrysler by German managers proved to be the only way out of a messy merger of equals.[1]

Many combinations like Daimler/Chrysler had to write off goodwill and make other financial provisions. As a result they now represent considerable potential and thus economic value.

When assessing the potential of the European Enterprise Model, it is important to be aware of some of the forces that are at play after a US-style takeover. In the immediate aftermath, the CEO is mired in conflicts about the interpretation of the agreement, in managerial infighting regarding restructuring and appointments, and in discussions about unpaid bills and other previously undisclosed legal obligations. It becomes clear that too many expectations were raised in the run-up to the agreement and it is not clear which commitments can be met. Furthermore the CEO has to cope with suspicious partners, customers and suppliers. He also has to deal with two companies, his own and the one taken over, in which everybody is waiting in trepidation for the inevitable cost cutting and lay-offs. In short, he faces the many different ways in which mergers can derail, and faces them all at once.

As empirical evidence shows, centrifugal forces take over in the majority of cases and original intentions and projected benefits disappear. Morale drops further, competitors take advantage, results disappoint and financial markets lose faith. At this stage, the CEO's optimism and commitment come back to haunt him. There is a feeling that he did not anticipate implementation problems because of a lack of experience, skill or interest and, worse, that he lost control. As a result the CEO is hardly in a position to supervise salvage operations. In many instances this is left to his successor who, almost as standard procedure, takes a considerable financial provision before wielding his axe.

Even if the CEO and his financially oriented team, flag-bearers of the American Enterprise Model, are given the opportunity to save the merger, they are scarcely equipped to make progress in what is a minefield of organizational integration and cultural change. Moreover management attitudes consistent with quick and aggressive expansion, again part of the 1990s heritage, are hardly conducive to the painstaking task of piecing together organizations in the atmosphere of anguish and distrust which prevails when mergers are in trouble.

In such situations, the European CEO and his team are well positioned to take the helm. The continuity of the company is at stake and financial orientation has to be replaced by emphasis on solving operational, commercial and organizational problems. The new CEO defines the values that should guide the organization, is clear about the business ideas on which the company will be built and defines the rules for decision making.

European management has the experience and credibility to redefine tasks and responsibilities. Managers are appointed on the basis of merit and not to reward those who stood by the CEO in testing times or to overcome resistance in the acquired company. The European CEO restores middle management, who take the brunt in US-style takeovers, to its rightful position.

The room for improvement is considerable. Some commercial and technical rationales for a merger are sound, and the focus can be on practicalities. Others need to be redesigned before a viable combined company can be built and yet others are so ill conceived that disentanglement is the most rational action.

The situation in recently merged companies is such that, under the right conditions, relatively simple steps can contribute significantly to an increase in sales and improved efficiency. Given the large number of mergers and acquisitions during the 1990s and assuming an 85 per cent failure rate – based on the latest work of Schenk and others – even a modest contribution from professional rescue operations could add significant value.

## Back to the drawing board

Another interesting area for adding value concerns the redesign of processes and procedures for innovation plus the generation and testing of new business ideas. Often opportunities arise from the benign or deliberate neglect of these. In the 1990s many managers were neither interested nor qualified to tackle the thorny issues that inevitably arise when innovators have to be both stimulated and guided. They had difficulty in settling the classic battles between research and marketing. In addition, research and development represented overheads and these were fair game throughout the 1990s. Schenk's studies show that research and development were one of the main victims of the merger craze.

Most renewal emerges from combining available technologies, and there is a huge reservoir of such permutations waiting to be tapped. Companies know more than they realize and removing organizational barriers of the kind described in Chapters 3 and 4 could produce pleasant surprises. Filling in the gaps in corporate know-how and intellectual property portfolios by acquiring a patent licence here and entering a joint venture there could add considerable value. Over the past years, markets for intellectual property have become far more transparent: communication barriers have come down and new brokers and deal-makers have set up business. The more important question is how the aforementioned reservoir of technological advancements can be exploited and not, at least for the foreseeable future, how technological development can be further accelerated to fill the reservoir.

The European CEO and his management team build new businesses on the basis of original combinations of tried and tested technologies embedded in a new offering to the customer. New technological findings in isolation add very little value; it is only by using this technology in a way that will appeal to customers that the company can create an economic surplus. The company that concentrates on leaps forward in terms of economic value enjoys a considerable competitive advantage. In biotechnology, for example, a patent is of little value in itself. To turn it into a genuine advantage generally requires licensing a number of patents developed by other companies, testing in animal models and finally studies in humans. Value is added at all these phases but by far the greatest jump is when the new compound proves its effectiveness on a scale that could yield statistically significant conclusions in so-called phase II studies ('multi-centre double-blind prospective trials'). After this, regulatory approval, production, marketing and the sale of the new drug could generate very substantial revenues, but large investment and operational costs put a ceiling on value creation. A parallel can be drawn with companies in other sectors who realize a jump in value when the results of the first large-scale market tests of a new product are favourable.

It is important to note that in each phase – but particularly that in which the most value is created – cooperation is of paramount importance. Nowadays there is hardly a patent application with fewer than four or five inventors. Building small molecules requires many different disciplines. Phase II trials are extraordinarily complex project organizations that involve scientists, medical staff and statisticians. Project management working together harmoniously with experts is the hallmark of the European Enterprise Model.

Spectacular changes can be seen in the organization of drug development. A paradigm shift in looking at disease – examining faulty combinations of genes – is leading to new forms of cooperation. Nothing can be achieved without the collaboration of chemists, biologists, mathematicians and computer scientists. Pharmaceutical giant Novartis is building a $300 million research facility to automate and systematically test new compounds, which is a fine example of cooperation between engineers and researchers. Another example is Amgen which is developing tests to identify patients that would benefit from its rheumatoid arthritis drug Kineret in a collaborative initiative by research and marketing departments.[2]

When it comes to stimulating innovation, the European CEO and his team do not have to cope with a number of organizational barriers intrinsic to the American Enterprise Model. As highlighted, the power and interests of the business unit and its position in the American Enterprise Model in particular act as a substantial barrier to innovation.

Ambitious financial objectives tightly connected to performance evaluation and remuneration systems force business units to reduce risk and to concentrate on the short term: the budget. Innovation sits uncomfortably next to short-term performance targets.

Innovation requires efforts beyond business unit boundaries and beyond the mandate of its manager. Generally some form of corporate sponsoring is required which often triggers adverse reactions. Business units have a vested interest in keeping overheads as low as possible. Furthermore, overt resistance to corporate initiatives helps to build the identity of the unit.

Another impediment is that business units lack incentives to make talented and experienced staff available for corporate projects. If they are forced to make manpower available for corporate projects, loyalty to the manager and an ability to defend the unit's interest are important criteria for selecting who is released. The business unit manager will want to assess potential repercussions for his unit as early as possible to smother threatening initiatives.

Finally, it is the business units that represent the interests of the largest and most profitable customers, and therefore it makes good business sense to direct investment towards these customers. This focus produces what Clayton Christensen, associate professor at the Harvard Business School, calls 'the innovator's dilemma'.[3] He looked at the impact of disruptive technologies on a variety of activities from the production of disc drives to mechanical excavators, and noted the following pattern.

Engineers in an established company which produces excavators discovered a new technique using hydraulic rather than cable-actuated parts. Mainstream customers had no use for this 'disruptive technology'. The demand was for large bucket sizes and this was initially beyond the capabilities of the new technology. It was therefore a rational move to direct innovation efforts to improving existing technology which was able to increase bucket size with the introduction of each new model. Meanwhile the new technology was taken elsewhere and another company found a profitable niche application. Hydraulic equipment was mounted onto tractors and proved very effective in digging trenches and doing odd jobs around the farm. Such a foothold supported further development of the hydraulic technology and over time this was able to deliver bucket sizes far beyond the limits of the traditional cable technology. Some of the established companies simply went out of business. Others made a belated jump to the new technology, only to discover that their competitors had a head start which they could never overcome.[4]

Johnson & Johnson is also facing some of the challenges associated with the strong position of business units. Over the past decade, this extremely successful all-American company has bought 52 firms for $30 billion and is now made up of 204 different businesses split into three divisions: drugs, medical devices and diagnostics, and consumer products. Each unit operates as an independent company with its own finance and human resources departments. Needless to say much of the company's success is attributed to this extreme form of decentralization.[5]

Like other pharmaceutical companies, Johnson & Johnson now faces new commercial realities. The big growth area in healthcare products is in the combinations of drugs, devices and diagnostics, for example the development of stents (used to keep clogged-up arteries open) coated with drugs to encourage blood flow.[6] Corporate sponsored research and product development coupled with close cooperation between business units is the way forward for Johnson & Johnson, but it is questionable whether the company can achieve this without squashing the entrepreneurial spirit.

All this requires cooperation across previously impenetrable organizational boundaries, and this is one of the strengths of the European Enterprise Model.

## Productivity revisited

The third area in which the European Enterprise Model is more competitive than the US model is multi-factor productivity. Improving productivity by investing in new plant and equipment is easy. It is more difficult to achieve productivity growth by improving management, organization, working methods and training. In Chapter 2 there was reference to a study that pointed at negative multi-productivity growth in the United States during the 1990s (with the exception of ICT hardware production). The emphasis on the quality of management and employees and their cooperation (part and parcel of the European Enterprise Model) will help to unlock very considerable potential at modest cost. A different approach to ICT and the motivation of employees can lay the foundation for growth in this area.

With regard to ICT, a healthy relationship between the company and its business units means that rational decisions can be taken in relation to company-wide and business unit-specific systems. Companies can reap the benefits of scale in terms of investment, system reliability, security and maintenance costs. Business units can run their applications on corporate hardware without compromising their commercial flexibility and customer service.

In the European Enterprise Model the need for managers to have industry-specific qualifications is recognized once more and insight into the opportunities offered by ICT is a requirement for all senior managers. New-style managers are interested in and feel capable of engaging themselves in the time-consuming and complicated redesigns of organizational structure, culture, training and decision making. This is the only way to combine ICT and social innovation to improve productivity.

This is a far cry from the managers of the 1990s who were ICT illiterate and paid scant attention to the true integration of information and communication technology in their organization. Again, the empowerment of business units did not help. Business unit management had every reason to fight for sizeable ICT budgets and for control over spending. This was justified on the basis of specific market requirements, but it also served to defend the realm and helped to put corporate head office and other business units at a distance. Potential savings at corporate level were sacrificed and the call on ICT professionals was increased at a time of considerable scarcity.

Both corporate and business unit managements were hard pressed to decide on ICT projects. Very few had the experience, the technical knowledge or the time to assume more than formal responsibility. In many companies and business units the design, selection and implementation of ICT projects were put in the supposedly safe hands of ICT professionals with their own separate budgets. Their technical orientation hampered the identification of commercial and operational needs. Interviewing potential users of systems to identify these needs and building systems to meet these demands seemed rational. However rapid changes in corporate priorities, a lack of understanding by managers with short-term contracts and an insatiable hunger for information put projects off course. Benefits could only be vaguely described, costs were very difficult to determine, projects were impossible to control and project evaluation was considered far too complicated.

Large numbers of ICT projects were not completed. Systems were installed that were never used. In some instances procedures and practices were adjusted to meet the requirements of the new computer systems. In general, the capacity and the willingness of people and organizations to absorb the new technology and to put it to good use were often overestimated. For many managers ICT was a source of embarrassment rather than a window to a new world.

The introduction of the European Enterprise Model implies the end of chief information officers and separate ICT managers in business units. The CEO and his team insist on integrated investment proposals, budgets and plans. Attempts to single out the ICT element of an investment and separate ICT operational cost from other costs is meaningless and produces quasi-control. Only basic services are exempt from this rule. Where possible the CEO and his team make sure that innovations that take hold in business units are disseminated across organizational boundaries.

The other foundation on which multi-factor productivity can be built concerns employee commitment. The European Enterprise Model satisfies important conditions to ensure motivation. Everybody is asked to make a contribution to a working community on the basis of his skills and experience, a contribution that is recognized and appreciated. Experts and middle managers hold the key to value creation and they can rely on their managers to guide and support them. They are part owners of the company and their financial rewards are at least partially linked to the increase in economic value that the company realizes. The emphasis is on sustainable growth with all the career opportunities this offers. The need to be a good team leader and a good team member puts considerable demands on employees, but tangible group results that support transparent corporate objectives are highly motivating.

Commitment also depends on respect for managers' skills, experiences and attitudes. Hands-on management in the renewal of the company stimulates employees. The legitimacy of management is further enhanced by the involvement of employees in the appointment of the supervisory board.

Alignment of corporate and business unit objectives allows a more agreeable working environment, with less tension and fewer conflicts. The rank and file perfectly understand that a company cannot continue unless it creates an economic surplus. A negative free cash flow is a much sounder basis for painful decisions than insufficient profitability. The three different corporate objectives – preserving the integrity of the organization, reinforcing the position of the company and renewal of the company – and the difficulty of trade-offs between these can be easily explained.

As in the American Enterprise Model, the European model does not guarantee lifetime employment. Depending on their value to the company, staff are given short-, medium- or long-term contracts. But under the European Enterprise Model employees are no longer interchangeable so it is important that both the company and the employee feel bound to these contracts.

This provides the company with incentives to support its staff and employees in making the best of the opportunity offered and to invest in their work. This leads to far fewer disruptions and avoids the complacency associated with a job for life as well as minimizing the risk of alienation that is common when employees can be made redundant at any time.

The American Enterprise Model is built on the premise that financial rewards are crucial in achieving results, and one incentive programme after another is designed to fire up employees. However as stressed in Chapter 4, such an approach is hardly conducive to cooperation, which lies at the heart of multi-factor productivity.

An even cruder but frequently applied instrument under the American Enterprise Model is large-scale redundancies. This seems to produce quick results, but whether the remaining workforce can carry the additional load in the medium and long term remains to be seen. And of course the majority of redundancy programmes leave management functions relatively unscathed. As highlighted in Chapter 3, rationalizations are drawn-out affairs, chaos reigns in their aftermath and the financial results are often disappointing.

Moreover the practice of firing employees when demand or profitability drops acts as a disincentive for companies to invest in training. Spending too much on workers who may have to be dismissed during the next economic downturn is bad business. It makes much more sense to keep jobs simple and well defined. If necessary, more complicated jobs can be split up. This facilitates internal transfers and makes hiring during the upturn quick and easy. From the perspective of the employee, job insecurity leads to little or no commitment to the company. The additional effort required to build relationships with colleagues will not be made. Training will be shunned. There is no incentive to be flexible, let alone helpful. Such attitudes are highly contagious and the basic ingredients for the improvement of multi-factor productivity become in short supply.[7]

## A new approach to services

The fourth potential source of value concerns improvements in marketing and sales 'from many to many'. It is generally assumed that the service economy has arrived, but the financial services industry, insurers, telephone companies and airlines are struggling, as many of their customers will testify.

The development of high-quality services and their delivery in a consistent manner in different geographical markets and to different categories of customers by large numbers of staff pose tremendous problems.

Swedish strategy consultant Richard Normann chooses a way forward that ties in very neatly with the European Enterprise Model.[8] Many service innovations are made possible by new ICT hardware and software. For example retail banks could not have extended their services and the speed of delivery without ICT. The quality of service also depends on scale. Each time a restaurant is added to a franchise, overheads per restaurant come down and the service becomes more widely available.

However real progress depends on social innovation, connecting unconnected parties, assigning new roles and aligning interests. Generally the service is produced at the moment it is consumed. An airline passenger occupies a seat that had he not shown up would have been lost for ever. Normann characterizes the relationship between a service provider and customer as a social contract. The cabin crew and the passenger co-produce the service. There is direct personal contact, and the quality of their interaction determines the value that is created in the perception of the customer.

Normann raises four questions that help to identify and to develop new services. The first question is how a customer could be induced to take over a larger part of the service himself in exchange for quality improvement and therefore value. The introduction of internet retail banking is a good example. Service is fundamentally improved as customers can handle most of their banking chores via the internet any time they want. The bank benefits greatly from the cost reductions that come from the huge decrease in administration. And all the information that used to be collected via various branches is now at the client's fingertips, representing further savings for the bank.

The second question is whether the service provider could combine different roles. Could he for example sell banking and insurance services at the same time? Timely bundling and unbundling of services creates value for the customer. Some clients acquire all their insurance policies from one company. Others seek the best proposition for each and every requirement.

The third question is whether previously unconnected parties could be brought together. The example of JCDecaux, the service company that puts up and maintains bus shelters free of charge in return for the advertising space they provide, has been mentioned earlier. This concept links municipal authorities, bus companies, passengers and advertisers in an innovative way.

The last question is whether dispersed energy can be focused. Individual owners of holiday homes are far less effective in renting their property than a service provider that combines the offerings, guarantees quality, creates economy of scale and sells via a number of channels.

Service is given by people and it is obvious that companies built around people are well positioned to make contracts with their clients. The mind-set required for customer service is the same as that needed for cooperation within a company. Attention is given to both the founding and the ending of relationships.

The much-lauded service offered by US companies is not what it seems, and improvement is difficult to achieve for the following reasons. US companies provide services that are specified to the last detail. Providers work from scripts that contain a number of customer questions and standard answers as well as leading questions that could enhance sales. As a result, employees have very modest mandates and unexpected questions cannot be properly handled. Any change in service requires costly training, whereas general guidelines would provide much-needed flexibility.

Secondly, the relationship between the company and its customers is antagonistic in the US model. Sales are made at the widest possible margin. 'Quality give-away' – for example selling gasoline with a higher octane than the specified minimum – is a deadly sin. Some oil companies go as far as deliberately selling inferior gasoline until the number of customer complaints reaches a certain predetermined level, at which point they improve the quality slightly. Customers try to squeeze as much as possible from their suppliers and are ruthless in the exploitation of their legal rights if a product does not meet required minimum specifications. This is consistent with competition as *leitmotiv* and with the will to win, preferably with a financial reward for those who prevail.

Finally, those who rose to prominence during the 1990s under the aegis of the American Enterprise Model are aliens in a world in which success depends on the proper reading of a seemingly irrational customer and the values that underpin his buying decisions and guide his interactions with providers. Those who take finance courses look down on behavioural economics. Those who are pushed to deliver quickly cannot take an interest in relationships that take time to develop.

# A WORLD OF PARTNERSHIPS

Managers have been streamlining the internal workings of their companies for decades. Much has been achieved but inevitably they are moving from large to smaller and smaller improvements. It stands to reason that crossing corporate boundaries is a promising route to further efficiency and other forms of value creation even though this is legally and organizationally far more complicated to achieve. Airports, airlines and air traffic control organizations for example have reached the end of the line in terms of what they can do as separate entities and major gains can now only be achieved via joint programmes. Joint operational control of ground movements, runways, parking and gate positions can, for instance, prevent delays of key flights and improve safety. The transfer of responsibilities, the design of a new control organization and the definition of the links between the three partners are complicated and require extraordinary management skills.

Companies can also book gains by assisting their business units in building a tailor-made set of partnerships. No option to create value need be excluded beforehand. Partnerships can range from temporary arrangements for small parts of the business to full integration of all activities in a new unit. They could relate to product development, production, sales, marketing and distribution or any combination thereof. Partnerships can also make a contribution to the financing of companies in terms of cash or services in kind. They also help to gain access to pools of management talent and experts, increasingly important at times when the war for talent is intense. Finally, partnerships bring new options as they can grow, broaden and deepen.

There are at least four promising areas that are worth exploring. Mergers can succeed if the process for their implementation is redesigned. New forms of partnerships can accelerate innovation. Opportunities arise when it is recognized that outsourcing services is a fundamentally different concept to the outsourcing of production. And finally, partnerships for product development, sales and marketing can be put on a new footing.

In each of these areas the distinctive features of a European Enterprise Model improve the competitive position of companies operating on this basis. The barriers that the American Enterprise Model throws up in establishing mutually beneficial partnerships will be summarized at the end of this chapter.

## A different type of merger

It would seem that the future belongs to those who can identify real commercial and technical synergies and to those who can offer a genuinely new approach to the merger and acquisition process. Given the dismal record of unfriendly takeovers, such an approach does not have to cater to this category. Serial takeovers can be excluded for the same reason.

Obviously management's exploration of mergers and acquisitions as a means to improve the position of their company in a structural way should be solidly rooted in a vision of the future for their industry and the rightful position of their company within it.

In the new approach, a preliminary step should be the design of a corporate decision-making process tailored to the possibility of a specific merger or acquisition. It is most unlikely that the decision-making apparatus companies already have in place is appropriate for such a special occasion.

The business idea for the merger of KLM and Alitalia in 1997 was twofold. Firstly, there was the combination of two hub operations, one at Amsterdam's Schiphol Airport and one at Malpensa Airport close to Milan. By combining these, the number of convenient connections between European cities and between Europe and intercontinental destinations could be increased way beyond what competitors Air France, Lufthansa and British Airways could offer from their single home bases in Paris, Frankfurt and London. Secondly, in establishing a link between the large Italian home market and the relatively large intercontinental network of KLM, Italian traffic to intercontinental destinations could be routed via Amsterdam instead of Frankfurt and Paris.

KLM only became truly interested in Alitalia when a number of conditions for cooperation had been fulfilled. A high-quality management team composed of airline professionals took over its reins. The new team struck an agreement with the unions that brought the Italian airline's labour costs down to competitive levels. It also secured state aid to bring order to the company's finances.

When the two parties decided to move ahead on the basis of the shared and viable business ideas, a number of joint teams were established. Each team was asked to identify and, where possible, quantify the additional value that joint operations would yield and to describe how this potential could be realized. Their brief was a merger of equals.

One team was charged with designing the integrated company in all its operational dimensions. In the case of airlines, this involves the amalgamation of both connection networks. On this basis a single timetable was drafted, tapping into high-yielding international traffic flows while optimizing aircraft use and taking into account maintenance schedules and crew rosters.

A second team took these results and designed the sales and marketing policies necessary to leverage the network to its maximum potential via a joint and, relatively speaking, smaller and cheaper sales force. The combination of increased revenues as the result of improved products (faster connections between cities with larger aircraft) and lower costs (better aircraft utilization, fewer aircraft and the corresponding reduction in crews) determined the additional operational value the new company would generate.

Other teams looked into potential savings for future investments. A joint investment plan for the fleet, reducing the number of fleet types and moving to larger aircraft, produced a lower level of capital expenditure and reduced overall maintenance cost. The same was true for ICT.

Yet other teams were responsible for the design of a new organizational structure and the integration of key planning units. Finally, there were project teams to identify and tackle communication and regulatory issues. Each team had to produce satisfactory results or the merger process would come to an end.

The managing directors of both airlines and their advisors were responsible for the terms of reference for the teams and the overall management of the process. They sought to satisfy the conditions for the implementation of the various teams' many proposals and aligned internal decision making with the merger process. Finally, they obtained the support of their shareholders, unions, anti-trust authorities and the two national governments involved.

During this process managing directors could concentrate on capturing identified potential as well as governance and financial issues. They could also focus on designing management and organizational structure and top-level appointments.

This is how KLM and Alitalia reached a unique agreement for the first cross-border merger in the airline industry, a merger that dramatically came apart in a sequence of events triggered off by the inability of the Italian government to handle a relatively minor environmental issue at Malpensa.

Despite this ultimate failure, the path that KLM and Alitalia followed was very different from the financially inspired mergers of the 1990s. The fate of the merger was put in the hands of teams composed of experts and middle managers. The favourable outcome depended on the quality of their cooperation, their creativity, their joint commercial and operational insights and the quality of their implementation plans.

## Joint innovation initiatives

Partnerships are a way to enrich research and development and to stimulate commercially viable innovation. It has been pointed out that the record of the 1990s is dismal in this respect. Acquisition of small innovative businesses by large companies and their subsequent absorption was the surest possible route to value destruction.

In a new era, the biggest gains will be made by large companies that can collaborate in a variety of ways to gain access to the intellectual property, expertise, services and products of small firms. Licensing from and to small companies with various degrees of exclusivity, contract research and joint research projects are more effective than takeovers. Take Swiss pharmaceutical giant Roche and the Danish–Dutch company Genmab for example. Roche has identified proteins on the surface of cancer cells that could serve as targets for either so-called small molecules or antibodies. Genmab meanwhile has the technology to build antibodies which connect with these surface proteins and destroy cancer cells while ignoring healthy cells. The contract gives Roche call options on a number of Genmab antibodies. Upfront down-payments and royalties on the sale of antibodies in case of success are agreed in advance. Roche and Genmab scientists have a common interest and work closely together in testing the antibodies in patients. If Roche, for whatever reason, wants to abandon a specific line of development it will return the call option to Genmab which is then free to draw its own plan. This sophisticated arrangement is now copied throughout the sector.

Large companies will also benefit by further broadening and deepening the scope of their potential partnerships to academic centres and governmental research laboratories. Companies that make skilful use of fiscal and other government incentives to stimulate innovation will also do well. Interestingly, the French government has announced an 800 million euro programme to stimulate innovation, and these subsidies can be applied for by any European company.

Another promising arena is cooperation with competitors. This includes joint ventures for pre-competitive research and the joint setting up of product standards. Many of the technologies of tomorrow will be too expensive and too risky for a single company to develop. Once a joint venture is successful in establishing a technology, the participants can start competing with applications. Philips Electronics is one of the pioneers in this field. The memory of the technically superior Beta VCR technology that did not become the industry standard for videos still lingers. In a change of strategy and to avoid battles on standards, Philips, STMicroelectronics and Motorola have set up one of the most advanced nanotechnology research centres in the world in France.[9]

Another social advance that will stimulate innovation is the so-called 'venturing out' of activities. More and more companies are placing promising units outside their own organizational constraints. Such ventures are often supported by a shareholding, the assignment of management or a supply and/or sales agreement with the parent company. The managers and the researchers that form the core of a new company believe strongly in their business idea, feel stifled by corporate management and are tired of competing with other business units. Venture capital firms are cash-rich and investment in large units helps to put major sums in companies that are far less risky than the average biotech start-up company. At least the units that are ventured out have a management, laboratories, researchers and intellectual property. Moreover their former parent companies have paid for all mistakes up to the sale. Investing in a limited number of large units also helps venture funds to support companies properly instead of spreading their attention over a large number of small units. The bulk of the venture capital invested in European biotech firms is invested in these more mature companies.[10]

At this point little is known about the factors that determine the success of such initiatives and how the partnership between parent and offspring will develop over time. It is however clear that the company that builds experience quickly will have the upper hand over its competitors.

## It looks the same but it isn't

Commercial and operational cooperation among companies has been going on for centuries and comes in many different guises. Sales companies carry their own and third-party products. The maintenance of a company's own equipment can be combined with that belonging to third parties. Joint purchasing programmes have been flourishing for some time. Optimizing the supply, manufacturing and delivery chain is also well established. Outsourcing of production is another well-trodden path. Yet new ground can still be broken in many different areas.

So far, in outsourcing production, most companies and their suppliers have relied on the standardization of components and intermediate products. Sufficient numbers of potential suppliers can only be reached and their offerings compared on the basis of unequivocal product specifications. Production runs can be made longer and economies of scale achieved only on the basis of a number of orders for exactly the same product.

A potentially major advance is the ability to adapt quickly to changes in demand and to respond to production interruptions as well as to accommodate product innovation. Swedish fashion chain Hennes & Mauritz caters to a large market segment of young people with low budgets but a keen eye for design. These customers focus less on quality because they know that fashions change quickly. Production runs for new models are modest but a very sophisticated management information system helps, within days, to differentiate between items that will and those that will not sell. Highly flexible production and distribution does the rest.

One of the requirements here is that all the parties in the chain gain insight into the flexibility of each other's production processes and are prepared to use this to improve the whole. This is very different from delivering the right quantities of products to the right specifications at the agreed time and place for the agreed price. The logical next steps are joint production and joint design of production facilities by manufacturers and suppliers.

All these opportunities require made-to-measure but flexible organizations, each with different experts, middle management, procedures and ICT support.

Outsourcing services, the largest growth area by far, is fundamentally different from outsourcing manufacturing on the basis of detailed specifications. This was already the case when the outsourcing of services was limited to data processing, administrative chores (such as the handling of insurance claims and credit card payments) and call centres. As stressed in Chapter 3, these activities can make or break a company because small mistakes add up in the eye of the customer.

But now companies are trying to go much further: Microsoft is outsourcing software development, Intel the design of chips, and Boeing engineering. This requires different forms of cooperation that have to be managed differently. The writing of software is difficult to monitor, and the quality is difficult to assess. Designs of plant and equipment are the outcome of numerous compromises with many departments playing their parts. The requirements of the customer have to be interpreted, customers change their minds and the originally conceived product needs to be adapted to fit ever-changing internal circumstances. In light of all these communication and coordination requirements, strong professional relationships have to be built across deep organizational divides. The building of trust is always relevant, but when it comes to outsourcing services it is paramount. The fact that China and India – countries with very different business cultures from the United States and Europe – are the largest suppliers of services complicates matters and puts even higher demands on those that have to negotiate and to manage the supply contracts.[11] Once more the fate of the company is in the hands of experts and middle management and their capacity to add value in collaboration with counterparts abroad.

## New frontiers

Opportunities for partnerships are not confined to production and logistic cooperation. At present, joint offerings to satisfy one or more client needs are still in their infancy but there are already examples of highly successful cooperations: Intel and PC manufacturers (two brands on one computer), Sara Lee and Philips (joint promotion of coffee machines and high-quality coffee), and Heinz and Lays (adding branded flavour to crisps).

In Chapter 3, some of the forces that will make the transfer and storage of data a commodity were discussed. The conclusion was drawn that the creation of lasting advantage is difficult where the economics of interconnectivity are irresistible. And now the full force of IBM is behind a concept where customers simply pay for the intensity and the duration of their use of infrastructure. But maximum connectivity implies maximum scope for cooperation as any panel of experts can sit together to discuss new business ideas. In the world of ICT product development the very last barriers come down as a result of new and reliable operating systems and the gradual opening up of Microsoft source code.

Of course there is also the quest for 'the next big thing'. Putting sensors on products to check their functioning and their whereabouts, using sensors to monitor pipelines and other remote installations and applying sensors to observe body functions are all possible and might add up to a new wave.[12]

However most commercial visionaries identify opportunities of a different nature. The creation of the smart home, the merging of IT with the whole entertainment and media infrastructure, the provision of security, wireless communication and data mining will all require cooperation beyond traditional industry boundaries. This applies to product development, sales, instalment and service. Is the smart home one package? And if so, who is going to sell it and via which channels? Who is going to install and maintain what, where and when, during and after the construction of the house? At present the picture is highly diffuse and building a position in this market will depend more on managerial acumen to engage in the right partnerships than on ICT know-how.

Looking back, American Enterprise Model managers have a poor track record in this area. Selling and servicing stand-alone PCs proved to be too difficult a task. The delivery and maintenance of internet connections is poor and cable services even worse. Stephen Roach, chief economist of Morgan Stanley bank, calculates that the average professional has to spend five hours a week to maintain his filing and e-mail facilities.

New service requirements go way beyond the simple products of the 1990s and need very different organizations. Only European Enterprise Model managers will be up to providing them.

# THE NEW FOUNDATIONS

The following conclusions can be drawn from this inventory of potential sources of value. The discovery and exploitation of new sources of value depend crucially on middle management and specialized professionals and the quality of their cooperation. It is middle management that has to revive units that are composed of the dispirited survivors of two merged companies. Researchers, product developers and marketing experts have to reach beyond endless incremental product improvement. Information technology experts and middle managers have to focus on changing work practices and not on the provision of software updates. Operational managers have to create the conditions for a lasting improvement of services provided by call centres and back offices. The middle managers and experts who form the work teams that develop and coordinate partner activities determine the fate of the partnership.

A second conclusion is that the contribution of management must become a derivative of the needs of middle managers and experts. Management has to create the conditions in which teams can function by providing and sticking to clear mandates, providing guidance, inspiration and moral support, and providing protection for individual members and the team as a whole. It also falls to management to follow up on the findings made by the teams and to shepherd valuable proposals through the decision-making process.

## Trust and cooperation

With so much hanging on cooperation, the most fundamental competitive advantage of the European Enterprise Model over its US rival is clear. The former provides an organizational setting in which trust can be built. Conversely, it is the destiny of the American Enterprise Model to cause considerable and irrevocable damage to trust and therefore cooperation.

Working in teams implies individual sacrifice in terms of time and energy. It also implies a degree of altruism in sharing experience and by making personal 'intellectual property' available to other team members. Moreover working in teams requires a division of tasks and responsibilities that at various points in time does not fit individual preferences. It also requires a belief that credit for the team's results will be shared fairly. Working in teams is a risky proposition in light of the widespread insight that mutual trust yields far better results, but that the damage resulting from a breakdown in trust could exceed the potential benefits. In addition, it is a fact of life that only one untrustworthy team member is sufficient to derail the team's progress.

At a fundamental level the building of trust depends first and foremost on basic trust or a trusting impulse, an attitude formed in early childhood that varies from individual to individual. Later on in life individuals deal with the uncertainty about the future behaviour of another person in a variety of ways. Previous experience in comparable situations helps, as do different forms of typecasting. Once initial contact has been established and a number of exchanges have been concluded in a satisfactory way, further progress depends on an individual's capacity to identify with the other party and to establish a form of social bonding. Eventually, when all goes well, the relationship can acquire an emotional dimension and social virtues such as communication, honesty, reliability and a sense of duty to others are self-evident.[13] At that point the relationship becomes so strong that considerable infringements of the informal rules are tolerated. All this takes time to develop.[14]

However the average young American with at least two years of college education can expect to change jobs at least 11 times in the course of his working life and to change his skill base three times. Such turmoil in professional and private lives is a price that has to be paid in a dynamic economy thriving on creative destruction. Technology dictates the pace. Change is always around the corner and, to limit exposure, payback times need to be short. Living with a short corporate time horizon, with aggressive competitors and demanding customers, employees need to be quick-footed, to embrace change and be competitive and entrepreneurial. Self-assertion is expected and dependence is to be avoided.

In the American Enterprise Model a high premium is put on change. Managers that deliberately and openly decide to do nothing are looked at with suspicion – even if their decision is based on proper analysis of the situation. The result is a high turnover of projects which simply do not allow management and employees the time to build trust, even if all those involved are capable and willing to do so.

Moreover the American Enterprise Model is based on individual targets and incentives. The increase in individual, largely financial, stakes decreases the likelihood of sacrifice. Expectations about the commitments other team members are prepared to make are low and individuals have every reason not to contribute more than the bare minimum.

Teamwork is further handicapped by the erosion in the confidence that individual members have in management and corporate leadership. Many employees have lost faith in the corporate strategy of their leaders, their competence and authenticity and their ability to be fair and consistent. They cannot help noticing how management protects itself against the possible adverse consequences of its own decisions.

Most of the corporate leaders that have embraced the American Enterprise Model see the breakdown of trust between employees and management as the inevitable by-product of measures such as cost cutting that are inevitable to keep the company going.

At the same time, the followers of the American Enterprise Model recognize that technology and market developments force cooperation, and it is considered self-evident that everybody is a keen team player. These expectations in combination with the cited impediments to genuine teamwork can only add to the anxiety people feel.

All in all, the only reasonable attitude individual team members can be expected to take is: do not commit; do not sacrifice. Diligent application of the American Enterprise Model has well and truly undermined trust and genuine cooperation at the very time that the economy dictates that these assets are more important than ever.

Looking back no one can calculate the value of lost opportunities. No one knows how many poor decisions over the past decades can be traced back to lack of teamwork. Even a modest contribution amounts to a very considerable sum, and that sum is rising.

To the contrary, the European Enterprise Model, explicitly focusing on people and the quality of their cooperation, has removed many impediments to the building of trust: not as a moral requirement and not because it ties in with the way people want to work (although this is also true) but first and foremost with an eye on the need to create economic value. The result is highly demanding – a world in which trust is built but inevitably also betrayed, with far-reaching personal and organizational consequences.

## Shaping partnerships

While partnerships offer considerable potential, they are difficult to establish and hard to develop by those whose attitudes are shaped by the American Enterprise Model. They are selected and trained to pursue well-defined objectives with well-specified resources as vigorously as possible. Control carries a high premium and the time frame is short. Performance can be measured and allocation of rewards is unambiguous.

Partnerships are different on all counts. The objectives of partnerships are likely to shift as priorities for both parties change over time. The amount and quality of resources that the partners bring to a venture are likely to deviate from time to time. Timely delivery can be defined in different ways. Competitive instincts need to be controlled and non-hierarchical personal relationships established.

Most importantly, control has to be shared and the full potential of the partnership can only be achieved over time. Both partners maintain different ways to evaluate and reward their managers and this is a perpetual source of uncertainty and conflict.

Since the distribution of power is very important in the American Enterprise Model it is relevant to note that one partnership creates three political force fields: the individual relationships between the joint venture and each of the parent companies, and the relationship between the parent companies themselves. All this requires patience, tolerance of ambiguity and an insight into the sensitivities and constraints of each of the three parties involved.

As circumstances change, markets are increasingly volatile and costs are harder to control, American managers – concerned about possible short-term bottom-line effects – have the tendency to focus on the crisis of the day and to secure the interests of their companies. As a result communication between the partners turns into negotiation. This is at the expense of the pursuit of future growth and prosperity for the partnership.

In negotiations to establish and run partnerships, American managers do not trust and do not expect to be trusted. Both partners have every right to pursue their interests vigorously, with all legal means available to them. It has already been mentioned in Chapter 1 that meetings can be acrimonious, with intimidation and personal attacks no exception, but these and other forms of adversity are considered virtuous as they mobilize creativity and assure both sides (and their lords and masters) that maximum effort has been made. 'Leaving money on the table' is unforgivable, a way to lose the respect of the opponent and a very poor starting point for the next negotiating round or meeting. There is also the implicit adage that both parties need to derive about the same amount of benefits from the partnership, even at the expense of the potential total gain.

High personal stakes, bonuses and options to which negotiators are entitled if they are successful play a detrimental role. They lead to tough negotiating stands and make discussions more emotional than necessary. Bigger damage is caused by the divergence of corporate and individual interests. Under such circumstances, four parties – the two companies and their negotiators – need to be satisfied before an agreement can be made. Intentions and breaking points become far more difficult to read, there is perpetual suspicion as to the true reasons for a particular stance, and as a result negotiations are more likely to fail. If they do succeed but personal ambitions have not been realized, the next round of negotiations has already been undermined.

Both sides understand that the other will use any change in circumstances and any shift in the preferences or weakening of their potential partner to their advantage. As a result, contracts need to be detailed to cover all eventualities, to explicitly exclude all undesirable actions by either partner and to guard against litigation. Detailed contracts mean rigidity at the expense of commercial and operational flexibility. Changes in circumstances lead to new negotiations to make amendments. In many partnerships there is always the distraction of ongoing consultations.

In the course of these discussions either party can drop out at any moment, including the very last moment. Both parties can increase initial demands and offers can be withdrawn. It goes without saying that both parties engage in concerted efforts to undermine the position of the opposing negotiator. If an opportunity for litigation arises, no party will hesitate to take advantage, particularly if the discussions have failed.

The high financial stakes of the individuals involved, the considerable organizational pressures, the will to win visibly and the lack of old-fashioned self-restraint all increase the likelihood of immoral behaviour. There is a large grey area to be exploited – outright deceit is not necessary to tip the balance. Confidentiality is hardly ever totally maintained; a nod and a wink to the press, the unions or the regulators can be highly effective. Manipulation of contractual conditions for completion is easy and therefore tempting. Contact with other parties might or might not violate any agreed exclusivity of negotiations.

The bottom line of negotiating US style is that distrust feeds distrust and partnerships can only continue if both parties are benefiting. If this is no longer the case, it has to be assumed that the partner, as a matter of principle, will let his own interests prevail to the detriment of the partnership. Temporary setbacks experienced by one of the parties cannot be bridged. An oversight by one of the parties cannot be left unpunished. In this light it would be irresponsible not to insist on a detailed contract in which all eventualities are covered and there are considerable penalties for non-performance.

Throughout the 1990s, companies operating on the principles embedded in the American Enterprise Model missed out on many opportunities to engage in partnerships. Any negotiation that fails for the wrong reason carries an economic cost: the difference in monetary terms to the next-best alternative. In a world in which partnerships become increasingly important and profitable, the overall costs will increase.

US-style negotiating and the US view of partnerships is the kiss of death if opportunities depend on nimble and flexible arrangements between companies. Partnerships fare much better in the European Enterprise Model.

The following is worth repeating. A crucial factor is a company's willingness and ability to break away from the traditional long-term detailed contract as the basis for its relationship. Impressive gains could be made if companies could tap into a large repertoire of cooperation models: for one or more partners; open or closed to additional partners; for the long and the short term; detailed or relying simply on a few principles; in one or more fields; with the same or with varying degrees of intensity; and finally, with no, modest or ambitious long-term objectives.

If companies nurture this new philosophy and deliberately build the skills and experience needed to work fruitfully with partners in many different ways, the varying and changing needs of the company as a whole and its business units can be accommodated more easily.

As mentioned, the new forms of partnerships should be based on three principles. Firstly, there has to be a basic legal arrangement that lays down the objectives of the partnership, specifies the resources that the partners will commit and fixes the duration of the contract. Secondly, there has to be a management structure to steer the partnership, to adapt it to changing circumstances and to resolve conflict. Thirdly, partnerships cannot function properly without mutual trust. Both parties need to know that their partner will meet both the letter and spirit of its obligations and will give due consideration to the interests of both organizations. The example in case is the takeover of KLM by Air France that was modelled on the basis of the Renault Nissan agreement. Air France KLM is a new company that controls Air France and KLM. Under this umbrella, a joint strategic management committee steers the cooperation of the two operating companies. Knowing that the capacity of organizations to absorb change is subject to limitations, and aware that conditions for change have to be created before it can be implemented, the committee sets priorities, monitors progress and makes adjustments to the projects if and when required. The hand of Cyrille Spinetta, the chairman of Air France KLM, is very noticeable and his very respectful treatment of KLM is setting the tone. The professionalism of KLM managers is appreciated and in many integration projects KLM practices prevail. The new company is ahead of schedule in realizing very substantial benefits.

In light of all this, the skills, experience and attitudes of the employees of potential partners become a critical consideration in deciding on working together. The same applies to the quality of management and decision making within the organizations involved. Management of the partnership and the quality of the cooperation among the experts of both parties determine how much value it will generate.

## TAKING STOCK

Believers in the American Enterprise Model cannot live beyond the presumed safety of a limited number of quantitative targets. They continue to believe that only a strategy of sticks and carrots works, and they need the security of enforceable legal contracts. As a result, they will never be able to bond with colleagues or truly understand their business partners.

The European Enterprise Model on the other hand is inherently suited for exploiting the new sources of value both in the area of internal growth and in the area of partnerships. Management is outward-looking and the priority is adding value and not bottom-line improvement. There is time for teams to build trust and bring relationships with partners to fruition.

# Epilogue

Whether the European Enterprise Model and other European Enterprise Models will develop and find broader application at the expense of listed companies must be seen within the European economic, political and cultural context.

There are at least four important features of Europe that will contribute to the emergence of European Enterprise Models:

- Europe is large and competitive enough to determine its own objectives and policies and shape its own private sector.

- Europe's full economic potential is far from realized.

- European cultural values are consistent with European Enterprise Models.

- The gradual emergence of a European world-view will feed the development of European Enterprise Models and vice versa.

# EUROPE CAN GO IT ALONE

Adair Turner (vice chairman of Merrill Lynch Europe and former director-general of the Confederation of British Industry),[1] Oxford professor John Gray[2] and others provide convincing evidence that different forms of capitalism can be highly successful. There is no reason why Europe cannot continue to value social cohesion and rely on the political process to correct the potential and actual harm caused by free markets. Equally there is no reason why the American Enterprise Model should set the world standard for public or private companies.

Turner points out that globalization is a myth in many important respects and that Europe has much more room for manoeuvre than is generally recognized. European trade with Japan, the United States, Canada, Australia and New Zealand amounted to a modest 6.3 per cent of European GDP in 1974 and, contrary to popular belief, actually decreased to 5.9 per cent of GDP in 1997. Rapid growth was confined to trade within the three trading blocks: NAFTA, the EU and ASEAN. Intra-European trade grew from 14 per cent of GDP in 1974 to 20 per cent in 1997, a rise that was matched by the growth of trade between the United States, Mexico and Canada (NAFTA) and by the South-East Asian countries (ASEAN).[3]

The opportunities to increase exports within any of the three regions are by no means exhausted. European countries are particularly well placed to do this. The effect of the introduction of the euro has been modest but that might well change now a period of slow economic growth is drawing to a close and a gradual shift from corporate restructuring to expansion becomes noticeable. Trade among old and new EC members is exploding. The often-heard claim that the world economy depends on the US consumer and his willingness to spend has been heavily oversold. Rises in demand are concentrated in the food, beverage and automobile sectors which are interesting for some European manufacturers but have very modest macroeconomic impact.[4]

Another indication that international trade is not as important for globalization as stressed by business leaders and politicians is the dominance of multinational companies. During the 1990s, no less than 70 per cent of world trade consisted of deliveries between units of the same firm. Oil supplies from Total Nigeria to Total France clearly belong to a different category from transactions between two independent companies. As such, the number of companies genuinely active in importing and exporting is much lower than trading volume figures suggest.

Moreover the vast majority of investments stay within country borders. Direct foreign investment growth worldwide is spectacular but started from a small base and, more importantly in this context, often stays within each of the trading blocks. Multinational companies, with a few notable exceptions in the oil and gas industry, still have their 'centre of gravity' in their region of origin.

The notion that an international labour market sets off globalization is equally inaccurate. Looking at the most mobile segment – graduate professionals – it is clear that the numbers are very modest. With the exception of Italians, less than 1 per cent of this labour segment works abroad and for many of these the situation is temporary. For example it is estimated that about 50 per cent of the Irish that emigrated to the US during the 1980s and 1990s have now returned. And the successful outsourcing of ICT hardware and software production to India is partially explained by the return of Indian entrepreneurs and technicians from abroad.

Economically the world is already multi-polar. The trading blocks have developed a sophisticated consultation and negotiating apparatus. They deal with each other on the basis of mutual respect of each other's might and will no doubt continue to pursue common interests.

## THE POTENTIAL OF EUROPE

An independent Europe has prepared, and is preparing, for the future. As explained in Chapter 2, the US and European economies performed equally well in the 1990s while large European companies fared better than their US competitors. In the 21st century, unprecedented intervention by the US government and Federal Reserve Bank plus a strong dollar (as the result of exceptional confidence in the US economy by foreign investors) were necessary to buy an economic upturn in the United States. Meanwhile growth in the United States is only modestly higher if statistical anomalies are removed from the comparison.

The question should be why the United States is not outperforming the EU by a wide margin. As outlined the United States was apparently unable to capitalize on its competitive advantages: a 50 per cent higher level of spending on research and development, closer links between academic institutions and businesses, an abundance of venture capital, liberal bankruptcy laws, a flexible labour market and a truly benign business environment.

Meanwhile Europe seems to be able to overcome its competitive disadvantages: a heterogeneous home market, 15 legal systems, 11 languages and a multitude of cultures. It has a common market for goods but there is no single market for services or labour. On top of this there is still a fine web of formal and informal restrictions on intra-European investment. It has to be kept in mind too that the introduction process of the euro was only completed on 1 January 2002 and the coordination of fiscal and economic policies of member states remains a shambles.

## Germany holds the key

Europe's relative success is all the more surprising because, ever since the late 1980s, Germany – traditionally its economic powerhouse and growth engine – has been pushed to its financial and economic limits. For historic reasons, West Germany had been the paymaster of European integration. After the fall of the Berlin Wall there was no choice but to move the seat of government from Bonn to the new capital, Berlin – at very considerable expense. Most important of all, Germany had to pay a hefty price for the integration of the DDR. The politically unavoidable choice of parity between the Deutschmark and the Ostmark destroyed the East German economy and it was inevitable that its 18 million people received very substantial financial support. At the same time, German infrastructure and the environmental policies of former East Germany had to be brought up to West German and EU standards. Finally, the German government had to provide financial incentives for direct investment to the former DDR to stem the rise of unemployment. Estimates vary, but total subsidies reached approximately 1,250 billion euros between 1992 and 1999. And up till 2004, 2 per cent of the GDP of former West Germany had been transferred to East Germany.

The fact that Germany, and as a consequence Europe as a whole, had to sacrifice economic growth as a result of this unavoidable and unprecedented largesse is hardly surprising. It was crucially important in the early 1990s to retain the support of West German citizens who had already been forced to accept significant tax rises to help finance reunification. Furthermore it is a fact of life that a political agenda can contain only so many items. All these pressures combined made postponement of vital budgetary, fiscal and social reforms unavoidable. While other European countries like Spain, the Netherlands, Denmark and Sweden worked on reforming their welfare states in a favourable economic climate, Germany had to start its restructuring at the onset of a recession.

'Agenda 2010' and Harz IV, the action programmes developed by Germany's Schröder government, met fierce resistance from all sides: employers, unions and the opposition. Nevertheless they were eventually accepted, albeit with many proposals watered down.[5] Recent surveys show that German companies have responded far better to the erosion of their competitive position than many observers thought possible. Meanwhile it remains a remarkable achievement that German exports continued to grow, recession or no recession, and irrespective of whether the euro's exchange rate was high or low. The explanation for this phenomenon lies in a remarkable combination of the slowest growth in wages in the euro zone and faster productivity growth than the euro-zone average in the years between 1999 and 2004.

The medium-term prospects for Germany are favourably affected by the entry of Eastern European countries into the EU. German companies have already invested in these new countries on a grand scale and will continue to benefit from their geographical and logistic advantages. On top of this the new member states are a source of young and well-educated talent.

The enlargement of Germany, its ongoing economic reforms and its position in Eastern Europe are all investments that will pay handsome returns. Germany will once more take the lead in the economic realm. The small but advanced economies closely connected to Germany's – Benelux, Denmark, Sweden, the Baltic States, Austria and Switzerland – will follow. The language barrier between these countries and Germany is low or non-existent and cultural differences are small. The result will be an integrated and innovative economy with 150 million wealthy consumers.

The combination of these countries will be a formidable force in Europe, the other large European economies will benefit and enhanced growth will provide the basis for an acceleration of European economic integration.

The EU has already made considerable progress in creating a common market for goods.[6] It is however revealing to note how many steps still need to be taken before the EU can deliver on its promise to create a single market for goods, services and people.[7] The free movement of goods still requires new procedures to achieve mutual recognition of standards among the member countries and more EU-steered European-wide standardization. Market integration of services is very limited and this is costing Europe jobs and prosperity as services represent an ever-increasing share of the EU's employment and GDP. A directive on the provision of services throughout the EU was expected in 2005, 13 years after European free traders claimed victory, but the Commission had to backtrack once again in the face of stiff resistance on the part on the large members.

The integration of European financial markets is another ongoing saga. There are successes such as agreement on the 'prospectus directive' as a result of which approval by the financial authorities in the country of origin is sufficient to sell the stock or bonds throughout the EU, but those are few and far between. New rules for pan-European public procurement are also still in the pipeline.

The so-called 'network industries' (energy, transport and telecommunications) need to become more efficient in the interest of the economy as a whole, but a fully open market for electricity and gas with proper guarantees for supply security will not be in place until 2007.

All this adds up to the conclusion that Europe can still claw defeat away from the jaws of victory. Having managed to compensate for many of its strategic disadvantages throughout the 1990s, and having survived a US onslaught during the early years of the new decade, foe and friend agree that time is now running out.

## Revaluation of alternative models

If the emergence of European Enterprise Models depends on companies without a stock market listing, there is a wide range of alternatives including co-operatives, large private companies and small and medium-sized enterprises (SMEs). The last category alone accounts for 70 per cent of the EU economy. Europe seems ready to take a fresh look at these models (which deviate very strongly from the American Enterprise Model). These too could help to accelerate economic growth.

The co-operative was the stepchild of the 1990s. Every company which was owned by suppliers or customers was an insult to the defenders of the American Enterprise Model. Co-operatives' ownership structure and their emphasis on continuity, governance, management and strong culture were all deemed hopelessly out of date. In terms of flexibility and speed of decision making, co-operatives left a lot to be desired. And of course they could not participate in the ever-popular game of mergers and acquisitions.

Today this picture has changed completely. The fact that co-operatives resisted the follies of the 1990s has greatly improved their market positions. Co-operative banks, such as Crédit Agricole in France, entered the new century in particularly good financial shape and are bound to expand.

A few years ago the EC identified co-operatives as an essential part of the European economic landscape and launched an initiative to support the region's 130,000 organizations and their 84 million members. A European co-operative statute is currently in the making to facilitate cross-border co-operation among and with co-operatives.[8]

Large private companies were considered the backwater of the economy during the 1990s. They were not in a position to participate in the good times. Protective of their independence, they had to rely on their cash flow and partnerships to finance expansion and as a result growth rates were modest. Their focus on the long term was seen as a fig leaf for inaptness. Advantageous major acquisitions could not be financed. There was always the problem of management succession. Family-controlled companies with a stock market listing such as Heineken were ferociously attacked by their minority shareholders for not following their competitors' strategies and for the supposed discount at which the shares were trading.

But the mood has changed and what was considered inaptness is now seen as foresight. Large private companies have no big expensive acquisitions to integrate and their corporate balance sheets are healthy. Owner–directors tend to have strong views on human interaction and their companies reflect that. Porsche is the envy of the world. Siemens, a company whose style is still shaped by one family, is a tough competitor of General Electric. The Mohn family, which has a controlling stake in Bertelsmann, finally stood up to its US-style CEO and fired him. In general, the strong corporate cultures of privately owned firms pay off for customers. The quality of their products is closely associated with the personal reputation of their owners. Private companies have unrivalled expertise in joint ventures and other forms of cooperation. This was developed as a way to circumvent lack of access to financial markets and is now an intangible, but nevertheless invaluable, asset. It would seem that large private companies are very well placed to capture the sort of opportunities described in Chapter 6.

But private European companies have great difficulty in complying with the new EU accounting standard, with its requirement to book goodwill as an investment to be depreciated over time. They are also under pressure to comply with a plethora of new financial regulations. The outside world is not taking lightly what it sees as the companies' resistance to transparency. Private firms' continuity too is constantly under threat because of inheritance taxes that often force the sale of the company with all the value destruction this entails.

Interestingly enough – and despite their considerable contribution to the economy – complaints by large private companies usually fall on deaf ears and neither the EU nor national governments are considering specific policies to support this segment of the economy.

The EU has however introduced a number of support programmes for SMEs. One is the European Charter for Small Enterprises.[9] This charter aims to promote consistency of EU measures to support SMEs with its general policies on the quality of legislation and regulation, taxation and a single market. It also provides links to programmes with comparable aims initiated by member states. The charter covers areas such as education and training for entrepreneurship, cheaper and faster start-up procedures, and the facilitation of access to broadband internet.

Particularly important for SMEs – and therefore for the foundation of European Enterprise Models – are EU plans to increase the availability of venture capital, improve the availability of skills and strengthen technological capacity of small enterprises. EU programmes to complement and coordinate initiatives by member states have been initiated in all three areas. The EC has introduced a Risk Capital Action Plan and adopted an Action Plan for Skills and Mobility. It has also made moves to increase SMEs' abilities to optimize ICT.

SMEs form the basis for the growth and for the development of European Enterprise Models. They can still choose their growth path, avoid the pitfalls of the American Enterprise Model and remain committed to the notion that economic value is only created by people.

## Capital markets will do their bit

As outlined, Europe is also independent in another crucial respect. In the United States, 75 per cent of the capital needs of companies is provided by equity markets, forcing the majority of US companies into a straitjacket of stock market regulation, analysts' expectations and the tried and tested American Enterprise Model. In Europe – where 75 per cent of financing needs is met from sources other than equity – the most appropriate governance and management model can be designed and laid down as part of shareholder and loan agreements in most cases.

Corporate need for finance varies over time, as does the quality of business ideas and managers. Expertise, outlook and policies vary from bank to bank. The supply of private capital is infinitely diverse, ranging from the modest 'business angel' all the way to the largest pension funds in the world. Each provider of capital has a different time horizon and looks differently at risk. Companies enter a multidimensional market and negotiate the best possible financial and organizational arrangement with their financiers on the basis of a shared strategy. As a result, Europe already has thousands of business models.

The challenge will be to improve on this very flexible system. Market transparency can definitely be improved. Banks such as the Rabobank and ABN AMRO in the Netherlands have clearing units where companies in need of finance and private investors in search of investment opportunities are brought together. Much more can be done on a European scale. A number of other approaches to improve private equity markets were highlighted in Chapter 5.

In this context it is encouraging to note that more and more companies are withdrawing from the stock market and that the amount of private equity has grown substantially over the past 10 years. Commitments of European venture capital firms rose from a very modest base in 1995 to investments to the tune of 20 billion euros in 2000, and then moved back to less than 10 billion euros in 2002. These figures are modest in comparison to worldwide investments (largely in the United States) of $10 billion in 1991 and $180 billion in 2000. However the 1990s produced a European infrastructure of seasoned and qualified venture capital firms. Evidently these investments are dwarfed by the equity invested in mature private companies.

The future looks even brighter. It is estimated that European venture funds are sitting on $32.4 billion in uninvested funds and the European Investment Bank adds to the credibility of the industry by weighing in with $1.7 billion as part of a broader EU initiative to support starting companies. Pension funds – many of them severely affected by the stock market crash – are increasing allocations to private equity funds for new and established companies. Finally, the political climate is improving in most EU countries, which is leading to a wide range of government initiatives in terms of financial, tax and other facilities.

Further growth of private equity funds will also be stimulated by recent research into the long-term return of this form of investment. There are now sufficient data to draw conclusions and it turns out that the return on private equity funds over a 10-year period is up to five percentage points higher than public equity. Returns are higher if they are corrected for the financing of high-risk start-ups as well as leveraged buy-outs, two investment categories that have a below-average return and that even stay below the return on public equity.

# DOING JUSTICE TO EUROPEAN CULTURAL ROOTS

Europe is very different from the United States and is likely to remain so, as basic values change only very gradually. Despite 10 years of economic revolution, unprecedented economic progress and the fact that many European business leaders were enthusiastic converts to the American Enterprise Model, the US world-view remains alien to broad sections of the European population.

Social psychologist Geert Hofstede has shed light on some of the cultural foundations that help to explain the success of the US and European Enterprise Models in their respective contexts.[10] His assessment of differences between nations and their consequences is based on a framework of five dimensions: power hierarchy, fear of the unknown, individualism versus collectivism, masculinity versus femininity, and long- versus short-term orientation. Research over the past 40 years concludes that Americans and Europeans were and remain strongly divided in two of these dimensions.

One is 'fear of the unknown', which is defined as 'the extent to which the members of a culture feel threatened by uncertain or unknown situations'. In all EU countries people score much higher than Americans in this category. The other dimension is individualism versus collectivism ('everyone is expected to look after himself and his immediate family versus integration from birth into strong, cohesive in-groups that provide protection in return for loyalty'). The widespread belief that Europeans are more group-oriented than Americans is confirmed by Hofstede's research.

Looking at corporate cultures, professors and consultants Charles Hampden-Turner and Fons Trompenaars use a conceptual framework of seven dichotomies.[11] This helps to analyse the different ways of creating wealth. In the context of this book and in light of the economically dominant position of Germany in Europe, it is most relevant to look specifically into similarities and differences between the United States and Germany, concentrating on four of the seven dichotomies:

- universalism vs. particularism;

- internal orientation vs. external orientation;

- analysis vs. integration;

- individualism vs. communitarianism.

On average, both US and German managers are more 'universal' than other nationals. They share the view that companies need rules, procedures and routines and that companies can only add value by being systematic. They agree that there are always exceptions and these have to be dealt with in the best way possible. However when there are too many exceptions, the integrity of the company is at stake and the rule needs to be revised.

Looking at the application of the American and the European Enterprise Models in Germany, it would seem that the American Enterprise Model's concentration on one universal objective – ie return on shareholder investment – and on the tuning of the organization to respond to customer demands, another universal concept, does not in itself produce cultural tensions.

The focus on free cash flow plus organizational structures geared to internal growth and partnerships with suppliers, customers and competitors – two of the universal concepts intrinsic to the European Enterprise Model – also provide a proper fit with German values.

In the American Enterprise Model the emphasis is on the law and legally binding contracts. This fits Americans. In the European Enterprise Model much emphasis is put on the rules of engagement within the company, in working together with partners and regulators. Leaders in the European Enterprise Model rule with the help of principles and try to strike a balance between flexibility and continuity. This emphasis is in line with German preferences as is protection of the integrity of the company in its broadest sense.

Americans and Germans are also more internally than externally oriented. Judgements, decisions and commitments are stronger impulses for action than signals coming from, demands formulated by, and trends in the outside world. This ties in with the crucial, albeit very different role, which CEOs play in both models. Americans and Germans hold strong-willed managers with a clear view on the tasks at hand in high esteem.

When it comes to analysis and integration, the European Enterprise Model is much closer to German values. Americans are analysts. They dissect problems and other phenomena, looking at facts, tasks, numbers, units, points and other specifics. They discover faults, find and implement remedies and, in doing so, they assume that the company as whole will benefit. Germans are more inclined to search for relationships; they search for patterns and put issues into a wider context. They need more time but once they have reached a diagnosis they can take on a number of interrelated problems in a coordinated way.

This is consistent with the rigorous demarcation lines between corporate activities in the form of business units that are part and parcel of the American Enterprise Model, the tendency to divide business units further and the very specific targets for individual managers. The European model comes with strong incentives to cooperate which helps to form an integrated view and organize joint action, which is how Germans cope with complexity. Moreover the European model suits companies that are aware of the variety of professional inputs that are required to arrive at comprehensive solutions. The surveys by Hampden-Turner and Trompenaars present evidence that the majority of Germans prefer to work in this manner.

The European Enterprise Model is also a better fit with the German business culture when it comes to 'individualism' and 'communitarianism'. Americans focus on the enhancement of individuals, their capacities and attitudes, rights and rewards. The individual can and should exercise control over his own destiny. The more control, the more successful he will be. Germans put more emphasis on the company as a community in which a number of social needs (considered as contributors to the wealth of a company) can also be met. Participation in society and in the company is a widely shared German priority. The welfare state exists to support social cohesion. Works councils are thriving institutions in small and large companies. Proposals to enhance the role of experts and middle managers are consistent with the way German companies work.

As one would expect many European values have found their way into Europe's legal systems and are anchored in its institutions. European law in general and particularly legislation governing contracts, commercial transactions and business enterprises is very different from that in the United States. In Europe the civic code provides certainty and protection for both strong and weak partners in transactions. Key principles such as 'good faith' have a broad scope and concepts such as 'good trading practices' and 'reasonableness and fairness' codify many business conventions that have proved invaluable over the centuries. In common law (the Anglo-Saxon system), the eternal search for precedent, the considerable leeway of judges and the seemingly endless possibilities for appeal all create uncertainty. Common law provides opportunities for the unwilling, the opportunists and the unscrupulous.

The fact that social democratic, Christian democratic and liberal priorities continue to dominate the political scene in Europe is another manifestation of profound and lasting differences with the United States. Europeans continue to value individual and social rights; they respect individual expression but the notion of the common good is also strong; they do not mind generous reward but not at the expense of social cohesion; they see merit in competition but believe there are many fields where cooperation yields better results. Decision making falls to those who have been granted the authority to commit the company and not to those who acquired power. Strife is detrimental; decision making with the help of a strong organizational hierarchy (as in France), or the proper introduction and application of rules (as in Germany), or consensus building (as in the Netherlands) is considered to be the superior approach.

## ARTICULATING A EUROPEAN WORLD-VIEW

Europe has made little progress in defining its common values, priorities and shared insights, and the question is whether an attractive and internally consistent European world-view will emerge that is powerful enough to penetrate governmental policy making and to shape the attitudes and priorities of special-interest groups. In the early 1980s, eloquent sceptics such as the Italian journalist Luigi Barzini saw a Europe 'that should, but won't, that must, but probably cannot, evolve a common will, speak with one voice, define its goals, defend itself and pursue a single foreign policy'.[12] So far, he has been right and US dominance is far greater than 25 years ago.

The US view of the world emerged as part of a political revolution with extraordinary politicians at the helm and plenty of highly visible business leaders to follow up. A European world-view will see the light of day in a very different manner.

The present generation of European politicians and managers has lost credibility. There are always fresh faces but their capacity to effect change is severely constrained by prevailing concepts, by the cultural dominance of large listed companies and by the fact that some politicians and government officials are still besotted with the US world-view and are still rolling out the American Enterprise Model.

As it happens, leaders are not essential in this turnaround. Contrary to the United States in the early 1980s, change in Europe can be evolutionary. Many of the potential building blocks of a European world-view have not been destroyed but have simply disappeared from sight. Principles, priorities and preferences and those holding them simply submerged when the political and corporate leaders of Europe bowed to pressure from the world of finance and presided over the import of the American Enterprise Model. It does not require a revolution to convince, coerce and mobilize large sections of society to turn the tables. Those who adhere to European values will gradually resurface and their political and commercial clout will gradually increase.

The articulation of the European world-view and its subsequent translation into government policies will receive impetus from three main sources. The first is what astute American observers such as Kagan[13] and Rifkin[14] describe as the European project: the use of ever-strengthening economic ties to end power politics, secure peace and create paradise. Agreement on the eastward extension of the EU and the drafting of a European constitution were watersheds on the road to a European identity. The direction cannot be reversed. Moreover the increasing number of political and trade disagreements with the United States sharpens minds. Common European values crystallize around these issues and reasons to defend them become more explicit. All this filters through to the general public.

On top of this, the daily grind of implementing EC directives, the legal battles for the European Court and the broadening scope of EC initiatives all help to define what Europe is about. The speed with which EC directives are translated into national law increased throughout the 1990s. The number of infringement procedures has remained stubbornly high, but one after another these have been brought to a conclusion. The number of industry standards has risen from approximately 2,000 in 1992 (the year the Internal Market was declared complete) to approximately 14,000 in 2002.

The second impetus for the emergence of a European world-view comes from the empowered individual. This new strong man is already flexing his muscles as a consumer: protesting against the manipulation of markets and the media, complaining about lack of service and demanding protection from the torrent of commercial messages fired in his direction. He takes aim at former utilities and the privatized monopolies many have become. He is cautious and suspicious – and has every reason to be so.

The empowered individual has also learnt to trust his political skills. The internet enables him to form peer groups around certain issues in his neighbourhood, municipality, and all the way to global issues. He supports special-interest groups that in turn are increasingly professional in countering political and corporate excesses.

As a shareholder and investor, the empowered individual learnt important lessons the hard way. He saw his financial advisors fail both morally and professionally. Many financial products were made complicated to hamper comparison with rival products. He has also lost confidence in the press as the self-proclaimed watchdog of the economy. Regaining his confidence will be beyond large parts of the financial community. The internet gives him access to all the basic data and independent advice.

The empowered individual also exercises pressure as an employee. It is a sign of the times that he actively seeks to reduce the duration of his corporate life by putting considerable sums away for early retirement. An increasing number of employees are also voting with their feet by starting their own business. Those who remain make their presence felt by defining and demanding a good working environment in the broadest sense of the word. They seek inspiring and productive professional relationships. They wish to grant authority to those who deserve it. They feel entitled to appreciation apart from remuneration. They long to trust and to be trusted and, old-fashioned or not, they want to be able to identify themselves with the company they work for.

Empowered individual Europeans will tune the companies they work for to new market demands and will demonstrate that a new way of working pays off in many different ways.

The articulation of a European world-view and the emergence of the European Enterprise Model is a two-way street. While an enterprise model will spread more quickly on a continent that is aware of its common heritage, companies that visibly operate on the basis of new principles will stimulate and direct the debate on European values: the third impetus for the emergence of a European world-view. With the demise of so many institutions and the dominance of economic life over other aspects of society, business is the strongest cultural force around. Companies need individual contributions from knowledgeable and socially capable employees. They can only survive if cooperating employees add sufficient economic value. They induce and enforce socially acceptable behaviour out of economic necessity, but in doing so act as one of the few remaining forces for the transfer of values and the defence of social cohesion.

In the end, the European project, initiatives by thousands of European groups with a common interest and the spread of the European Enterprise Model will anchor a European world-view in the public consciousness and will influence the attitudes, priorities and behaviour of Europeans. Politicians and civil servants will take their cues from the grass-roots and the European world-view will find expression in policies, laws and regulations that support value creation.

Ironically, three of the proudest achievements of the US-led economic revolution of the 1990s – the spreading of the spirit of innovation, the emergence of the empowered individual and the explosive growth of the availability and use of information and communication technology – are precisely the developments that will contribute to the demise of the American Enterprise Model in Europe.

## AND FINALLY ...

Europe's strengths will manifest themselves, but the first tenet of forecasting will apply: change will take much longer than expected but, when it happens, it will proceed at a much faster pace than imagined and will eventually reach far beyond the limits that can be seen now.

However, the emergence of European Enterprise Models could accelerate if the United States stumbles. Confidence in the US economy is brittle. At present, the value of the dollar is propped up by the central banks of China, Japan and South Korea. The moment these banks can no longer carry the risk of their very considerable investment in US treasuries and start to diversify their portfolio, the corrosion of the dollar might turn into a collapse. Imports will become more expensive and inflation will go up. Interest rates will need to rise to counter inflation and to lure new investors to finance the triple deficit. Higher interest rates imply lower corporate profits and less investment, and once again lay-offs will be seen as inevitable.

The US consumer will be hit in three different ways: rising prices, higher costs of servicing his considerable debt and higher risk of unemployment. All this will be at a time that he has to increase his negligible savings to cope with higher health and retirement costs. A deep recession is unavoidable if indeed the seemingly perpetual increase in spending of American consumers merely levels off.

At such a juncture, very little of the appeal of the US world-view or the American Enterprise Model will be left and Europe will prevail by default. At the same time, the negative political and economic repercussions for the world economy cannot be overestimated, not because these economies are so intertwined, but because such a situation will lead to irrational investment and disinvestment decisions by the European believers in the American Enterprise Model. The belief that the United States will become an economic burden to the world for a long time will turn into a self-fulfilling prophecy.

It is the final indictment of those who built and defend the American Enterprise Model that in their recklessness they have created a world that is so much out of control that such a sequence of events – and many other pathways with comparable outcomes – is entirely plausible.

The proponents of the American way of doing business defend the law of the jungle under the guise of the rule of law. They presided over a period of great opportunity, but the average American has not made any progress and will have to live with the consequences of the exuberance of a few. The wrong objectives were pursued, a technological revolution was squandered and economic value was destroyed at unrelenting pace. Power and wealth were amassed to the detriment of social foundations for corporate and economic development. The defenders of the American Enterprise Model have maintained a system in which, insidiously, invisible cost and indefinable but frightening risks are transferred to the anonymous, innocent and vulnerable shareholder, employee and consumer. In short: to the citizens of the world.

Only Europe can turn the tide.

# Notes

## CHAPTER 1

1. Frölke, Viktor (2002) Enron Global Crossing, Adelphia, Tyco, ImClone, Omnicomm enzovoorts: De zachte onderbuik van het kapitalisme, *NRC Handelsblad*, 15–16th June
2. *BusinessWeek Online* [accessed 31 July 2002] The CEO/CFO Swear-In Watch, http://www.businessweek.com/investor/content/jul2002/pi20020731_9500.htm
3. *Economist.com* [accessed 30 July 2002] Congress's crackdown becomes law, http://www.economist.com/agenda/displayStory.cfm?Story_id=S') H%24)RQ%2F*%200%22%24 %0A
4. Schmitt, Eric (2001) American dream update: More and more and mortgages, too, *International Herald Tribune*, 7 August
5. Pfanner, Eric (2002) Fed chief's outlook upbeat. But Greenspan warns scandals are 'destructive to capitalism', *International Herald Tribune*, 17 July
6. Rubin, James P. (2002) Good work in Kosovo: Start honoring the nation-builders, *International Herald Tribune*, 22 October
7. Roberts, Richard and Kynaston, David (2001) Whatever happened to Will Hutton's vision of 'a less degenerate capitalism'?, *New Statesman*, 17 September
8. Stein, Charles (2002) Deflation: Yes, it could happen, *International Herald Tribune*, 15 August

9. Cornwell, Susan (2002) Mixed results for business as US Congress breaks, *Reuters*, 20 October

10. *Economist.com* (2002) In search of honesty, 15 August

11. Labaton, Stephen (2002) SEC's troubles pile up at 'worst possible time', *International Herald Tribune*, 2 December
    Weil, Jonathan and Wilke, John R. (2002) Study by US Senate details SEC's failure in regulating Enron, *Wall Street Journal Europe*, 7 October

12. Peterson, Jim (2002) A role few want to audition for, *International Herald Tribune*, October

13. Norris, Floyd (2003) SEC chooses Fed banker to head accounting panel, *International Herald Tribune*, 16 April

14. Norris, Floyd (2003) Warning to banks that aided corporate fraud, *International Herald Tribune*, 30 July

15. Morgenson, Gretchen (2002) Regulators set plan to cooperate, *International Herald Tribune*, 4 October

16. *NRC Handelsblad* (2003) Na misleiding beleggers Wall Street: Record-boete banken VS, 29 April

17. McGeehan, Patrick (2003) Bucks still stop at chiefs' offices. Executive pay is called 'totally out of line' with performance, *International Herald Tribune*, 7 April

18. *International Herald Tribune* (2003) Worthless promises? Was American bosses' first certification of accounts a nonevent?, 24 March

19. Peterson, Jim (2003) Financial markets need a holistic cure, *International Herald Tribune*, 30–31 August

# CHAPTER 2

1. Deutsche Bundesbank Monthly Report, *Discussing the growth and prosperity gap between the United States and the Euro area*, May 2002

2. Lequiller, François (2001) The new economy and the measurement of GDP growth, *Institut National de la Statistique et des Etudes Economiques*, February

3. East, Steven H. (2002) Modest recovery in real growth should continue. Low nominal growth and high debt levels are challenges, *Economic Outlook*, Friedman Billings Ramsey, December

4. *Department of Labor, Bureau of Labor Statistics Data* [accessed 17 December 2002] Labor force statistics from the current population survey 1992–2002, http://www.bls.gov

5. Leonhardt , David (2002) Jobless but no longer looking for work: US unemployment data understate a large and growing problem, *International Herald Tribune*, 1 October

6. *US Department of Justice, Office of Justice Programs* [accessed from 18 December 2002] Prison statistics, http://www.ojp.usdoj.gov/bjs/prisons.htm

7. *The Economist* (2002) Prison and beyond: A stigma that never fades, 10 August

8. *The Economist* (2002) Europe's work in progress: Why does Europe's productivity growth lag so far behind America's?, 16 November

9. Browning, Lynnley (2003) US rich get richer, and poor poorer, data shows, *International Herald Tribune*, 25 September

10. Wolff, Edward N. (2000) *Recent trends in wealth ownership, 1983–1998*, Jerome Levy Economics Institute of Bard College

11. Bernstein, Jared [accessed 4 November 2002] It's full employment, stupid: Even a slight rise in unemployment clobbers the bottom half, *Prospect* [Online], http://www.prospect.org

12. *Het Financieele Dagblad* (2003) Toezicht verbetert economie, 29 October

13. Roach, Stephen [accessed 30 July 2003] *BOSAP, PPS and the productivity scam*, Morgan Stanley Economists, http://www.morganstanley.com

14. *The Economist* (2001) A spanner in the productivity miracle: Statistical revisions show how America's recent productivity boom is less remarkable than was once thought, 11 August

15. Testimony by William C. Dudley, chief US economist, Goldman, Sachs & Co., US Senate Budget Committee, 27 June 2001

16. McKinsey & Company [accessed October 2001] MGI Report: US productivity growth 1995–2000, *McKinsey Global Institute* [Online], http://www.mckinsey.com

17. Gordon, Robert J. (2000) *Does the 'new economy' measure up to the great inventions of the past?*, Working Paper 7833, National Bureau of Economic Research, Cambridge, MA

18. *The Economist* (2001) Statistical illusions: Europe's productivity growth has been almost as rapid as America's, 10 November

19. Rhoads, Christopher [accessed 19 January 2004] U.S., EU productivity gap is widening, *Wall Street Journal* [Online], http://online.wsj.com/public/us

20. *The Economist* (2001) Irrational pessimism: None of the explanations for the euro's weakness stand up, 8 December

21. de Haas, Bruno (2001) Leugens vervloekte leugens en bedrijfswin-sten, *Het Financieele Dagblad*, 30 August
22. Leering, Raoul (2002) Feiten keren zich tegen de dollar. Europese beurzen kunnen profiteren nu beleggers zien dat er nooit een Amerikaans winstwonder is geweest, *Het Financieele Dagblad*, 4 May
23. Pickford, Derry (2003) *Employee stock options: A closer look*, Smithers & Co. Ltd
24. de Haas, Bruno (2002) Verstoppertje spelen met optiebeloning, *Het Financieele Dagblad*, 11 April
25. Morgenson, Gretchen (2002) Pension gains count, losses don't, *International Herald Tribune*, 15 November
26. *The Securities Class Action Clearinghouse* [accessed 12 January 2003] Federal securities fraud class action litigation, *Stanford Law School* [Online] http://www.securities.stanford.edu
27. Haenen, Hein (2002) Beleggers in VS willen hun geld terug: Verzwijging of misleiding brandstof voor hausse aansprakelijkheid-sclaims, *Het Financieele Dagblad*, 12 November
28. Wayne, Leslie (2002) An old foe takes aim at Wall Street, *International Herald Tribune*, 7 October
29. Leering, Raoul (2003) Dollar schiet geen gat in tekort, *Het Financieele Dagblad*, 11 October
30. *The Economist* (2003) The head ignores the feet. The Bush administra-tion seems indifferent to the budget crisis in the states: It may not be able to be so for long, 24 May
31. *Independent Strategy* [accessed 29 January 2002] Will US private sector leverage bring the equity market crashing down?, http://www.instrategy.com
32. Osler, Carol and Hong, Gijoon (2000) Rapidly rising corporate debt: Are firms now vulnerable to an economic slowdown?, *Current Issues in Economics and Finance*, Federal Resevre Bank of New York
33. Kuttner, Robert (2003) The great American pension-fund robbery, *BusinessWeek*, 8 September
34. *The Economist* (2002) Ticking bomb. Unfunded benefit promises to retired employees are now too big to ignore, 16 November
35. Ignatius, David (2002) Get serious about the threat of a credit collapse, *International Herald Tribune*, 16–17 November
36. Bank for International Settlements [accessed 8 July 2002] Seeds of concern, *BIS 72nd Annual Report*, http://www.bis.org, 8 July 2002

37. Thornton, Emily, Coy, Peter and Timmons, Heather (2002) The breakdown in banking: Trust is eroding, and profits may follow as business models falter, *BusinessWeek* [Online] http://www.businessweek.com

38. Haspeslagh, Philippe, Noda, Tomo and Boulos, Fares (2001) Managing for value: It's not just about the numbers, *Harvard Business Review*, 7222

39. *The Vanguard Group* [accessed 25 September 2002] Facts about the investor literacy test, http://www.flagship3.vanguard.com> Personal Investors

40. Hulbert, Mark (2002) Another failing grade for analysts, *International Herald Tribune*, 22 October

# CHAPTER 3

1. *CBO* [accessed 29 January 2003] 'Historical budget data' in The budget and economic outlook: Fiscal years 2004–2013, http://www.cbo.gov

2. Walsh, Edward [accessed 30 May 2003] OMB details 'outsourcing' revisions: Unions denounce new rules aimed at competition, *Washington Post* [Online] http://www.Washingtonpost.com

3. OECD Privatisation Database (2001) *Privatisations in OECD countries by main sector*, 53

4. Kurstjens, Bas (2002) Privatiseringsplannen Frankrijk lopen vast, *Het Financieele Dagblad*, 13 September

5. Becker, Elizabeth (2003) Political shadow over WTO talks, *International Herald Tribune*, 16 September

6. *International Herald Tribune* (year) US agenda on trade advances with deals, 26–27 July

7. *AFL-CIO* [accessed June 2003] Bushwatch: The complete file, http://www.aflcio.org

8. Norris, Floyd (2003) Steady earnings are an unrealistic idea, *International Herald Tribune*, 29–30 November

9. *Het Financieele Dagblad* (2003) Stork halveert aantal divisies in drie jaar: Markt prijst strategische focus, 14 August

10. *Het Financieele Dagblad* (2002) Fusies en overnames verder in slop: Waarde daalt harder dan aantal deals; EU passeert VS in transactievolume, 26 September

11. Bolte, Geerhard (2003) *Managementblunders: 50 onthutsende missers geanalyseerd*, Het Spectrum Utrecht

12. *BusinessWeek* [accessed 14 October 2002] Mergers: why most big deals don't pay off, http://www.businessweek.com

13. Ravenscraft, A. and Scherer, F. Michael (1987) *Mergers, sell-offs, and economic efficiency*, Brookings Institution, Washington DC

14. Bartel, J.C.K.W., van Frederikslust, R.A.I. and Schenk, H. (Ed.), (2002) *Fusies & acquisities: Fundamentele aspecten van fusie en acquisities*, Elsevier Business Intelligence, Dordrecht

15. Schenk, Hans [accessed June 1999] Large mergers a matter of strategy rather than economics, *Rotterdam School of Management* [Online] http://www.fbk.eur.nl

16. Schenk, Hans (1996) Fuseren of innoveren?, *Economisch Statistische Berichten*, 81 (4050)

17. Schenk, Hans (2000) Policy implications of purely strategic mergers, in Wolfram Elsner and John Groenewegen (Ed.), *Industrial policies after 2000*, Kluwer Academic Publishers, Dordrecht
    Schenk, Hans (2001 ) Megafusies: kern van de recessie?, *ESB*, 6 April

18. Reynolds Fisher, Susan and White, Margaret A. (2000) Downsizing in a learning organization: Are there hidden costs?, *Academy of Management Review*, 25 (1)

19. *Het Financieele Dagblad* (2003) 'Kaasschaaf bij bedrijven is uitgewerkt' KPMG: ga structureler te werk, 20 August

20. Cameron, Kim S. (1994) Strategies for successful organizational downsizing, *Human Resource Management*, 33 (2)
    Cameron, Kim S. (1994) Guest editor's note: investigating organizational downsizing – Fundamental issues, *Human Resource Management*, 33 (2)

21. Couwenbergh, Pieter (2003) Niet zingen voordat de klus is geklaard, Unilever wil nog niet praten over vervolg on 'Weg naar Groei strategie', *Het Financieele Dagblad*, 14 February.
    Couwenbergh, Pieter (2003) Hardloper Unilever raakt buiten adem, *Het Financieele Dagblad*, 30 October

22. Poiesz, Theo and van Raaij, Fred (2002) *Synergetische marketing, Een visie op oorzaken en gevolgen van veranderend consumentengedrag*, Pearson Education Benelux, Amsterdam

23. Rigby, Darrell K. (2001) *Management tools 2001: An executive's guide*, Bain & Company Inc., Boston, MA

24. Lohr, Steve (2003) Is technology business still a growth industry? Result could shape economy as a whole, *International Herald Tribune*, 17–18 May

25. Carr, Nicholas G. (2003) IT doesn't matter, *Harvard Business Review*, 3566, 27
Roach, Stephen [accessed 18 July 2003] How's business?, *Morgan Stanley* [Online], http://www.morganstanley.com

26. de Jongh, Hans (2003) Banengroei VS nog lang niet in zicht: Economen zijn veel minder optimistisch dan regering-Bush, *Het Financieele Dagblad*, 9 September

27. *Biotechnology Industry Organization* [accessed 12 August 2003] US Biotech Revenues 1992–2001, http://www.bio.org

# CHAPTER 4

1. *Towers Perrin* (2001) Worldwide total remuneration (2001–2002), 1 April

2. Bennis, Warren and O'Toole, James (2002) Don't hire the wrong CEO, *Harvard Business Review*, May–June

3. Couwenbergh, Pieter and Haenen, Hein (2003) De ceo beteugeld, *Het Financieele Dagblad*, 22 February

4. Wiersema, Margarethe (2002) Holes at the top: Why CEO firings backfire, *Harvard Business Review*, December

5. O'Brien, Timothy L. (2003) AOL chief's exit leaves company's future clouded, *International Herald Tribune*, 14 January

6. O'Boyle, Thomas F. (1998) *At any cost*, Vintage Books, New York

7. *See* note 4

8. WorkUSA (2002) *Weathering the storm: A study of employee attitudes and opinions*, Watson Wyatt, Washington DC

9. Hodgson, Paul (2003) *CSX compensation policies and incentive plan: A multi-year perspective*, The Corporate Library, January

10. Beer, Michael (2003) Building organizational fitness, in S. Chowdhry (Ed.), *Organizations 21C*, Financial Times-Prentice Hall, New Jersey

11. *The Economist* (1999) Thank you and goodbye, 28 October

12. *See* note 4

13. Information from www.mca2000.org/tower_00.ppt.

14. Vlasic, Bill and Stertz, Bradley A. (2000) *Taken for a ride: How Daimler-Benz drove off with Chrysler*, William Morrow, New York

15. Jensen, Michael C. (2001) Corporate budgeting is broken – let's fix it, *HBR On Point*, 813X

16. *Het Financieele Dagblad* (2001) Rijkman Groenink stelt ambities bij: ABN Amro slikt doelstelling voor de beurskoers drie leden raad van bestuur vertrekken, 17 August

17. *Het Financieele Dagblad* (2001) 'Zonder Omwegen' valt duurder uit: ABN Amro ziet nog geen economisch herstel in 2002, 15 February

18. *Het Financieele Dagblad* (2003) Rijkman Groenink wil weer ondernemen: Na de saneringen is er nu weer ruimte voor investeringen..., 14 February

19. *Het Financieele Dagblad* (2003) Hoe moet Moberg dit bedrag opmaken?, 5 September

20. *Het Financieele Dagblad* (2003) Financieel herstel Ahold bepaalt hoogte bonus Moberg, 25 November

## CHAPTER 5

1. van der Heijden, Kees (1996) *Scenarios: The art of strategic conversation*, John Wiley & Sons, Chichester

2. Magretta, Joan with Stone, Nan (2002) *What management is: And why it's everyone's business*, HarperCollins Business, London

3. Normann, Richard (1991) *Service management: Strategy and leadership in service business*, second edition, John Wiley & Sons, Chichester

4. Fentener van Vlissingen, Paul (1995) *Ondernemers zijn ezels*, Balans, Amsterdam

5. Ante, Spencer E. (2003) The new Blue, *BusinessWeek*, 17 March

6. *The Economist* (1998) Europe's American dream. [...] Change in Europe may come more slowly than some expect, 19 November

7. Green, Stephen, Hassan, Fred, Immelt, Jeffrey, Marks, Michael and Meiland, Daniel (2003) In search of global leaders, *Harvard Business Review*, special issue August

8. *See* note 7

9. Argyris, Chris (1985) *Strategy, change and defensive routines*, Pitman, Boston, MA

10. Beer, Michael and Cannon, Mark D. (2002) *Promise and peril in implementing pay for performance: A report on thirteen natural experiments Harvard Business School*, paper 02-064

11. Beer, Michael and Katz, Nancy (1997) *Do incentives work? The perceptions of senior executives from thirty countries*, Academy of Management, AOM reference number 125677

# CHAPTER 6

1. Edmondson, Gail and Kerwin, Kathleen (2003) Stalled: Was the Daimler–Chrysler merger a mistake?, *BusinessWeek*, 29 September
2. Weintraub, Arlene (2003) Five hurdles for biotech, *BusinessWeek*, 2 June
3. Christensen, Clayton (1997) *The innovator's dilemma: When new technologies cause great firms to fail*, Harvard Business School Press, Boston, MA
4. *See* note 3
5. Barrett, Amy (2003) Staying on top: Can he keep up the growth?, *BusinessWeek*, 5 May
6. Carey, John and Arndt, Michael (2003) Combo medicine, *Business-Week*, 7 April
7. Lynch, Lisa M. (1997) *Do investments in education and training make a difference?*, paper for USIS Stockholm
8. Normann, Richard (1991) *Service management: Strategy and leadership in service business*, second edition, John Wiley & Sons, Chichester
9. Kleisterlee, Gerard (2002) Interview, *USAToday.com*, 18 November
10. Capell, Kerry (2003) Spin-offs: biotech's growth hormone, *Business-Week*, 3 March
11. Engardio, Pete, Bernstein, Aaron and Kripalani, Manjeet (2003) The new global job shift, *BusinessWeek*, 3 February
12. Hof, Robert D. (2003) The quest for the next big thing, *BusinessWeek*, 18–25 August
13. Fukuyama, Francis (1995) *Trust: The social virtues and the creation of prosperity*, Hamish Hamilton, London
14. Nooteboom, Bart (2002) *Vert–ouwen*, Academic Service, Schoonhoven
15. Sennett, Richard (1998) *The corrosion of character: The personal consequences of work in the new capitalism*, W.W. Norton & Company, New York

# EPILOGUE

1. Turner, Adair (2001) *Just capital: The liberal economy*, Macmillan, London
2. Gray, John (1998) *False dawn: The delusions of global capitalism*, Granta Books, London

3. *See* note 1

4. *Bureau of the Census* [accessed 24 September 2002] US Department of Commerce, US trade in goods 1978–2001, http://www.ita.doc.gov

5. *Umsetzungsfahrplan* [accessed 9 April 2003] Agenda 2010, Bereich Wirtschaft und Arbeit, http://www.bundesregierung.de

6. Europese Commissie (2002) *Scorebord van de interne markt*, 11, special edition November

7. European Commission (2003) *Internal market strategy. Priorities 2003–2006*, COM 238, Brussels, 7 May

8. European Commission (2001) *Co-operatives in enterprise Europe*, Draft consultation paper, Brussels, 7 December

9. European Commission (2003) *On the implementation of the European Charter for Small Enterprises*, COM 21, Brussels, 13 February

10. Hofstede, Geert (2001) *Culture's consequences*, second edition, Sage, Thousand Oaks, CA

11. Hampden-Turner, Charles and Trompenaars, Fons (1993) *The seven cultures of capitalism*, Piatkus, London

12. Barzini, Luigi (1983) *The impossible Europeans*, Weidenfeld & Nicolson, London

13. Kagan, Robert (2003) *Paradise and power: America and Europe in the new world order*, Atlantic Books, London

14. Rifkin, Jeremy (2004) *The European Dream: How Europe's vision of the future is quietly eclipsing the American Dream*, Polity Press, Cambridge

# Index

ABN AMRO bank    110, 195
accounting industry    15, 23–24, 26
acquisitions    52–53, 68–70, 91, 97, 98, 126
    see also mergers
Adelphia Communications    15
Ahold    65, 68–69, 112–13, 158
Air France    60, 127, 184
airline industry    80, 102, 107–08, 171
    KLM-Alitalia merger    141–42, 172–74
Albert Heijn    65
Alitalia    141–42, 172–74
Allen, Robert    95
alliances    91, 97, 123, 144
    see also partnerships
American Enterprise Model    20–23, 27, 56,
        142, 155, 180
    characteristics and core propositions
        21–22, 125–26, 127
    consequences and costs    85–119
    corporate results    35–42
    demise of    2–7, 12
    limitations    5–6, 7, 63–78, 83, 158
    shortage of ideas that could lengthen    6,
        78–83
    success of    3–4
    successful export of and emulation by
        European companies    3, 8, 22, 55,
        56
    survival of    7–8, 157
American Management Association    73
AOL Time Warner    15, 41, 53, 90
Apple Computers    123
Armstrong, Michael    95
Arthur Andersen    2, 15, 26
Arthur D. Little    79, 103
AT&T    50, 95

Bain & Company    67, 78, 79, 100, 101, 103

balance sheet    11, 49, 134
Bank for International Settlements    46
banks
    European    148–49, 195
    and internet    169
    US    15–16, 75, 96–100
        and analysts    25
        and CEO    99
        and mergers/acquisitions    97–99
        role in decision-making process of
            companies    99
        selling off corporate and consumer
            debt    46–47
Barzini, Luigi    199
Beer, Michael    95
benchmarking    101, 102
Bennis, Warren    88
Berger, Roland    136–37
Bertelsmann    41, 158, 193
biotechnology    83, 163
Blair, Tony    23
'bleeders'    66
boards
    and American Enterprise Model    90, 133
    and European Enterprise Model    10,
        132–33, 136–38
Boeing    39–40, 177
Boonstra, Cor    66, 89–90
Booz Allen & Hamilton    79, 94–95, 103
Boston Consulting Group (BCG)    69–70, 79,
        100, 103
brands    73–74, 75
Brenninkmeijer family    131–32
Bristol-Myers    40
Britain    58, 60, 62
British Airways (BA)    99
    merger with KLM    97–98
British Steel    53

budget
   federal (US)    58–59
   UK    59
Bureau of Labor Statistics (US)    36
Bush, President George W.    2, 5, 17, 18, 23, 56,
   59, 62, 83, 87
business schools    6, 22, 123
business units
   and American Enterprise Model    5, 6–7,
      66–67, 73, 86, 103–18, 198
      and corporate head office    7, 104–05
      and performance planning    108–11
      reasoning behind introduction of and
         benefits    103–04
      and targets    108–10, 111–12
      tensions between    7, 107–08
      tensions between CEO and managers
         7, 104, 105–07
   and European Enterprise Model    11, 139,
      152–53, 164
   and ICT    166
*BusinessWeek*    23, 69

C&A    131
Cadbury    50
CalPERS    40
Carr, Nicholas    81–82
Case, Steve    90
Cempella, Dominico    142
CEOs (chief executive officers)
   American Enterprise Model    6, 21, 26, 67,
      86–95, 114, 147
      and aftermath of acquisitions/mergers
         160–61.
      and business unit manager    7, 104,
         105–07
      and destabilization of companies    6,
         89–90
      dismissals of    94–95
      distance between management team
         and    90
      earnings    39
      elevation of to star status    6, 85, 86–88
      expectations of    92–93
      and investment bankers    99
      and pursuit of shareholder return
         92–93
      remuneration packages and golden
         parachutes    94
      and SEC demands    23
      undermining of capacity to control and
         credibility    88–89, 93–94
   European Enterprise Model    11, 132, 137,
      138, 144, 146, 152, 159, 161
      and aftermath of acquisitions/mergers
         161–62
      and board    10
      qualities of    139–41
Cheney, Dick    87

Chicago school    48
China    43, 158, 177, 202
Christensen, Clayton    164
Chrysler    160
Cisco    127, 157
Citigroup    2, 16, 26, 40
Clinton, President Bill    57, 63
co-operatives    192–93
Coca-Cola    76
commodity trap    74, 75
competition    20, 21, 103
Computer Associates    15, 16
consultants/consultancy firms    6, 78–79, 83,
   85–86, 96, 100–03, 118
Consumer Price Index (CPI)    33
consumer spending    43, 47
cooperation and European Enterprise
   Model    12, 123, 124, 163, 165, 179–81, 187
   undermining of by American Enterprise
      Model    180–81
core activities
   focus on    66, 101
corporate head office and business units    7,
   104–05
Credit Agricole (France)    193
Credit Suisse First Boston (CSFB)    16, 37, 39,
   40, 97
CSX    94
cultural roots, European    196–99
customer relations management (CRM)
   79–81
customer segmentation    75–76
Cutler, Stephen    16

Daimler-Benz    106–07
DaimlerChrysler    160
DASA    106
debt    53
   corporate    5, 44–45
   credit card    82
   private    5
decision making
   decentralization of in American Enterprise
      Model    21, 86, 104
   and European Enterprise Model    150
Deloitte & Touche    100
depreciation ratio    41
derivatives    45–46
Deutsche Bank    97, 144, 160
Deutsche Bundesbank    31
Deutsche Post    60
Deutsche Telekom    60
DiamondCluster    67
Digital Equipment Corporation    123
direct foreign investment    13–14, 42, 189

dismissals and European Enterprise Model 145
Doha Round　61, 62
dollar, US　84, 202
Donaldson, William　24
Dow Chemical　50
downsizing　70–73
Dresdner Kleinwort Wasserstein bank　39, 97
Drexel Burnham Lambert　45
Dunn, Doug　90
Durables Index　33

East Asia　44
Ebbers, Bernie　70
EC directives　200
economic crisis (US) (2002)　15–16
　reaction to and remedial action launched 2, 4, 16–17, 18, 23–24
　recovery and restoring of confidence 17–19, 48
economic disparity　32, 34
economic policies in US and Europe　57–63
*Economist*　23
economy, US in 1990s　3, 4, 17, 18, 27, 29, 30, 31–35, 41–2, 47, 189
employees
　and American Enterprise Model　22, 114, 168
　and European Enterprise Model　149–51, 167–68
employment　34
empowered individual　201
Endemol　41
Enron　2, 15, 19, 26, 40, 79, 103
equity markets　148, 194
ethnic minorities　32, 71
euro　188, 190
Europe
　competitive disadvantages　190
　cultural roots　196–99
　economic policies　57–63
　features contributing to emergence of European Enterprise Model 187–202
　potential of　189–96
　and trade　188
　US criticism of　56
　world-view　14, 199–202
European Charter for Small Enterprises　194
European Enterprise Model　50, 79, 121–56
　competitiveness of　12–13, 157–85
　features of Europe that will contribute to emergence of　187–202
　foundations of growth　121–27
　and governance　132–38
　and internal growth　12–13, 159–70, 185
　and managers　11, 138–43, 161, 166
　and ownership　8–9, 127–32
　principles and features　7–12

reasons for prevailing　158–59
　rise of　7–13
European Investment Bank　148, 195
European Stability Pact　60

federal deficit　4–5, 43
Federal Deposit Insurance Corporation　45
Federal Reserve Bank　29, 30, 44, 45, 84, 189
financial advisors　85–86, 96
financing
　and American Enterprise Model　21–22, 64–65, 95–96, 147–48
　and European Enterprise Model　128–30, 147–49, 194–95
FitzGerald, Niall　77
food industry　76, 77
France　58, 60, 63, 175
France Telecom　60
free cash flow
　focus on in European Enterprise Model 10, 11, 49–50, 124, 133, 134, 152, 159, 197
free trade　61–62

GDP (gross domestic product)　31, 37
General Electric (GE)　39–40, 72, 91, 142, 149
Germany　31, 37, 58, 190–92
　differences between United States and 197–98
　integration of DDR　190
　privatization　60
　tax cuts　58
　trade unions　63
Giant Food　69
Global Crossing　15, 40, 79, 103
globalization　1, 188–89
Goldman Sachs　16, 36, 40, 96
Gordon, Robert　36–37, 42
Governance and European Enterprise Model 132–38
government involvement　57–59
Gray, John　188
Greenspan, Alan　121
Gulag Archipelago　118–19

Halliburton　16
Hampden-Turner, Charles　196–97, 198
*Harvard Business Review (HBR)*　50, 81, 95
hedonic method　31, 32
Heineken　193
Heinz　177
Hennes & Mauritz　176
Herkströter, Cor　117
Hewlett-Packard　154–55
Hofstede, Geert　196
Honeywell　142
Hoogovens　53

IBM　127, 141, 157, 177

ICT (information and communication
      technology)   4, 35, 81–82, 83, 123, 177
   and European Enterprise Model   13,
      165–67
   investment in   41, 42
   outsourcing of to India   189
   and productivity in American companies
      30, 36, 37
   and service innovations   169
IKEA   112
ImClone Systems   15, 140
IMF (International Monetary Fund)   56
Immelt, Jeffrey   72, 149
incentives, financial   86, 122
incomes   32
India   177, 189
individualism
   versus collectivism   196
   versus communitarianism   198
industrial relations   62–63
inflation, US   17, 29, 31, 33
information and communication technology
   *see* ICT
ING   64, 97
innovation   74–75, 123, 142
   and European Enterprise Model   12,
      146–47, 162–65
   and partnerships   13, 174–75
Intel   40, 177
intellectual property   162, 179
interest rates   5, 30, 43–44, 47, 82
internal growth and European Enterprise
   Model   12–13, 159–70, 185
*International Herald Tribune* (*IHT*)   46
internet   41
   and empowered individual   201
   and retail banking   169
investment, US   40–41
Investor Responsibility Research Center
   (Washington)   26
Iraq war   43, 58

Jager, Dirk   52
Japan   20, 43, 158
JCDecaux   127–28, 169–70
Johnson & Johnson   165
joint ventures   13, 151, 174–75
JPMorgan   2, 96–97
JPMorgan Chase   26, 40, 46
junk bonds   65

Kagan, Robert   200
Kets de Vries, Manfred   71, 91, 118
KLM
   and Alitalia merger   141–42, 172–74
   merger with BA   97–98
   takeover of by Air France   184
KPMG   100

labour markets
   and globalization   189
law, European   198–99
lawsuits, shareholder   40
lay-offs   6, 70–73, 82, 168
'leveraged buy-out'   65
Levy, Chris   52
*Life* magazine   67–68
Linden, Christopher   52
'line of sight'   146
Lisbon strategy (EU)   42
Lloyds Bank   50

McDonough, William   24
McKinsey   36, 78, 79, 100, 103, 151
Maljers, Floris   89, 90
Malpensa Airport (Italy)   141–42, 172, 174
management agenda (European Enterprise
      Model)   143–55, 178–79, 185
   of financing   147–49
   of innovation   146–47
   organizational development   149–52
   performance planning and evaluation
      152–54
   and remuneration   154–55
   setting standards and designing rules
      143–45
managers   123, 124
   and American Enterprise Model   22, 86,
      113–18, 119, 140
      relationship with CEO   7, 104, 105–07
      and remuneration packages   7, 86, 104,
         116
   and European Enterprise Model   11,
      138–43, 161, 166
market leadership   73–77
market liberalization   60–61
Marshall, Colin   99
matrix organizations   103
Mercedes-Benz   106–07, 160
mergers   5, 13, 68–70, 91, 97, 126, 160
   dealing with aftermath of   12, 160–62
   and investment banks   97–99
   and partnerships   13, 172–74
Merrill Lynch   2, 16, 25, 96
Mesa Group   81
Messier, Jean-Marie   93, 158
Microsoft   39, 177
Middelhoff, Thomas   158
middle management   115, 123, 178–79
Moberg, Anders   112–13
Montgomery Ward   72
Monti, Mario   142
Morgan Stanley   46, 96
motivation, employee   167
Motorola   175
multinational companies   188, 189

Nakasone, Robert 90
nanotechnology 175
NASDAQ 16, 17
National Association of Securities Dealers
    (NASD) 25
National Bureau of Economic Research 36
National Institute of Standards and
    Technology 41
NDP (net domestic product) 32, 37
Netherlands 60, 62
Network Associates 16
new products 74–75
New York Stock Exchange (NYSE) 2, 4, 16,
    25, 130
Nike 67–8
Normann, Richard 169
Novartis 163

Office of Comptroller of the Currency 45
oil companies 170
O'Neill, Paul 23
option schemes 39, 65
Organisation for Economic Co-operation and
    Development (OECD) 59
organizational development
    and European Enterprise Model 149–52
orientation
    internal versus external 197–98
O'Toole, James 88
outsourcing 6, 30, 53, 57, 59, 67–68, 176–77
ownership
    and European Enterprise Model 8–9,
    127–32

partnerships 123
    American Enterprise Model 181–83
    European Enterprise Model 10, 11, 13,
        144, 147, 148, 171–78, 183–85
    benefits of 171
    and joint innovation initiatives 13,
        174–75
    and management team 147
    and mergers 13, 172–74
    and outsourcing 176–77
    principles based on 184
pay-for-performance systems 154–55
pension funds 39–40, 45, 65, 148, 195
Pepsi-Cola 76
Peregrine Systems 16
performance planning/evaluation
    and American Enterprise Model 86, 104,
        108–11
    and European Enterprise Model 12,
        133–37, 145, 152–43
petroleum industry 64–65
pharmaceutical multinationals 70
Philips Electronics 66, 89–90, 144, 175, 177
Pieterse, Rob 92
Pischetsrieder, Bernd 146

Pitt, Harvey 24
Poiesz, Theo 74
portfolio of activities 10, 66, 133, 134
poverty 32–33
PricewaterhouseCoopers 67, 100
private capital
    financing of European companies 9, 14,
        129, 130–32, 195–96
private companies 192, 193–94
privatization 5, 21, 59–60
Procter & Gamble 52, 77
Producer Price Index (PPI) 33
productivity
    Europe 36, 37
    and European Enterprise Model 13,
        165–68
    and mergers 70
    US 3, 4, 17, 29–30, 35–37
profit and loss statement 49
profit per share 38, 51, 63, 65
profitability
    Europe 38
    US 4, 5, 38–40, 49, 51
Public Company Accounting Oversight Board
    (PCAOB) 23–24

Railtrack 60
Reagan, Ronald 3, 19, 20, 57, 62, 101
recession (2001) 30, 45, 53, 55, 78
recruitment
    and European Enterprise Model 145
redesign, corporate 66–68
redundancies
    and American Enterprise Model 168
remuneration
    and European Enterprise Model 12, 151,
        154–55, 159
    and managers in American Enterprise
        Model 7, 86, 104, 116
retail sector 82, 83
Rhineland Model 124–25
risk taking
    emphasis on in American Enterprise
        Model 21
Rite Aid 16
Roach, Stephen 35, 178
Roche 70, 174
Roland Berger Strategy Consultants 136–37
Royal Dutch Shell 51, 117
rules 197
    designing of in European Enterprise
        Model 143–45

S&P (Standard & Poor's) 500 38, 39, 40, 73
Sarbanes-Oxley Act 2, 17, 23–24, 26
Schenk, Hans 70, 162
Schering Plough 149
Schrempp, Jurgen 106, 107, 160

SEC (Securities and Exchange Commission)
2, 4, 15, 16, 17, 19, 24, 25, 26, 39
Senn, Josef-Fidelis   146
services   114
    and American Enterprise Model   170
    and European Enterprise Model   168–70
    outsourcing of   176–77
shareholder return/value
    destruction of   5
    pursuit of   3, 17, 21, 48–53, 51, 53, 63, 68,
        83, 85, 92, 95, 105, 122, 125
shareholders
    and American Enterprise Model   30, 127
    and European Enterprise Model   128
Shell   51, 96, 117–18
Siemens   50, 193
single market, European   191–92
small and medium-sized enterprises (SMEs)
    70, 192, 194
Smithers & Co   39
Snow, John   94
software acquisition/development   31, 41
South Korea   202
Spinetta, Cyrille   184
Spitzer, Eliot   16, 25
STMicroelectronics   175
standard of living   18, 29, 32–33
standards
    setting of in European Enterprise Model
        143–45
standards, industry   200
Stanford Law School   40
stock market crash   16, 30, 36, 148
stock markets   14, 26, 52, 82, 155, 195
stock price   51, 52, 82
stocks, lowering of   64
Stop & Shop   68–69
sustainability   135
Swissair   79, 103
syndicates   46–47
Syntac   70

takeovers *see* acquisitions
targets
    and business units   108–10, 111–12
taxes   21, 30, 43, 57–58
teams
    and European Enterprise Model   11, 151,
        179, 181
technological development   122, 162–63
Thatcher, Margaret   19, 20, 62, 101
Third World   56
Time Warner   41, 53

total quality management   79
trade   61–62
    European   188
trade deficit, US   5, 42–43
trade unions   62–63, 125
Trompenaars, Fons   196–97, 198
trust
    and European Enterprise Model   179–81,
        184
Turner, Adair   188
Tyco   15, 70

UBS Warburg   38
unemployment   47
    in 1990s   17, 29, 33, 34
Unilever   65, 74, 77, 89
unions *see* trade unions
United States
    competitive advantages   189
    corporate results   35–42
    criticism of Europe   56
    differences between Germany and
        197–98
    economic crisis/scandals and remedial
        action (2002)   2, 4, 15–17, 18, 23–24
    economic policies   57–63
    economic recovery   17–19, 48
universalism versus particularism   197
Uruguay Round   61

value creation   123, 124, 136
value-based management   49–50, 124
van der Hoeven, Cees   69, 112, 158
venture capital firms   175, 195
'venturing out' of activities   79, 175
Vivendi Universal   41, 158
Volkswagen AG   146

Walt Disney   41
'Washington Consensus'   56
Watson Wyatt Worldwide   72, 93
wealth, individual   32–33
Welch, Jack   72, 91, 142
Werner, Helmut   106–07
Wharton School of Business   73
Wiersema, Margarethe   90, 95
world-view
    American   3, 4, 19–20, 56, 57, 63, 93, 196,
        199–200
    European   14, 199–202
WorldCom   15, 70
write-offs   4, 41
WTO   62

Xerox Corporation   16, 123